FARMERS' RESEARCH IN PRACTICE

ILEIA READINGS IN SUSTAINABLE AGRICULTURE

Farmers' research in practice
Lessons from the field

Edited by Laurens van Veldhuizen, Ann Waters-Bayer,
Ricardo Ramírez, Debra A. Johnson and John Thompson

INTERMEDIATE TECHNOLOGY PUBLICATIONS 1997

Published by Intermediate Technology Publications
103/105 Southampton Row, London WC1B 4HH, UK

A CIP catalogue record for this book is available from the British Library

ISBN 1 85339 392 4

Printed by SRP, Exeter UK

Contents

A provocative exploration into what triggers off innovation by farmers. The author finds the instinctive notion of 'situational knowledge' more practical than the conventional approach through problem analysis. In his experience, the latter does not lead to real solutions. He still regards the scientific approach as valid, but only as one 'window' of exploration among many others. Examples from Nepal and from the Swiss Alps illustrate that the most important skill needed in agricultural development is the ability to facilitate interactive situations that bring together the pragmatism of rural people and the analytical skills of scientists.

A closer look at the logic and methods of informal experiments by Malian farmers revealed how difficult it is to separate experimentation from farming practice. Case examples show that farmers explore new things or test hypotheses, but particularly that they do 'move–testing' experiments: taking action and watching closely to see what happens. To practise farming means to act, to judge, to learn and to adjust in a series of informal experiments.

The nature of farmer experimentation in Central America is the focus of this contribution. It confronts readers with the challenge: do we really know how to understand farmer experimentation? Farmers' voices are heard through numerous quotes rich with insight, anecdotes and everyday common sense. The author describes the mechanisms used by agricultural technicians to strengthen farmer experimentation based on local know–how and priorities.

A range of experiences are described in this contribution from the Punjab in India where farmers' initiatives have led to effective collaboration with researchers at the state agricultural university and research station. The researchers are supporting experimenting farmers to carry out their own research and promote the production and distribution of local seed varieties. They are also using participatory video to document their interactions and share their experiences with others. The researchers have learned from farmer innovations in bird control, new uses for grain crops and an alternative seedling medium for muskmelon. Participatory research experiences with farmers in a Green Revolution setting makes this contribution unique.

Adding technical options

experimentation with farmers demonstrated the weaknesses of conventional top–down extension systems. The next challenge will be to institutionalise this innovative approach in a large, governmental extension service.

Improving experimental design

Researchers' initial investigations of the transition from slash–and–burn to permanent agriculture suggested that mechanisation was not economically viable for smallholders along the western part of the Transamazonian highway in Brazil, in view of present landuse patterns and the market situation. Regardless, the farmers wanted to try out animal traction, and asked researchers to support their experimentation. This is an example of a negotiated partnership between a large regional farmers' organisation and an interdisciplinary team of university–based researchers in action research with the aim of helping the farmers draw their own conclusions about the suitability of mechanisation. At the same time, it gave the researchers greater insight into the motivations of the experimenting farmers.

This chapter describes World Neighbors' experience in Bolivia whereby farmers were trained to design and manage experiments and carry out basic statistical interpretation of results. Farmers' acquired know–how empowered them to experiment on their own and to take on the role which in the past was reserved for technicians. In addition, the experience yielded concrete outcomes in terms of yield increases in staple crops through the utilisation of green manures and varieties suited to different altitudes.

The authors disprove the myth that 'research is done by scientists in their laboratories and farmers work the land'. A group of 23 potato growers in the Netherlands established their own laboratory to closely monitor nematode infections in their lands. This enabled them to experiment with alternative control methods and assess their impact. The use of synthetic inputs was thus reduced dramatically. They feel that their success depends on their keeping the size of their group limited, despite the growing demand from neighbours for the service.

Sustaining the process

Acknowledgements

The idea for this book grew out of discussions with practitioners of Participatory Technology Development (PTD) during our advisory and training work overseas and during meetings of the St Ulrich Group, an informal network of PTD promoters based in Europe. The motivation to compile experiences in supporting farmers' own research was heightened by our encounters - often by chance - with experimenting farmers, many of whom were working in relative isolation.

The enthusiastic response by numerous researchers and development fieldworkers throughout the world to our call for experiences showed us that the farmers need not work alone; there are many 'outsiders' who are eager to support them and have already begun to support those farmer-researchers they can find. We thank the many people who submitted abstracts or even entire articles about their experiences and observations. We are sorry that there was not room to include them all in this collection.

Many people from the ILEIA team and the ILEIA network gave their time in reviewing the contributions. Our thanks go to Carine Alders, Wolfgang Bayer, Christian Gaborel, David Gibbon, Wim Hiemstra, Uwe Kievelitz, Clive Lightfoot, Eli Lino de Jesus, Coen Reijntjes, Niels Röling and Guy Trebuil. Niels also helped to put the contributions to the book in context by preparing an overview for us of the theory of farmer innovation..

We have tried our best to give credits for the photographs accompanying the chapters. Special thanks to Mapatano Mulume for maintaining the correspondence between eastern Zaire and the Netherlands, and managing to send photographs of the farmer research brigades that continue their experimentation during the current political unrest in that area. One of his photographs has been used for the front cover.

We would also like to thank Ann Long for her assistance in language editing, and Lila Felipie, Regina Ruane and Carmen Rodriguez from ILEIA for their extremely capable administrative support at a time of much flux within the organization. They achieved the seemingly impossible task of keeping communication open and ordered between five editors based in four countries but often travelling elsewhere. During the period of gestation of this book, Lila also managed to produce her baby in much less time then it took us to produce ours.

Finally, we are grateful to Jan Hiensch for preparing the camera-ready copy for printing, and to Neal Burton from IT Publications for being so calm, patient and helpful during the long period of editing the text and polishing the final version.

The editors, Leusden, April 1997

Introduction

This book is about farmers' own research. In many parts of the world, farmers are seeking ways to improve their farming systems and to adapt their practices to changing agroecological and socioeconomic conditions. The contributions to this book give evidence of how farmers adopt, adapt and formulate new ideas and innovations, try them out in different settings, evaluate and assess the results, and make decisions about their potential value for improving the way they farm. All of these experiments, no matter what methods they employ, are referred to here as farmers' agricultural research. This is a considerable expansion of the conventional understanding of agricultural research, which is usually limited to scientifically designed, highly methodological and closely controlled experiments and investigations carried out on national and international agricultural research stations and in the field.

This book is also about the efforts of people in governmental extension and research organisations (GOs) and in non–governmental organisations (NGOs), development agencies and community–based organisations that work together with farmers and support them in a process of what we call Participatory Technology Development (PTD). This is a broad term encompassing all forms of interaction that combine the knowledge and skills of farmers with those of outside facilitators in creating sustainable improvements in farming systems. The contributions to this book consist mainly of case studies of recent or ongoing efforts to achieve genuine collaboration in agricultural development. The authors give honest accounts of the successes, the failures or false paths, and the lessons learnt by both farmers and PTD facilitators in this process.

A review of experiences of successful collaboration between farmers and outsiders (research scientists, extensionists, development workers) in improving farming technologies and systems (ILEIA 1989) revealed that these experiences involved some basic aspects which can be depicted in a PTD framework (Jiggins and de Zeeuw 1992). This consists of the following clusters of activities:

- getting started: establishing contact, gaining basic information, clarifying agenda and agreeing on future collaboration
- situation analysis: gaining a joint understanding of local problems and resources
- looking for things to try: identifying promising solutions or new opportunities for improving agriculture
- trying things out: experimenting with, and adapting, new ideas in trials that are planned and implemented by farmers, with the support of outsiders, and that are designed and evaluated jointly by both parties according to agreed criteria

---

[1] Authors whose articles appear in the book are referred to here by name alone (e.g. Ishag et al.), whereas references from the literature appear with a date of publication (e.g. Hamilton 1996).

- sharing the results: letting other farmers, research scientists and development workers know what was achieved and how, primarily by means of farmer–to–farmer exchange and workshops
- sustaining the process: stimulating local organisation and linkages with other farmers and agricultural services, so that farmer–led agricultural improvement can continue without the direct support of external facilitators.

It is important to note that PTD reflects a systems approach which goes beyond the development of specific farming techniques. It aims to enhance farmers' capacity to adjust their farming system, indeed their entire livelihood system, to changing conditions. It is focused on farmer–led analysis and experimentation, which is strengthened by the farmers' social organisation and linkages with a multitude of other actors.

Why is PTD important?

The contributions to this book give evidence of the efforts made by farmers in all parts of the world to improve their farming systems. Several chapters offer examples of farmers who, without external support, develop new practices, test ideas from other places, adapt their present methods and assess the impact on their lives (e.g. Bajwa et al.; de Waal et al.). In addition, Aresawum Mengesha and Martin Bull's description of FARM–Africa's work in Ethiopia and Natasja Oerlemans and her colleagues' analysis of the importance of farmer study groups in the Netherlands present illuminating cases of farmers who initiated their own experiments with little or no encouragement from external authorities. These cases illustrate how merely providing an opportunity for farmers to meet other farmers, posing thought–provoking questions during meetings, workshops and field visits, and presenting a few alternative ideas or options can be all the stimulation needed to spark farmer experimentation, often without even mentioning the concept itself (Hagmann et al; see also Connelly and Wilson 1995).

The accounts of farmers' concepts of and approaches to experimentation presented by Arthur Stolzenbach, based on experiences in West Africa, and Henri Hocdé, based on experiences in Central America, reveal how little we, as outsiders, know about indigenous knowledge creation, and how much we have yet to learn (Scoones and Thompson 1994; Long and Long 1992; Marglin and Marglin 1990). What is clear is that scientific and indigenous information represent different kinds of knowledge systems and expertise. Participatory research practitioners believe that linking scientific experimentation methods with indigenous forms of experimentation can enhance the quality of research carried out by both farmers and scientists (Röling and Wagemakers 1996; Okali et al. 1994; Jiggins et al. 1996).

Some ways in which the research scientists and extension agents can gain from collaborating with experimenting farmers include:

- acquiring deeper insight into problems and potential solutions from the farmers' viewpoint and discovering possibilities not previously contemplated, which can be further investigated in jointly designed and managed trials

- learning the concepts and methods that farmers employ in their experiments, making it possible to work with them on the planning and evaluating of trials of relevance to them, both on–station and on–farm
- gaining greater awareness of the differences between the priorities and objectives of the farmers and those of the scientists and therefore being able to adjust the content, design and evaluation criteria of scientific trials accordingly, thus ensuring that the farmers' priorities are at the top of a common research agenda
- increasing the understanding of local agroecological and socioeconomic conditions and how introduced technologies can be better adapted to them
- identifying technology components that must be studied more rigorously, or the need to find alternative solutions by observing farmers' modifications to introduced technologies and discussing these modifications with them.

Improving the exchange of ideas and information among farmers, research scientists and extensionists can improve the technology development process for farmers, especially those in complex, diverse, marginal environments with limited resources. It can help focus formal research on questions of practical importance for agricultural development and make more effective use of the scarce time and expertise of scientists, farmers and extensionists.

Farmers' research

Farmers sometimes engage in their own research partly because they are not receiving what they want through the formal agricultural research and extension services. The existing paths for information coming from research centres via extensionists to farmers (and, ideally, back to the scientists again) are too slow, and farmers' priorities get lost along the way. The responsiveness of scientists to farmers' needs is therefore often limited (Oerlemans et al.).

Lack of support from formal research is, however, only one reason why farmers experiment. For generations they have tried out new techniques, developed new cultivars and hybrids, devised effective means for battling pests and diseases, created complex irrigation and drainage works, developed new farming systems and much more, long before official agricultural research and extension services existed. There is every reason to assume that they will continue to do so in the future.

Farmers experiment for a variety of reasons, including problem–solving, adaptation of existing technologies, curiosity and sometimes in response to peer pressure (Millar 1994; Rhoades and Bebbington 1988). Understanding what stimulates innovation can help us understand why, in some instances, innovative farmers begin experimenting even when they have very limited contacts with other like–minded people. Röling (pers. comm.) has identified a number of circumstances and events which may 'trigger' innovation:

- acquaintance with a novel idea which seems to be a possible answer to a latent or pressing problem

- becoming aware of a problem, perhaps arising from changing conditions, and looking for ways to solve it
- coming up with new ways to put technology to work in response to market possibilities
- accidental or playful discovery and curious exploration
- putting the prototype of an existing technology to work, thus allowing the technology to be applied in local conditions
- being pressured to conform to norms or regulations
- making an analysis of different actors, the communication networks they share and the objectives and needs they share.

Some of the chapters highlight these 'triggers' for innovative farmers (Scheuermeier; Hocdé), others focus on the collaboration that emerges when outsiders gain contact with such farmers (de Waal). These farmers often express very clearly their own interest in involving research scientists, extensionists and other actors in their research activities. The following are some positive features of such collaboration:

- tackling farmer–defined issues and developing technical options under more controlled conditions than can be achieved in farmers' fields, scientists can help explain farmers' results and seek potential solutions to problems encountered by them (Mellis et al.)
- collaboration helps spread the farmers' results, including the publication of farmers' experiments in more formal journals (Ruddell et al.)
- all important actors are more likely to accept the results, because farmers' experiments are given legitimacy (Oerlemans et al.)
- innovations, new information and alternatives can be fed back to farmers for incorporation into their own research through farmer–to–farmer extension, field–days or exchange visits between farmer groups, farmer–researcher workshops or more conventional extension procedures (Hagmann et al.; Ishag et al.).

Not only farmers, but many agricultural extensionists and some research scientists have also been dissatisfied with the conventional approach to technology adoption and diffusion. They feel that it has not allowed them to meet the real needs of farmers, particularly of those with limited access to external inputs to increase production. The search for alternative approaches has led to increased attention to the farmers' own knowledge and innovativeness, to farmer–to–farmer extension and to on–farm experimentation, notably within Farming Systems Research programmes (Scarborough 1996). Such alternative approaches have given outsiders the opportunity to see farmers actively engaged in research and extension and to discuss and understand their rationale with them, and have greatly increased the sensitivity of outsiders to farmers' own research capacity and to possibilities for enhancing it. The value of these interactions in increasing the effectiveness of formal research is also being more widely recognised.

Understanding farmers' research requires a willingness by outsiders to learn from local patterns of innovation and from local ways to bring about experimentation. The following metaphor proposed by Levine (1996) challenges some assumptions which scientists need to address.

I want to take very seriously the idea that agriculture is like cooking. ... Cooking is some-thing that (almost) all of us have to do throughout our lives to stay alive - yet can we say that we 'are all experts'? Or that, if we do not copy the cooking on some television pro-gramme, it is because we are stupid or 'constrained by tradition'? Are we 'all constantly experimenting'? And how? ... The analogy can be taken in many different ways. If I want to try a new brand of flour to bake a cake, I won't bake two, one to have as a control. So when it fails, how do I know it was the flour, and not the oven? I have no problem in saying that I am experimenting with a new brand of flour. But at the same time, if a researcher asked me what experiments I had performed in the last year, would I say that I switched brands of flour last week? Our concept of 'experimenting' is also so much looser than we are led to believe for as long as we are thinking about agriculture: it both includes and excludes try-ing out a new brand of an ingredient, depending on who I am talking to and when. So, a farmer who tells me he doesn't experiment, but happily points out five new species he is try-ing out for the first time, is not necessarily lying, denying, hiding or doing anything that I wouldn't do in exactly the same circumstances... . (abstracted from Levine 1996: 55-56).

Farmers' ownership of the research agenda

The contributions to this book cover a range of understandings regarding the importance and implications of who initiates and controls the research process, who participates in it and how relationships between farmers and outsiders are established and evolve. The methodo-logical implications of how these interactions originate are profound, for it is a question of how to promote collaborative research endeavours that can give farmers the lead in the inter-action and do not impose pre−defined methods, activities, timeframes, indicators or out-comes.

Sceptical observers have challenged the basic approach to PTD on the basis that it follows a scientist's logic, not that of the average farmer. They have argued that scientists and farm-ers often use different frames of reference when thinking about experimentation. The scientists' thinking is often 'out of time', in that they have the luxury to run their experiments in controlled environments, even when conducting on−farm trials. By contrast, the farmers' performances can only occur 'in time', as they are embedded in particular agroecological and sociocultural contexts which involve changing conditions to which the farmers must make a series of rolling adjustments (cf. Stolzenbach). For the scientist, what counts is replication and comparison. For the farmer, what counts is fitting available resources to changing circum-stances well enough to make it through the growing season (Thompson and Scoones 1994; Richards 1989).

In his chapter, Ueli Scheuermeier draws on recent field experiences in the Nepalese Himalayas and the Swiss Alps to compare and contrast farmers' and scientists' notions of agricultural technology development. He contends that farmers rarely follow a logical sequence in their experimentation from situation analysis and problem definition to research design, as suggested by the PTD framework. Instead, they appear to pursue a more pragmat-ic and adaptive approach to problem−solving. He concludes that the most critical skill needed to promote agricultural development is the ability to create interactive situations which combine rural people's pragmatism with the analytical skills of scientists.

While it is difficult to dispute the fact that farmers and scientists have different frames of reference and follow different analytical paths to reach their desired objectives, there is growing evidence of effective farmer–scientist collaboration within a PTD framework. In their case study from Colombia, Jacqueline Ashby and her colleagues in the IPRA project describe their attempts to support community–based committees to manage adaptive research activities. They tell of their efforts to identify experimenting farmers, ascertain whether their research benefits the community, discover what linkages with external agencies are needed, identify the necessary financial mechanisms to support local research initiatives, and select methods that are most effective in leading to locally relevant research outcomes. Their experience demonstrates the importance of farmers and researchers jointly defining the core concepts, basic principles, key methods and performance indicators that guide their research. It also shows how a structured PTD project can strengthen the capacity of farmers' groups to take ownership of the research process.

Many programmes and projects that are committed to participatory agricultural development are struggling to find a balance between serving farmers' interests and their own agenda. The cases in this book have been selected with a bias towards examples of farmer–initiated research. We have been more strict in the selection of cases designed by 'outsiders', be they national or international scientists or development agents. Ownership of the learning process by farmers is a central concern, with a view to ensuring practical relevance and continuity of the activities undertaken.

Promoting local ownership of the research process can lead scientists to support farmer-defined experiments even when they believe them to be of little scientific merit. Such is the example of animal traction research in the Brazilian Amazon, where Heribert Schmitz and his colleagues agreed to work with farmers to investigate a technology which they themselves did not believe was appropriate. From their point of view it was more important to build trust and a sense of common purpose with the farmers than to try to impose external ideas which local people would have found unacceptable. Hence, although their initial research efforts proved unsuccessful (as the researchers expected), the process had established enough rapport to enable them to undertake other, more scientifically viable experiments. The importance of such efforts as an entry point is echoed by other authors in the book.

Jurgen Hagmann and his collaborators regard entry–point activities as important for drawing farmers and scientists together. They may seem to have a somewhat top–down connotation in the context of an externally–initiated development project, but entry–point activities are equally important for making hitherto conventional researchers aware of the excitement and personal satisfaction of PTD.

Some contributors to the book, including Peter Gubbels, who describes the strengthening of community capacity to carry out participatory agricultural technology development in Mali, and Samia Osman Ishag and her colleagues, who discuss farmer–to–farmer extension based on local experimentation in the Sudan, argue that providing only very limited or no material and financial inputs during the initial activities will ensure that only genuinely interested farmers (and, we might add, research scientists) will participate. Moreover, it will increase the likelihood that the activities are suitable for farmers with limited means, a point that Ashby and her colleagues also make.

It is often claimed that rapid and easily recognised results during entry–point activities are a key to assuring farmers' involvement and maintaining their commitment to an externally initiated process. This is possible if the initial research activities are clearly defined, well focused and carefully managed. With time, however, if the interaction continues to be led by external researchers, the collaboration can become extremely complex and time–consuming, and can expose farmers to unacceptable levels of risk. During the later stages of an external–ly–initiated PTD process, it is primarily the farmers who will have to judge what level of risk they are prepared to take. They are the ones who will assume the ultimate decision–making responsibilities for the research in their fields and herds. It is also they who must decide on how they want to compensate group members for risks taken.

PTD facilitators also use entry–point activities to gain the commitment of scientists to the process of supporting farmers' research. Examples are found in the cases discussed by de Waal and his associates engaged in village–based cassava–breeding in southern Tanzania and by Bajwa and his colleagues involved in supporting innovative farmers in the Punjab in India. In both cases, the willingness of scientists to collaborate with farmers was gained when the scientists began to recognise the relevance of farmer–initiated efforts for their own research work.

Complementarity with conventional research

Bringing farmers and outsiders together into a common research process, and building on farmers' own capacity to generate technologies and modify practices (i.e. PTD) can comple-ment conventional scientific forms of experimentation. The latter tends to aim for long–term goals, has more generic applications and has a tradition of methodological rigour. The com-plementary strengths of PTD help to fill gaps in conventional research by providing rapid results to site–specific conditions, and by providing farmers with better tools to sustain the process of adapting to change.

The bridging of farmers' and outsiders' perspectives is a challenge to both parties, as it requires each group to make compromises. In the best of cases, these compromises are artic-ulated in joint definition of objectives, activities, roles and responsibilities, and outcomes which allow both parties to learn and explore important parts of their agendas in which their interests meet. Mistakes made during the initial stages of PTD may not be detrimental to the collaboration if the partners, particularly the outsiders, openly acknowledge the lessons learnt from them (Hagmann et al.). Moreover, coming to a joint definition by farmers and outsid-ers of what both parties consider to be a 'successful' outcome of these first activities may be more important than short–term solutions to specific problems. The cases from Brazil (Schmitz et al.) and Colombia (Ashby et al.) highlight how joint learning was valued over and above the short–term concrete results of the individual experiments.

At the same time it is not so much the complementary nature but the differences which are emphasised by those people trying to introduce a PTD approach into conventional project and programme settings. PTD contrasts with top–down, 'transfer–of–technology' (ToT) approaches in which the farmer is perceived as a passive receiver of technologies generated elsewhere (Ruttan 1996; Leeuwis 1993). The Training–and–Visit (T&V) system of extension – and more recent derivations of it, such as that promoted by Sasakawa–Global 2000 – measure success in terms of numbers of 'adopters' of a technology and yield–increases in the products being promoted. As farmers are not part of the technology development process, no reference is made to their enhanced research capacity as an outcome (SG2000 1993-96; Jiggins et al. 1996). Hence, one of the criticisms of the ToT approach is that it leaves the farmer ill–equipped to make adjustments in the light of inevitable site–specific differences, environmental or institutional change, or market fluctuations that occur after a technological package has been 'transferred' (Moris 1991).

Who are the farmer–collaborators in PTD?

A major question which is raised by some authors in this book (e.g. Gubbels; Ishag et al.; Stolzenbach) is whether a PTD approach, with its emphasis on participatory experimentation, is advocating that farmers become 'para–extensionists' and 'para–scientists'. Is it necessary that farmers abandon their traditional ways of discovery and learning and that they set up small controlled experiments, limiting the number of variables, making replications, and separating out control plots or animals? Many agricultural development programmes struggle with the question of whether and how farmers' own research practices need to be improved. However, evidence from the field, reflected in the contributions to this book, shows that PTD practitioners throughout the world answer these questions in many different ways.

The PTD framework mentioned above clearly integrates research and extension dimensions. Efforts are often limited initially to a selected number of farmers, so–called 'farmer–experimenters' or 'research–minded farmers'. Certain concerns emerge from the cases reported here.

- Who are these farmer–experimenters or research–minded farmers? How can they be identified by outsiders wanting to enter into PTD collaboration? To us it is clear that these farmers are not to be confused with what used to be called 'progressive' farmers in theories of diffusion of innovations (Ruttan 1996; Moris 1991; Rogers 1983). The latter are known for being responsive to messages from agricultural extension, often because they have the resources needed to apply the new technologies being advocated. Yet farmers who are 'less responsive' to such extension messages, often because they do not have the necessary resources, can be found to be very active in trying out new practices in their own farming system (cf. Sperling and Scheidegger 1995).
- How are the farmer–collaborators in PTD selected? Agricultural development programmes with a research emphasis may struggle with the representativeness of the local people selected. Some of the difficulties in guaranteeing representative participation in research activities are described by Ashby (1993). Programmes with an extension thrust may be more concerned with finding people who can play a key role in further spreading

methods of supporting farmers' research (Hocdé; Ishag et al.) rather than technological packages. Beyond the local level, with a view to greater sustainability of technology development activities, programmes may need to involve other actors such as local craftsmen and traders (Mellis et al.).

• In all cases, the links between the initial farmer–experimenters and other farmers in the village are important. It is clearly advantageous to involve the wider community from the start. The activities are then likely to have wider social acceptance and the findings of individual experimenters will be more accessible to a larger group (Gubbels).

Well–founded decisions about these issues can be made only if the external actors in PTD are conscious of the heterogeneity within a village. They need to be able to differentiate between socioeconomic groups (e.g. by means of wealth–ranking) as well as between men and women, between people with different cultural backgrounds, and between people with different professional specialisations (e.g. between pastoralists and crop farmers). This will allow some insight into the local patterns of power and control which determine the 'representativeness' of a community experimentation group and the possible impact of their work. Unfortunately, the contributions to this book are not strong in providing examples of differentiated approaches in PTD to respond to wealth or gender differences within a community. Describing their work with farmer–led research on animal traction in Kenya, Mellis and his collaborators acknowledge that, had wealth–ranking been done, their project's approach to technology development could have been better targeted.

Developing local capacities and institutions

The success of PTD programmes cannot be proved merely by presenting outcomes such as a more appropriate variety, an improved method of soil conservation, a new agricultural tool or a new way of organising labour inputs. It is not only the solving of one particular problem that matters. New problems will inevitably arise. A PTD programme can be judged as successful only if the farmers have benefited from their collaboration with outsiders in such a way that they are better able to handle these new concerns. A fundamental goal of PTD is, therefore, to strengthen the capacity of farmers and their communities to innovate, to find or create solutions in various other situations than the particular situation in which the initial PTD experience was gained.

This capacity to innovate is composed of several elements, such as self–confidence, analytical and experimental skills, leadership qualities, organisational development, horizontal and vertical linkages and the ability to mobilise resources. Some of these elements reflect the capacities of individuals, e.g. self–confidence (Aresawum and Bull) or analytical skills (Gubbels), whereas others refer to collaboration among farmers and building up local institutions (Ishag et al.; Ashby et al.) and better communication linkages (Mapatano).

An important element of any programme aimed at strengthening local capacities to innovate is the development of local institutions. Gubbels shows how, in Mali, existing village organisations are being transformed as they grapple with the new challenges. They become more formalised; roles are spread among more people who take up leadership responsibilities through their involvement in farmer–led experimentation. It is therefore not surprising that there is general support for some form of group approach rather than for working with individual farmers (e.g. Mellis et al.; Ashby et al.; Ishag et al.; Mapatano; Wettasinha et al.; Oerlemans et al.; Broekema et al.). This is especially the case at the informal or semi–formal level of horizontal learning and sharing of experiences. Farmer groups clearly help individual members in addressing key challenges. The benefits for outsiders in terms of work efficiency are self–evident.

Complex choices have to be made in considering the further strengthening and institutionalising of the more informal groups:

- Is there a need to formalise groups at all? This sometimes leads to increased conflicts regarding financial and management issues. A number of the cases presented here advocate formalisation to ensure the sustainability of the activities, based on their own successes (Ashby et al.; Gubbels; Hocdé; Oerlemans et al.). Some authors further endorse this strategy to create local groups which can manage decentralised research funds (Ashby et al.) or can become a recognised partner in policy debates (Oerlemans et al.).
- Is the focus in organisational strengthening put on developing production techniques, or must it be wider than this? At the informal stage of group formation, farmers' activities are often oriented to this type of technology development, but it seems doubtful whether this is a strong enough basis for a more formal farmer organisation (Gubbels).
- What types of organisation need to be created or strengthened and at what levels (group, village, region) in order to support the farmers' own research? To what extent should outsiders try to influence who is involved at these different levels; specifically, what role should outsiders play in ensuring representation of otherwise marginalised groups, such as women or pastoralists?
- What is the role of existing farmer organisations at regional and national levels? In some cases, technology development is part of the agenda of such organisations (Ashby et al.; Schmitz et al.; Oerlemans et al.), but often they dedicate themselves rather to lobbying and advocacy. What role can these lobbying activities play in supporting farmer–led technology development?

From the experiences documented here and elsewhere, several general conclusions can be drawn:

- With a view to strengthening local capacities to innovate in agriculture, supporting farmers in developing appropriate institutions or reinforcing existing ones is an integral part of the PTD process.
- Within one village, various organisational forms or institutions commonly co–exist, often with some overlapping in their membership: e.g. interest groups around vegetable gardening or small livestock development, a group of farmer–researchers collaborating with outside researchers, a larger farmer association to coordinate marketing or advocacy activities. Some of these may be traditional forms of organisation, and others created under external

influence. How can 'organisational burnout' be prevented, as can so easily occur when many supporting NGOs and GOs create multiple organisations which are not mutually accountable, each organisation with different purposes and activities, all in the name of 'institutional strengthening'? The institutional dimension requires attention right from the start of PTD activities (Gubbels; Mellis et al.) and needs to be based on insight into existing local institutions which have an influence on agriculture and on agricultural technology development. Outsiders need to look beyond the most obvious institutions, such as village chiefs, local government administrations or specialised farmer groups, to become aware of other important influences on local 'cosmovision' such as religious leaders, soothsayers, ceremonies, rituals and local arts of communication (cf. Millar 1994; Haverkort and Millar 1992; Salas 1994).

• Some form of sense of community or ethic of community service or 'working together makes us stronger' exists in many parts of the world and plays an important role in ensuring sustainability of efforts in agricultural development (Hagmann et al.; Diepenbroeck et al.; Gubbels).

In addition to local institutions, the role of other stakeholders in agricultural technology development merits attention. Mellis and his colleagues highlight the need to involve other actors beyond community−level stakeholders. The theoretical foundations for the social organisation of innovation are well documented (e.g. Engel 1995), but PTD practitioners have thus far exhibited relatively little concern for this dimension. A notable exception in this book is the account of efforts in Zaire to create linkages between groups of farm-er−researchers in different villages, so that information about farmers' findings and methods of farmer−led technology development can be shared more widely (Mapatano). The Zairian efforts have been built thus far primarily on indigenous forms of communication, expanding farmer−to−farmer exchange and celebration to a regional level in the form of farmer fairs. But other forms of communication such as radio and video−recording could also be considered.

A guide to the field cases

A review of the cases presented in this book suggests that four main options are possible for supporting farmers' research:

• Grasping farmers' research: outsiders seek to learn from farmers' ongoing experimental activities and make these known to other farmers and within their own institutions.
• Adding technical options: outsiders offer a wider range of ideas and information than was available to the farmers hitherto, so that they have more to choose from when seeking solutions to try out.
• Improving experimental design: outsiders make suggestions to farmers on how to improve their experimental set−up to be more systematic. Outsiders also assist in increasing the analytical capabilities of farmer−researchers by entering into a dialogue with them, allow-

ing them to incorporate other levels of understanding into their indigenous knowledge systems. Suggestions given are not necessarily alternative techniques, but alternative ways of explaining causes and effects.

• Sustaining the process: this involves stengthening local organisational capacities to analyse, experiment, document and communicate innovation. One unique case presented by Oerlemans et al. shows that farmer groups also intervene in policy development by demonstrating the implications of new policies through direct experimentation.

The articles in this book are grouped according to these four options. The staff of the Punjab Agricultural University in India (Bajwa et al.) demonstrate the first option within a conventional institutional setting. The research scientists started their PTD activities by learning about how farmers experiment, innovate and share information with each other. Learning what farmers are already doing is further explored by Scheuermeier, who seeks to understand what triggers off innovation by farmers. Stolzenbach describes how, in the case of Mali in West Africa, it is often difficult to separate experimentation from ongoing farming practices. Farmers' research was conducted literally 'in practice', as in the title of this book. Hocdé describes a comparable effort in a Central American context, where trained facilitators gave farmers methodological advice with a purposeful commitment not to interfere in the content of the experiments. In this sense, Hocdé's article bridges the first and second options described above.

Most cases, however, illustrate a certain tension or shift between the second and third options. Aresawum and Bull relate how the FARM–Africa project in Ethiopia supported farmers' research by bringing 'research–minded' farmers into contact with a number of ideas and options from other farmers and, to a small extent, from the extension system. Replicability of the experiments was not a major concern to the project, and decisions about how to carry out the experiments were left completely to the farmers. Ishag and her colleagues describe the shift they experienced from a conventional integrated rural development project, to a more modest but also more sustainable approach of promoting farmer–to–farmer extension based on local experimentation.

The case from Tanzania presented by de Waal and colleagues is an example of the third option: a farmer's understanding of his own cassava–breeding experiments was enriched by the inputs from a visiting geneticist. The relationship which developed between the farmer and the geneticist was respectful and paced according to the farmer's agenda. Providing insight into the biophysical and ecological processes that underlie a farmer's practices and that explain his observations also helps farmers better to focus their research efforts (Hagmann et al.; Bentley 1994; Levine 1996).

Another example of the third option is the case from the Bolivian Andes, presented by Ed Ruddell and his colleagues. Bolivian Quechua and Aymaran farmers were proud to learn and apply statistical analyses to interpret the results of their own trials. The reasons they gave for their interest in learning about more systematic ways of experimentation included:

• a desire to better understand and assess new practices so as to have greater confidence when talking with other farmers about their findings, in their role as farmer–extensionists

- an interest in comparing their results with those of other farmers, also in other villages
- wanting their work to be more accessible and acceptable to outsiders, including scientific researchers; this would lead to wider recognition.

Another example of putting scientific tools in the hands of farmers is reported from Australia, where the farmers were given access to computer modelling and rainfall simulation facilities previously used exclusively by researchers. Using these tools, the farmers could gain invaluable insights for judging the value of alternative agricultural practices, as they were able to explore the possible outcomes of the practices in a risk−free situation. The experience of the extensionists and researchers in this interaction with farmers is reflected in the title of a recent book on the case: *Learning to learn with farmers* (Hamilton 1996).

A contrasting experience is the Mali case presented by Gubbels. Having learned through their collaboration with World Neighbors (WN) to do small−scale systematic experiments since the 1980s, farmers indicate that they benefited in many ways from this collaboration. Nevertheless, most of them did not continue to apply the more systematic methods of experimentation, as they did not feel it to be worth the trouble. The efforts made by WN to strengthen local institutions to maintain this process, however, turned out to be a cor-ner−stone in extending new ideas and technologies between farmers.

While Gubbels' case may bridge the third and fourth options, the case presented by Ashby et al. in Colombia fits well within the last option in terms of the institutionalisation of the local agricultural research committees or CIALS.

A completely different turn is taken by farmers in Brazil (Schmitz et al.) and the Netherlands (Oerlemans et al.). In both cases, the farmers opted to 'hire−in' researchers for the more systematic experimental work on their farms. In these examples, the farmer−led research is still clearly controlled by farmers, but the actual implementation is entrusted to professional researchers. This appears to be an approach that both farmers and research-ers find acceptable, as it meets the priorities of each group, while building on their respec-tive skills and knowledge (cf. Osborn 1995; Bebbington 1991).

We have deliberately included two contributions from the Netherlands, as we were struck by the parallels with the cases from the South. As in other parts of the world, a stronger role for farmers in technology development is being advocated in Europe. The economic posi-tion of the Dutch farmers and the specific technologies with which they are experimenting may be different, and the institutional context may be more structured and formalised. Yet it is obvious that, here too, farmers need to play a key role in the search for sustainable forms of agriculture, not only in defining the agenda for research and extension but also by intervening directly in the policy arena (e.g. to ensure that a viable step−by−step reduction of pesticide use is made possible).

Better monitoring by farmers of what happens on their farms, supported by their selec-tive experimentation, can make an important contribution to changing damaging agricultu-ral policies and practices. In Europe, as elsewhere, a shift in the extension approach from adoption by farmers to learning by farmers needs to take place. The discussion of the role of informal and formal farmer learning groups in the Netherlands (Oerlemans et al.) is mirrored in many of the contributions from the South (e.g. Ashby et al.; Gubbels; Hocdé; Mapatano).

References

Ashby, J. 1993. Identifying beneficiaries and participants in client−driven on−farm research. *AFSRE Newsletter* 4 (1): 1-3, 10.

Bebbington, A. 1991. Farmer organisations in Ecuador: Contributions to Farmer First research and development. *Gatekeeper Series*, 21. London, International Institute for Environment and Development (IIED).

Bentley, J.W. 1994. Stimulating farmer experiments in non−chemical pest control in Central America. In: Scoones, I. and J. Thompson (eds), *Beyond Farmer First: Rural people's knowledge, agricultural research and extension practice*. London, IT Publications, pp 147-150.

Connelly, S. and N. Wilson. 1995. Flexible experiments. *ILEIA Newsletter* 11 (1): 15.

Engel, P. 1995. Facilitating innovation. PhD thesis, Wageningen Agricultural University.

Hamilton, A. 1996. Learning to learn with farmers. PhD thesis, Wageningen Agricultural University.

Haverkort, B. and D. Millar. 1992. Farmers' experiments and cosmovision. *ILEIA Newsletter* 8 (1): 26-27.

Jiggins, J. and H. de Zeeuw, 1992 Participatory Technology Development in practice: Process and methods. In: Reijntjes, C., B. Haverkort and A. Waters-Bayer (eds), *Farming for the future: An introduction to low−external−input and sustainable agriculture*. London, Macmillan, pp 135-162.

Jiggins, J., C. Reijntjes and C. Lightfoot. 1996. Mobilising science and technology to get agriculture moving in Africa: A response to Borlaug and Dowswell. *Development Policy Review* 14: 89-103.

Leeuwis, C. 1993. Towards a sociological conceptualization of communication in extension science. *Sociologia Ruralis* 33: 281-305.

Levine, S. 1996. *Looking for innovation: Post−war agricultural change in Niassa Province, Mozambique*. MSc thesis, Wageningen Agricultural University.

Long, N. and A. Long (eds). 1992. *Battlefields of knowledge: The interlocking of theory and practice in social research and development*. London, Routledge.

Marglin, F. and J. Marglin (eds). 1990. *Dominating knowledge: Development, culture and resistance*. Oxford, Clarendon Press.

Millar, D. 1994. Experimenting farmers in Northern Ghana. In: Scoones, I. and J. Thompson (eds), *Beyond Farmer First: Rural people's knowledge, agricultural research and extension practice*. London, IT Publications, pp 160-165.

Moris, J. 1991. *Extension alternatives in Africa*. London, Overseas Development Institute (ODI).

Okali, C., J. Sumberg and J. Farrington. 1994. *Farmer participatory research: Rhetoric and reality*. London, IT Publications.

Osborn, T. 1995. Participatory agricultural extension: Experiences from West Africa. *Gatekeeper Series*, 48. London, IIED.

Richards, P. 1989. Agriculture as a performance. In: Chambers, R., A. Pacey and L.A. Thrupp (eds), *Farmer First: Farmer innovation and agricultural research*. London, IT Publications pp 39-43.

Rhoades, R.E. and A. Bebbington. 1988. *Farmers who experiment: An untapped resource for agricultural development*. Lima, International Potato Center (CIP).

Röling, N.R. and M.A. Wagemakers (eds). 1996. *Sustainable agriculture and participatory learning*. Cambridge, Cambridge University Press (in press).

Rogers, E. 1983. *Diffusion of innovations*. 3rd ed. New York, Free Press.

Ruttan, V.W. 1996. What happened to technology adoption–diffusion research? *Sociologia Ruralis* 36: 51-73.

Salas, M.A. 1994. "The technicians only believe in science and cannot read the sky": The cultural dimension of knowledge conflict in the Andes. In: Scoones, I. and J. Thompson (eds), *Beyond Farmer First: Rural people's knowledge, agricultural research and extension practice*, London, IT Publications, pp 57-59.

Sasakawa Global 2000. 1993-1996. *Annual reports*. Tokyo, Sasakawa Africa Association.

Scarborough, V. (ed). 1996. Farmer–led approaches to extension: Papers presented at a workshop in the Philippines, July 1995. *Agricultural Research and Extension Network Papers* 59 a, b, c. London, ODI.

Scoones, I. and J. Thompson (eds). 1994. *Beyond Farmer First: Rural people's knowledge, agricultural research and extension practice*. London, IT Publications.

Sperling, L. and U. Scheidegger. 1995. Participatory selection of beans in Rwanda: Methods and institutional issues. *Gatekeeper Series*, 51. London, IIED.

Thompson, J. and I. Scoones. 1994. Challenging the populist perspective: Rural people's knowledge, agricultural research and extension practice. *Agriculture and Human Values* 11 (2-3): 58-76.

Grasping farmers' research

Creating turtles' resection

1. Let's try it out and see how it works

Ueli Scheuermeier[1]

How do ideas happen? How does a farmer who is known for his or her innovations actually proceed? Is it in the same way the scientifically–trained researcher or extensionist has been taught to proceed: analyse the situation, define the problem, decide on the criteria for a good solution, set up a hypothesis for your trials, conduct the trials, analyse the results, check on the hypothesis, make an assessment? When I try to remember the times I have been in close contact with innovating farmers, I start to realize there might be aspects of creativity which we have not yet touched upon with our scientific procedures. What then can we learn from the way farmers go about exploring new ideas? Surely this ought to be highly relevant to the

[1] Ueli Scheuermeier, Alexandraweg 34, 3006 Bern, Switzerland. E–mail: uscheuermeier@access.ch home address. c/o S. Brunhold, LBL Department of Development Cooperation, 8315 Lindau, Switzerland. E–mail: eza@lbl.agri.ch.

way in which participatory technology development is practised? Let us look, then, into some situations which I have experienced personally.

Four anecdotes of innovative farmers

Sprinklers for tomatoes

Gom Bahadur Gaha was sitting in my office asking me whether I could help him get hold of a sprinkler or two. Now where on earth did he get this idea of sprinklers from? I knew him as a small farmer in the hills of Nepal, barely surviving with his family on the marginal and steep land where he has recently settled. Sprinklers were out of the question for him, since they had to be imported, and furthermore you need water pressure, which he was not going to have. This was just too high and costly a technology for his kind of situation, which we had analysed in our project.

Before telling him so I fortunately asked him where he had got the idea. "I have a relative a few hours walk away. He is presently watering a sloping field full of tomato plants, and hopes to start selling tomatoes in three weeks time." Tomatoes, now, before the monsoon, on the Butwal market? Sounds like that farmer is going to make money. I'm interested and we arrange a trip together to visit this relative of his. Sure enough, the same situation as Gom Bahadur's, only this farmer did not even have a single square foot of terraced and irrigated rice. He was a below-subsistence-level farmer, topping up his income with labour in the rice-fields down on the plains. But there was the sprinkler, tied to a stick which he stuck into different parts of his field every two hours or so. And a simple polythene pipe ran all the way up the hill, crossed two gullies wrapped round a thick wire, and ended finally in a tiny stream running down the mountain, some 300m of pipe in all. I was amazed. We started discussing how he got this all set up. "About 15 sprinklers were handed out to poor families by an NGO programme, but nobody really knew what to do with them", the farmer told me. "I asked my brother who accompanies trucks down to India what he could make out of it, and he showed me the trick with the pipe. Last year I made a small plot with some vegetables, and for the first time we had tomatoes and cucumbers before the rains. So this year I decided to plant this whole field with tomatoes. I know they will be harvested by the time the first rains come, so the field will be ready for the maize. I hope it works out nicely, because I have taken credit from the small-farmers' credit scheme to buy the pipe. If the tomatoes come out right, I'm sure we can sell them in Butwal. It is off-season now, and prices are high. My brother has found a shop in India where similar sprinklers can be had". And that is where Gom Bahadur immediately placed his order for a sprinkler. A year later it turned out that this particular farmer had repaid his credit to the savings scheme, plus the loans he had taken at tremendous costs from money-lenders, and had thereby put his family back into economic independence.

How could we have been so wrong in our assessments of the project? We had invested a lot of effort in analysing the situation of these farmers. We had established that their problem was the vicious circle of poor land, below-subsistence production, lack of cash, and seasonal migration of the men. We had checked this with some of them, and they had agreed. We were searching for solutions, a lot of the efforts going into giving the men opportunities to stay at home. The option of micro-irrigation with polythene pipes had actually also been looked into, but the costs and the risks were considered too high. Here I was with obvious proof of the opposite. Seasonal migration had even possibly been the most important impulse to making it work: that brother working as a truck loader.

Ranching with Scottish Highlanders in the Alps

What's this? I had seen Scottish Highland cattle in photographs, but I had never seen these small, long-horned animals with their shaggy long red hair for real, and certainly not in an alpine pasture. Obviously only the bull was pure Scottish, the cows looked like the normal grey cows of the Alps, though a bit smaller, and there were a number of very healthy calves jumping about. But wait a minute, this doesn't look like milk production, does it? Good milking cows are the pride of every alpine farmer, and rightly so. But the farmer who had accompanied us to his herd gently scratched the head of a cow who had come near to him, and laughed at our surprise.

"Well you see", he said, "this makes a lot more sense to us than what we were doing before. My father was a full-time farmer. But when I took over, it was clear that we couldn't make a living from farming alone, since the farm is just too small. So I work outside in a construction firm. My wife also works part-time. You can't keep milking cows that way. So we switched to ranching for beef. And this here is by far the best combination: Scottish bulls with Tirolean dwarf-cows. They are sturdy, they survive, and the butchers pay nearly double the price than for the meat of normal calves, because the combination seems to make for a very fine-grained meat. We didn't know that at first, but we're glad. We also didn't know that the calves would grow so fast".

But how and where did he get the idea, and how did he develop it? "Well, actually I don't remember any more when exactly the idea cropped up. I just remember we were a few of us in the bar, and one guy said he was either having to stop milking or stop farming altogether. We all of us laughed and said we would rather stop farming altogether than be a farmer with no milking cows, because farmers with sheep just simply aren't farmers, are they? Anyway, somehow, somebody set up a joke about having Scottish Highlanders. This joke kept circulating in a few heads until one day a neighbour came along with a magazine article about these cattle. I was intrigued, and we wrote to the author. We also asked the extension service, but they said they knew nothing about these cattle. Anyway, the idea slowly evolved. At first we thought to cross them with our big brown cattle and see what happened. But then another neighbour had the idea of trying it with the disappearing breed of Tiroleans. Nobody liked them any more because of their small size, and their consequent lower milk-producing capacity. But they are highly adapted to our mountains, and somewhat sturdier. We formed a group, and got past the tremendous administrative hassle to get a bull or two, and started breeding, just to see whether this joke would work out, though for some of us it no longer looked like a joke. When we saw how enthusiastic the butcher became about the cross-bred calves, my wife started asking why we didn't quit milking and have a herd of Tirolean cows and a Scottish bull? It was only then that I started to consider the proposition seriously. So now we're on our way. The research station has started to show an interest and we're setting up a research programme with them to see whether we should go for developing our own breed, or whether we should try to exploit the heterosis effect in the calves. And the extensionists have started to get interested in the economics of it. But I can already tell you...", and with a final pat on the head of the Tirolean cow he had scratched, he added: "I would never go back to milking unless of course I had a bigger farm, or maybe not even then".

Giant mulberries made small

Manbir Rana was showing me his fruit-tree nursery, which he had built up with the aid of the project in Nepal. For two years now he had been running it on his own, having been trained in grafting techniques of citrus and apple. His nursery was fine, and he had started to sell independently of the project to the surrounding villages; it had already become known that the plants from Manbir usually did not die off, providing, of course, no goat got near them. Suddenly, I saw young grafted plants which looked like mulberry, but obviously couldn't be, because mulberries are propagated by cuttings and not grafted. What was this?

"Ah well", he explained, "I'm just doing a little trial. I'm trying to find out whether it is possible to graft the big jungle mulberry onto the normal mulberry. You see I did four with tongue-grafting, four with lip-grafting, four with bud-grafting, and four or five others in various ways. Tongue-grafting seems to work best".

"But why?", I asked. "What's the use of this, and what is 'jungle-mulberry'?" "I'll show you", he said. Off we went into the high forest, where Manbir showed me a huge tree; sure enough, lying around under the tree were the remains of very large mulberry fruits. It seemed the monkeys had been through the tree-tops. "You see, this type of tree bears very big fruits very similar to the mulberries we have around our fields for fodder purposes. The fruits are very sweet, and the kids know each and every tree and come together to pick up the fallen fruits from the ground. Unfortunately, the tree grows so tall, it is very difficult to reach the fruit up there. Watching the kids I suddenly had an idea. I climbed up and got myself a branch and then grafted it onto the small mulberry, which never grows tall even if you never cut it for fodder. I'm trying to see whether it might be possible in this way to have a smaller tree with those same big sweet fruits. We shall see. Maybe it works, maybe it doesn't. If it works, I have absolutely no doubt about the interest in the villages for planting such grafted trees. You should come here when the kids try to bring down fruit by throwing stones!"

Home-made rower-pump

I was rowing a rower-pump and I couldn't believe my eyes. Water was coming out of a well about six metres deep with a fairly decent splash, and away it trickled to some vegetable plots nearby. The farmer was grinning in delight, and his kids ran around squirting the water from the discharge pipe, even his wife interrupted her weaving to come and have a look at this outsider who wouldn't believe they had a working rower-pump. Well, well, well, I knew exactly what a rower-pump was and how it worked. And some time back, I had actually had the idea to somehow get hold of rower-pumps because they could make a big impact on the income of many poor households on the river plain, which had no irrigation water. However, the engineers in the technical training centre in the capital had all told me that the pumps had to be imported because certain vital parts could not be produced in the country. So I forgot about them, and frankly didn't believe the people who had come to tell me there were rower-pumps working in the neighbouring district. But here I was, with a rower-pump produced in the village itself, and I myself was rowing it.

The manager of the local branch of the Agricultural Bank had been told the same thing by the engineers. Soon after having arrived at his new post, he had made a tour through the store of the bank, and had found a machine nobody understood, but which was said to be an imported pump. He found a clever farmer who said he would like to find out how it worked. Unfortunately I could not meet this farmer, so the bank manager explained what happened next. After a few weeks he went to see the farmer, who was pumping water. The bank manager immediately saw the potential this could have, and asked at headquarters where more such pumps could be found. "Sorry", was the reply. "They have to be imported and cannot be produced in the country." He did not give up, but went to the farmer and asked him if he could copy the machine. Well, he would try. "I then found some funds to buy materials that the farmer needed for copying the machine. We both agreed they had to be readily available materials, without having to bother headquarters for supplies. So he went to work. He replaced the steel pipes with polythene pipes, which took several attempts to figure out. Some parts in the valves he simply cut in hard wood instead of cast iron which wasn't available. The biggest headache proved to be the surge-chamber, but eventually it turned out that we could even replace the steel with an earthen pot stuck on top of the pipe, with a wet cloth as a seal. So now he's produced somewhere around 20 such pumps in the last year, which we immediately financed through credit for small farmers out on the plain. It has turned out to be a very good investment. The credits are all being paid back, and these people are making a decent cash-income for the first time in their lives selling vegetables in the local market."

Well, I had something to say to those engineers who had told me they couldn't produce rower-pumps cheap enough because they needed imported cast-iron parts. They too were surprised, and after my explanation of how these adapted pumps were constructed, they insisted that this kind of model would definitely have up to 30% less efficiency. "So what", I replied, "that information is absolutely irrelevant for the actual workings of the system out there in the plains, with the delighted farmer and his splashing kids."

What triggers the innovative process?

Innovative processes are triggered by trying out new things and not by analysing the situation. Before starting to try out something, did any of these farmers analyse their situation rationally? They certainly knew about their situation, but did they consciously and fully analyse it before doing something? I don't think so. I believe it is much more helpful to assume that the expertise farmers have about the system they are living in is largely of an intuitive nature. In other words, they never need to analyse fully their system, and do not work with the notion of system in the sense in which the scientist uses the term. But they constantly assess chances and ideas against the backdrop of their intuitive understanding of their own situation. By intuitive I mean that it is much more helpful to ask "what would happen if this or that thing were possible", than to ask "tell us how you make a living". This is situational knowledge as I understand it; that is, only when I imagine a particular situation, can I start to understand what changes this imagined situation would make to the circumstances in which I am living. A precise question or a precise challenge, an interesting piece of new information, or a precisely defined supposed chance triggers the knowledge about the probable interactions with all the relevant variables in the system.

On the other hand, a 'let's fully understand this system first before we suggest any sort of action' approach, tends to draw a blank. Of course, in retrospect, the villagers will always be able to point out clearly the workings of the situation which led them to take a certain course of action. Their explanations usually make a lot of rational sense. The alpine farmer, in particular, could point out very neatly the systemic reasons why he is ranching now. This seems, however, to be a rationality emerging only after the fact. When I ask, "How did the idea of doing it in this new way actually develop?", the process no longer appears to be so analytically straightforward.

I'm now quite sure the process is largely intuitive, has to be intuitive, because there is no way a rational analysis can cover all the complexities and heterogeneity of any given livelihood system. So how do ideas happen? Not, I believe, by starting from a rational analysis of the 'system' or larger situation. I believe it more likely to be the other way round: that sudden ideas throw light on a system or situation from various angles. The workings of the system become known by trying to find out the effect of any practical idea against the backdrop of the situational knowledge of the farmers.

Discovering interesting things that work

The concept of 'problem' follows much the same logical pattern as that of system or situation analysis. Did Gom Bahadur Gaha define his problem clearly before he started figuring out how to use a sprinkler? Which 'problem' did the alpine farmer have clearly defined in his head, before he started getting interested in Scottish bulls? What was the 'problem' that prompted that bankmanager to look for a clever farmer to rebuild the pump with other materials? Did Manbir have a 'problem' nicely formulated before he climbed that tree to get that grafting material? I doubt it. Of course, in retrospect it is easy to define a problem which can then justify the actions having been undertaken, and doing so is very helpful for understanding how the system works.

But it was not problem definitions which led to solutions, it was the ideas and their implementation which in retrospect help us now to define the problems. I know this contradicts everything I was taught during my training in scientific procedures, but during my contacts with innovative farmers I had to change, and learn to appreciate their ways of doing and exploring.

Or maybe we should get rid of the word problem altogether? Maybe what was going on in these examples was not the solving of any 'problem' whose definition was based on an accurate 'situation analysis'? I'm sure most readers would find similar examples in their own experiences or even in their own innovative behaviour. Maybe it was rather the discovery of an interesting thing which tickled the curiosity of a farmer. And while doing the things required for stilling that curiosity, s/he comes across the opportunities for change that the new thing might bring to the system s/he is living in, and immediately the situational knowledge triggers all sorts of reinforcing arguments in terms of 'problems' and 'systems-workings' in support of continuing the exploration of the new thing.

Useful concepts

The power of using the right wording is evident in our work and I no longer believe in talking the language of 'situation analysis' and 'problem identification' when working with farmers (and often not even with extensionists or administrators). To me, the way we have been trained rationally to perform problem analysis is a particular approach that reductionist science has developed and is too limited in real-life situations. It is maybe all well and fine when we function as disciplined scientists, but that is not the way any one of us thinks and acts in daily life. Maybe the best ideas in science do not come this way, either. Certainly villagers do not think and act like that, and neither should they be asked to. When we tell farmers they should first analyse a problem before figuring out an experiment, we are running the same basic academic model as the positivist researcher. That is a pity, because then we leave out the rich situational, experiential and other knowledge of villagers, which can best be triggered through concrete ideas for action. I have therefore switched over to talking in terms of 'exploration' and 'knowledge sharing' with increasingly better results, getting situational knowledge and science to interact.

So where does that leave scientists, researchers and extensionists with a background of reductionist and positivist science? I am convinced those scientific skills still have a use, even when interacting with villagers. Our knowledge may likewise contribute to defining clear-cut problems and analysing situations. We must remain capable of setting up trials and of describing systemic interactions in a retrievable manner. However, we must regard reductionist science as only one, albeit important, window for viewing and reflecting upon the livelihood systems which villagers operate. It will remain an important window but not the only window. And it can and will lead to important innovations. Villagers have another view, and perceive their lives from their own situational knowledge, which produces all kinds of interesting ideas and information. This view, too, is important, and my experience suggests that it leads to breakthroughs which would be impossible looking through the science window only (remember the engineers telling me it was impossible to construct a rower-pump without cast iron). The challenge for both villagers and outsiders is to be able to communicate through their different windows. This will lead to an even more enhanced learning process. The example of the rower-pump is a good one: the physics of it are somewhat complicated, and it would never have been developed without solid scientific engineering. Imagine, however, if the developing engineers had been in close contact with some innovative village craftsmen when they were building the first prototypes. No doubt the blueprints then would not have insisted on cast iron parts for the valves. The pump would have spread much more quickly, and that bank manager would never have been given the reply that it was too complicated to produce in the country.

What does this mean for conducting PTD?

I suggest here that participatory technology development (PTD) cannot tap the vast resources of village knowledge and experience if it sticks to the academic procedure of situation analysis, problem definition, experimental design. For me PTD is *not* that. PTD is the method which allows all kinds of people, outsiders and villagers, to generate ideas and explore their importance and usefulness for their own livelihood situations and circumstances: what's this? can we make it work? let's try it out and see what comes of it, maybe it will turn out to be useful.

The challenge for the scientifically trained in PTD is to nurture and encourage ideas, including their own, so that eventual and existing farmer experiments will elicit the maximum information about livelihood situations and the changes these may undergo as a result of implementing ideas. For this they need to learn to explore like villagers. They need to be open to all kinds of knowledge and see this as valid.

The challenge for villagers in such PTD is to think an idea through while implementing it, thereby reflecting in a more systematic way about their livelihood situation in order to make short-cuts in the learning process. For this they need to learn to formulate their intentions in a clearer way.

There are challenges for all those involved in developing PTD methodology. Cross cultural communication, for scientist and villager, is not easy. It requires good 'people skills', which technical scientists are perhaps not the best placed to develop; these are maybe more abundant among extensionists whose success in the field depends on them. But for all concerned, the most crucial skill is the ability to create and facilitate interactive situations in such a way that the explorative pragmatism of villagers can be married to the analytical skills of scientists.

2. The craft of farming and experimentation

photo: Arthur Stolzenbach

Arthur Stolzenbach [1]

[1] Arthur Stolzenbach, De Zevenhoeven 26, 1963 SG Heemskerk, The Netherlands.

The heart of participatory technology development (PTD) lies in strengthening the capacity of farmers to experiment and innovate. To do this, however, PTD practitioners must have some idea of how farmers already experiment and develop new technologies.

For some years, World Neighbors (WN) has been working with farmers in Sanando, a semi–arid region of Mali (see the chapter by Gubbels in this volume). Following the approach described by Bunch (1985) and Gubbels (1988), WN has introduced simple inno-vations, stimulated and assisted farmers to experiment with them, and organized meetings of farmers from different villages to discuss the results. WN felt, however, that if the field staff do not understand the logic and methods of the farmers' own experiments, i.e. those that are defined, controlled, implemented and evaluated by farmers using their own inputs and doing their own observations, there is a danger of imposing 'better' ways of experimenting that do not fit the local sociocultural context and would be dropped as soon as the support pro-gramme withdrew. I was, therefore, asked to investigate the nature of farmer–experimentation in the villages where WN was active.

Since the aim of the research was to explore new concepts and build new hypotheses, qualitative methods were used, mainly unstructured interviewing. During the initial inter-views, it emerged that, in the Bambara language, the farmers have a word, *shifleli,* that means 'doing something and looking closely at the results'. This seemed to be fairly close to my idea of experimentation. Trained as an agronomist, I regarded an experiment as an action under-taken with the explicit purpose of learning from it. Consequently, it should be undertaken in such a way as to be able to learn the most from it.

I continued the interviews, using two strategies: (1) asking farmers directly if they had ever done *shifleli.* If they had, we discussed the whens, hows and whys of the practice; (2) follow-ing the history of crops and trying to reconstruct how changes in farming practices had taken place. The assumption here was that experimentation, in no matter what form, can lead to changes in the techniques applied. By asking about crop histories, I could discover experi-menting activities in an indirect way, even if the farmers were not conscious that they had been doing what I would consider to be experimentation. This approach led mainly into dis-cussions with older men; in Sanando they are the ones who manage the farm and cherish agricultural knowledge. Initially, I tried to find out about the nature of *shifleli* on the basis of some clear cases. However, as I continued my investigations and regarded *shifleli* within the wider context of innovation, various new dimensions of farmers' experimentation emerged, and I was forced to relativize some of my initial concepts.

The nature of *shifleli*

When farmers were asked what they meant by *shifleli,* they most commonly spoke about close observation, showing or proving something to others, checking what others say, and comparing something known with something unknown. The range of topics was broad, and grew mainly out of the farmers' appreciation of changing circumstances and opportunities. For example, one test involved seeking the right sowing date for a variety of cowpea (*Vigna unguiculata*). This date is important because cowpea is highly susceptible to a severe lack or surplus of rain, especially at the time of flowering. Another farmer tested to see if post–harvest losses in his granary could be reduced by treatment with a certain insecticide. Most *shifleli*, however, involved the testing of new crop varieties.

When asked about the most important aspects of *shifleli*, the farmers were vague, specifying not much more than that it had to be something useful for real–life, practical situations. Nevertheless, in their stories about change and, indirectly, about cases of *shifleli*, certain implicit criteria emerged. These appeared to be linked closely with different kinds of experimentation, distinguished by Schön (1983) in his study of the rationality of practitioners. Each kind has its own logic and criteria for success and failure. Schön distinguishes between:

- exploratory experiments: doing something new just to see what will happen, without any attempt to predict the results
- hypothesis–testing experiments: taking action with already some expectations about the results of the action. The purpose is to test the assumptions underlying the expectations. The experiment succeeds when one or more of the competitive hypotheses formulated to explain the same phenomenon is proved inferior
- move–testing experiments: taking action with the purpose of making a desired change in the environment. Schön gives the example of a chess player who moves his pawn with the purpose of protecting his king, although he cannot oversee all the consequences of this move. The experiment is successful if the results of the action, with all its consequences, are considered positive, even though the underlying hypotheses and assumptions may be incorrect and the results may be quite different from those expected. The move is nevertheless confirmed. For example, if the chess player accidentally checkmates his opponent by this move, he would not withdraw the pawn because the result is not what he had expected.

These different aspects of experimentation become clearer if we look at some specific cases of *shifleli*.

Experimenting with fertilizer

Solo Keta had sown two plots with groundnuts. The plots differed only in the application of fertilizer: none in one plot, and mineral fertilizer in the other. In the fertilized plot, the vegetative growth of the groundnut plants was much stimulated, as Solo had expected from what he had seen earlier, when cereals had been fertilized. In this case, however, he became anxious that, after flowering, the gynophore (the downward–stretching stalk that contains the growing seed) might not be able to reach the soil and then would not produce seed. He intervened by earthing up the plants in the fertilized plot. After the harvest, Solo was very satisfied with the higher yield on the fertilized plot. The taste, however, did not please him. This would not be a major problem if he were to sell the groundnuts, but the market for cotton was more interesting so, in the end, he decided not to continue applying fertilizer, because it was not worth the cost and the additional work of earthing up.

Farmers' research in practice: Lessons from the field

Experimenting with varieties

The first time a farmer of Koyan saw sunan *(a short variety of millet) in a field, he went to speak with the owner, who told him that this particular variety could be harvested early and yielded well. Since the farmer had noticed that the length of the rainy season had decreased in the last few years, he was very interested. He asked for and received a handful of seed to try out. Back home, he decided to sow at the closest spacing used by the people of his village when sowing millet: four hand widths. The new variety indeed produced well; the farmer commented, however, that 'the taste is not so good, nor the colour. When it is cooked it is somewhat black.' As he thought that the yield could probably be improved by increasing the plant density, he reduced the spacing of seed the next year. This time, he sowed large plots. Each year, he reduced the spacing a little bit more, until one year the spacing had become too narrow. In the end, the optimum spacing for sowing in his fields proved to be more or less two hand widths.*

When Solo Keta started his groundnut experiment, he was taking the first step gradually to changing the way he managed his farm. He soon had to reconsider the effects of his action and intervene during the process in order to achieve his vaguely defined goal of 'achieving better groundnut production by applying fertilizer'. This move–testing experiment was completed when he negated the results, with all the consequences, and decided not to continue with the idea. The farmer from Koyan did his move–testing experiment in response to a perceived change in climate, in order to see if he could harvest earlier. After the new millet variety had been harvested, cooked and eaten, he affirmed his move. He then changed the goal to finding the optimum spacing between plants and continued his move–testing experiments.

The actions of Solo Keta and the farmer from Koyan can also be explained as exploratory experiments that cause farmers 'to appreciate things in the situation that go beyond their initial perception of the problem' (Schön 1983). They were confronted with new things they had not foreseen. Solo had not realized that the ovaries of the plant might not be able to reach the ground. The farmer from Koyan had thought that, besides trying a new variety, there might also be room for improvement by changing the planting distance.

Both cases involved also some aspects of hypothesis–testing. The farmers based their initial statements of the problem on numerous assumptions and (implicit) hypotheses, which had to be reframed during the course of the *shifleli*. Solo's hypothesis that fertilizing groundnuts would increase the yield was confirmed. But his assumption that fertilized groundnuts could be cultivated in the same way as non–fertilized groundnuts was not. The Koyan farmer's assumption that a four–hands' sowing distance for the short millet would give the best results was questioned. This led to a new hypothesis that 'closer might be better'. He waited for the next season to change the treatment, but Solo changed the treatment during the course of one growing season. By earthing up, he proved his hypothesis that fertilized groundnuts yield more.

This contrasts radically with the scientific approach to testing an hypothesis, which consists in trying to disprove it. The farmers are themselves part of the situation they are studying and have direct and immediate interest in improving that situation. Agronomists have to describe their methods and findings in a way that conforms with formal scientific norms. Learning and decision–making are separated in the scientific model of problem–solving. First, detailed analyses are made to gain insight into the situation. Experimentation can begin only when the reality has been simplified to such an extent that a clearly defined problem is separated out. To the farmer, these analyses are often too rigid and long; his/her interest is in understanding what is happening in the real and complex circumstances of production.

What makes an experiment successful?

Experimenting farmers try to understand the situation by changing something and reflecting on the results. In both of the above cases, it is clear that the most important criterion for success was that the new technique, with all its consequences, should improve the farmer's situation. Although, in their attempts to improve their situation, the experimenting farmers deliberately tried to prove their assumptions, this does not mean that they created self–fulfilling prophecies. The environment resists total manipulation and gives feedback, to which the experimenting farmers were receptive.

When farmers have tested a technique once on a small field, they usually gain enough information to decide whether to reject the technique or to test it the next year on a larger field, possibly under slightly different circumstances. They look for explanations when the new technique does not work out to their satisfaction. Factors that unintentionally have a positive influence on the results are not regarded as disturbing interferences. Whether the farmer can find an explanation for negative results will influence further action, as in the case of Salia Diarra:

Repetition of an experiment

Salia Diarra is one of the few farmers who sometimes repeats an experiment on a small scale before deciding whether or not to reject a variety. If a new variety performs well in his first small–scale test, he then sows it on a larger scale, irrespective of the reasons for the success. If the new variety performs poorly and he cannot explain why, he rejects it. If it performs poorly but he can attribute this to unfavourable conditions, he repeats the experiment on a small scale. Schematically, his decisions can be presented as follows:

Assessment of the results of experiment	Explicable with local knowledge?	Further action
Desired	no	variety accepted
Undesired	yes	variety rejected
Undesired	no	test

43

In the above example, the move–testing aspect of experimentation was more important to the farmer than the hypothesis–testing. In contrast to scientific experimentation, the changes during the course of farmers' experiments are not regarded as faults but rather as the very essence of the success of the experiment (Schön 1983). Especially in regions like Sanando, where farming is characterized by variability and unpredictability, it is more important to be able to reframe the problem to the changing situation, and to act accordingly, than to test a hypothesis thoroughly.

How farmers explain their results

From a scientific viewpoint, a major difficulty of field experiments is that the results are affected by numerous circumstances that cannot be controlled. In Sanando the outcome of farming, and of farmers' experiments, is heavily influenced by such factors as soil fertility, erosion, damage by birds and insects, and variability in the quantity and timing of rainfall. Agronomists try to separate out the effects by using statistical analysis and by designing and implementing the experiments according to the requirements of this type of analysis. If, in the course of the experiment, something changes that does not fit into the way they framed the problem and chose the factors for the experiment, a valid analysis cannot be made.

Although farmers change the way they execute their experiments while they are doing them, they often claim that they can explain the factors that determine the results. A strength of farmers' experimentation is their frequent observation of their crops during the entire growing season. Experimenting farmers in Sanando observe parameters such as vigour and colour of the stem, leaf colour, plant height, size of seed, and times of germination and ripening. Looking back at the end of the season, they can point to a multitude of factors that could have influenced the yield. For instance, if the lower parts of the stems were reddish rather than dark green/greyish during their early growth, the soil fertility is probably low; also the kinds of weeds that grow indicate the soil–fertility status. A weakness in experimentation by farmers, however, is the limitation of their perception to directly observable phenomena.

To explain causes and effects, the farmers commonly make comparisons between different locations and treatments and also between variations within a treatment. For instance, if the average yield of a plot is not satisfactory, but plants in some places appear to be growing and yielding well, farmers conclude that the primary factor limiting growth is not the rain but rather soil fertility; if the yield is low in the entire field, rain is more likely to have been the limiting factor. The farmers regard spontaneous variation as a source for interpretation of the results. Interpretation is easier if comparisons can be made with reference plants or plots, as in the following case:

Comparison with a reference

Lassana has one variety of beans that is very sensitive to rain. If, during flowering, there is a cloudburst, the flowers will drop and the crop will not yield. If there is a shortage of rain, the sunlight will wither up the flowers and the crop will not yield. Lassana deliberately

makes use of this characteristic: 'Because this is the most delicate variety, I am able to know
why another variety has not yielded, by referring to this one.'

Experimenting as performance

The above four cases of *shifleli* could be easily identified as such, because they were isolated in place and/or time from the main production process. But then I found myself seeing
more *shifleli* than the farmers did, for instance, in Adama Diarra's yard:

'Just' mixing varieties

This year, Adama told me, he had done shifleli *in a corner of the garden. Indeed, in this*
small area, he had sown beans of a new variety. On the other side of the garden, however,
he had sown last year's beans with double spacing between rows and, one month later, in
between these rows, he had sown another variety of his beans. But, although he had never
before mixed two varieties of beans and sown them in between each other, he did not con-
sider this to be shifleli, *because he 'already knew the varieties from last year'. This year he*
had 'just tried to spread the time of harvest'. By chance, he had two varieties at his disposi-
tion and he had found it 'interesting just to mix them'. After some discussion, he agreed with
me that 'indeed, you can call it shifleli *if you want to'. He probably did not classify this lat-*
ter case as shifleli *because it was completely integrated into the production process and*
because it was more driven by intuition than by an explicit desire to learn. It was 'just
experience'.

In this case, defining an experiment as purposeful action for learning creates problems,
because Adama had different purposes at the same time with the same actions. Where
does an experiment start and where does it end? Maybe it never ends, and it is arbitrary to
set a limit. Experimentation is inherent to agriculture, because to practise agriculture means
to act, to judge and to adjust. For example, as soon as the rains start, a farmer tills the soil,
and if it looks as though the rains will continue, he sows. If the rains stop a few days after
germination, he may have to re–sow the fields. Maybe he will now choose another (perhaps
faster–growing) variety, or maybe he has no more seed and will let the field turn into pasture.

Thus, the farmer is improvising on a repertoire of different intertwining themes. Richards
(1989) calls this 'adaptive performance'; the process of improving this performance is
'learning'. Experimentation is a means of learning through practice. Even when farmers do
not design experiments deliberately, they frequently find themselves in spontaneous situations from which they learn merely by observing and discussing. It often happens, for example, that two farmers with adjacent fields cultivate the same crop, each in his own manner.
Different people working in the same field may cause different 'treatments': children may
sow with shorter spacing because they have short legs, or 'because they did not understand
the instructions properly'. A farmer may apply manure to only half of a field because he did
not have enough to cover the whole field. An open attitude to such situations, and keen

observation of the results, can lead to new insights. The need for explicit experimentation should not be over-rated.

Experiments as a setting for learning

Since the nature of farming is adaptive performance, farmers' experiments, even when deliberate, are not very systematic from a scientific viewpoint. The ambitions of participatory research to improve farmers' experimentation or conduct experiments that can serve both the farmer and the agricultural scientist appear to be over-optimistic, at least in the case of Sanando. Farmers and scientists have different goals. 'Scientification' of farmers' experiments would miss the point (van der Ploeg 1987). Flexibility and adaptive performance, both essential qualities of successful farming, do not always combine well with systematization.

In addition to providing an opportunity to develop and explore farming techniques, however, experimentation can also serve as a linkage mechanism to improve communication. When demonstrating and discussing their experiments, farmers are stimulated to make their knowledge (and its implications) explicit and, thus, exchangeable. This is important because the farmers' informal research is usually known only within the household or, at most, the extended family; and ethnic, class, gender or other differences may block a wider exchange of knowledge. The experience of WN in Mali shows that development organizations can serve as intermediaries, bringing experimenting farmers in contact with each other and with scientists.

Conclusions

The experimental activities of farmers can have, by the same actions and at the same time, the functions of exploration, hypothesis-testing and move-testing. Since agricultural production is more important to the farmer than research, move-testing takes precedence over the rigidity of hypothesis-testing. As the farmers judge their moves against their own norms and interests, their assessment of their experiments is highly subjective. Without being able to foresee all the consequences, farmers take decisions and actions to achieve their goals, and reflect on the results in order to improve their situation. This adaptive performance is based on reflection about chains of related operations and events during the production process. The management of a farm can be seen, in effect, as a series of (informal) experiments. Unlike scientists, farmers do not follow strictly a pre-established design for implementing their experiments. A crucial element is their ability to reframe the problem and to act in accordance with the changing situation. They do not regard these changes as faults; because of the prevalence of move-testing and because spontaneous variation provides valuable information, the changes can be the essence of the success of an experiment.

Experimentation must, therefore, be considered as a continuous innovative element in the craft of farming. If it can be isolated in time and space from the production process, it is given a name, like *shifleli*. If it is completely integrated into the production process, then it is 'just experience'. Farmers' experimentation has its own strength. A critical look must be taken at attempts to change it by introducing scientific methods, because the differences between farmers' and scientists' research extend far beyond differences in methods. The most important function of linking up with farmers' research in PTD is to promote social learning: to remove barriers to the exchange of knowledge between farmers and scientists and among farmers themselves.

References

Bunch, R. 1985. *Two ears of corn: A guide to people-centered agricultural improvement.* Oklahoma City, World Neighbors.

Gubbels, P. 1988. Peasant farmer agricultural self-development. *ILEIA Newsletter* 4 (3): 11-14.

Ploeg, J.D. van der. 1987. *De verwetenschappelijking van der landbouwbeoefening.* Wageningen Agricultural University.

Richards, P. 1989. Agriculture as a performance. In: Chambers, R., A. Pacey and L.A. Thrupp (eds), *Farmer first: Farmer innovation and agricultural research.* London, IT Publications, pp 39-43.

Schön, D.A. 1983. *The reflective practitioner: How professionals think in action.* New York, Basic Books.

3. Crazy but not mad

Henri Hocdé[1]

You have almost certainly heard about farmer experimentation going on somewhere or other. What is this phenomenon precisely? Should you want to verify in the field what you have heard, and you visit a plot where such experimentation is being carried out, you will be surprised: there are no visible signs of it. In most cases there is no neatly defined and squared–off area, and the experimenting farmers will not show you the tables, graphs and curves required to justify the title of experiment. The traditional signals that mark out 'experimentation' escape them. Should you continue your investigation, and discover supporting

[1] Henri Hocdé, (Researcher) CIRAD France, Member of the Dirección Ejecutiva Regional del Programa Regional de Reforzamiento a la Investigación Agronómica en Granos Básicos PRIAG. Convenio CORECA–UE/IICA, ALA 88/23, AP.55 Coronado 2200, Costa Rica.

specialists, they will not be professional researchers, but *técnicos*, the communicators, trainers, extension workers and promoters. Should you then call such work experimentation? Your curiosity is provoked. Something is certainly there. Let's take a further look.

In general, the farmer explaining his experiment is decisive, motivated and convinced, full of ideas and dynamism, someone who analyses his own work, wants to talk, to communicate, to learn and to teach. He tells you about himself, his plot, his neighbour, perhaps his group. His neighbours see him as an accomplished worker, industrious, honest, observant, curious, daring, conciliatory, a believer in God, not scared of failure, enterprising, a good father, self–confident, a leader, but not as experimenter or researcher.

What then is this process of experimentation? Is it a new fashion, like many of the others sent to Central America by some international institution or aid project from up North? or the tactic of some financial agency or international donor to frighten professional researchers into the belief that the new trend will take away their jobs and displace them from their traditional field of action? Perhaps it is a revival of anthropological romanticism from a new NGO generation? Is it a temporary phenomenon or is it the beginning of a more profound movement, of which we see only the tip of an iceberg?

When experimentation does not rhyme with farmer

We define two categories of actors related to farmer experimentation: the insiders, the farmers themselves, the agents directly involved in the process of farmer experimentation; and the outsiders, all those others who surround them.

To the outsiders, the mention of 'farmer experimentation' brings a variety of reactions: from surprise, query, fear, ironic smile, scorn, indifference, to enthusiasm, even conviction. Comments and questions such as the following are commonplace:

> *I have a university education and for me experimentation is measuring and comparing. Do the farmers who experiment use the same mental process as the researcher?*

> *I am confused about participative research and farmer experimentation. I know what the first one is, but the second is not clear to me. It gives the impression that the farmers are doing it by themselves whether the experts are present or not.*

Some expect the focus of farmer experimentation to be limited to the particular and to pertain only to the exclusive needs and use of the individual farmer, such as experimentation with domestic pesticides or herbicides, or a planting stick (*espequeadora* or *espeque)* used with animal traction, or a groover for perimeter potato–planting. These would qualify for many outsiders as farmer experimentation. They are the inventions of farmers, not the products and inventions that experts would devise or put on the market. Outsiders would not expect to put in this category experimentation with the introduction of a new crop that might generate a complete change in the production system. Take the example of a double problem such as *mustia* in beans and land erosion in a plot with a first planting of beans, followed by a second crop, maize. The solution chosen by the farmer, from his own tests, was a triple change: first planting of maize plus a combination of a second crop of beans with management of maize stubble. This provided a system where half the plots used the initial crop sequence, while the other half used the second sequence: maize followed by beans which climbed up the maize stalks. This solution entailed a complete change in the entire system of farm management.

There are outsiders who believe that the process of farmer experimentation should be strengthened, the scientific spirit of farmers be encouraged. They think that farmer experimentation stimulates an enrichment of farmers' collective intelligence, promotes their sense of criticism and sharpens their observation. They believe that, through experimentation, sustainability will become a component of farmers' culture and not only a survival strategy.

What do the insiders say? Everywhere in Central America farmers who have been experimenting on their own, or who have formed groups to continue their research with the support of extension and other services, tell a similar story. They do not see themselves as educated:

> *[We] farmers are not learned, much less in mathematics. Land is therefore our copybook, and the machete and the hoe are our pen. We try to take some measurements in order to compare.*

Or they mention their shortcomings:

> *In the beginning I tried new things in a disorderly manner, and at the end of the experiment I realized that I had not written anything down. Now I want to do things more systematically; I want to make comparisons with traditional ways. I want to write down data, carry records from the preparation of the land to the harvest so as to have exact information, to be surer and to tell others.*

They comment on their newly found knowledge and skills:

> *The ones who made me, a farmer, experiment are you my farmer friends, who visit me today. Who will benefit from this knowledge? My sons. What we can leave our children is knowledge and better land. The advances made in experimentation have helped us realize that we are capable of making changes, and of being more observant, capable of diversifying crops, of discovering new mixed-cropping systems, of organizing fields according to ecological conditions, preparing natural insecticides, forming groups to plan experiments and carry out follow-ups and evaluations. Our experimentation work is a complete process.*

This debate of ideas and contrasting opinions is not limited to Central America, my own place of work. It is being raised in the international research centres, financial agencies, external aid bodies, in short, in most fora. Many of those responsible for important research centres (such as the International Service for National Research (ISNAR) and the Northern universities) believe, and write, that to improve research it is preferable to assign funds and financing to the producer organizations and associations instead of to their own profession-al bodies. This way would provide the producer associations with real research capacity, which would enable them to negotiate with research centres.

What can we learn today about this still embryonic process?

My aim in this chapter is not to analyse in detail the numbers of farmers experimenting in Central America, either alone or with the support of others, or to dissect the strengths and weaknesses of their diverse experimentation. I concentrate instead on what I believe to be the main force lines of this process.

Let us look at what we understand by the terminology. Different expressions are used for a similar concept. One speaks of initiators, or of leading or experimenting farmers, but basi-cally they all amount to the same thing: they are farmers (individually or in groups) who have a way of operating in order to find solutions to their own problems. They have stopped wait-ing for salvation to come from outside their own sphere (whether from the expert, the state or commercial firms); but what, we might ask, is the novelty? Farmers have practised such a modality since the dawn of agriculture.

Farmer experimentation, first of all, denotes the farmer's own will, a certain attitude on the part of the farmer. It is he or she who will decide, despite the climate or any other circum-stance. The experimenting farmer behaves in a manner which proclaims: "I observed, I real-ized, I believe that, and therefore I am going to do". Such behaviour originates from a prob-lem that affects a farmer's crops or animals. S/He visualizes what could have caused the problem, s/he proposes an action to attack the cause and, finally, s/he observes closely if the test s/he conceived has worked. What s/he uses is in fact the scientific approach! In this sense, the experimenting farmer stands apart from the traditional or classic promoters of change, categories invented by an increasing number of institutions, with names as diversi-fied as agricultural representative, para–technician, front–line worker, facilitator, liaison pro-ducer, validating producer. Such farmers are already part of a conscious process of experi-mentation, although at times their practice tends to hide this. The same can be said of cer-tain experts, but in reverse. By being tied down to a rigid experimental carpentry, many lose sight of the actual investigative process.

For many years, Central American farmers have carried out their experiments discreetly, sometimes secretly and quietly, hiding them from the various experts who supposedly pro-vided them with technical assistance. Today, however, many such farmers are in the process of formalizing their work, in so doing, engaging the talents of the more progressive technical personnel. The farmers' initiatives are becoming increasingly better known, and it is here that the innovation to which I refer lies.

Farmer experimentation can achieve two important goals:

- It can solve a farmer's problems, though often only partially. The experimenters demon-strate a margin of improvement and technical progress in small– and medium–scale farm-ing. They are seeking to reduce costs and thus use cheaper technologies. Many of them no longer go to town to buy basic foods. They have improved their homes and fixed their fences. They survive. With more favourable economic policies, many of them could enter into an accumulation process.

- Through their experiments, farmers generate and increase the range of important technological options available to them. Availability is, without doubt, the most important element for them. It is not enough for them to know that this or that technique has been validated and retested; they have to be able to afford it in order to be able to apply it on their own plots. The options open to them may relate to soil conservation, the use of legumes for green manure and/or cover crops for human and animal consumption, improving the fertility of their arable land (using stubble or manure), fertility (breakdown of different source of nitrogen), comparing basic grain varieties, using commercial crops and products for diversifying, animal traction (equipment and animal training), pest control (domestic pesticides and seeds treatments) or the production of seed.

Such experimentation allows farmers to create new cropping systems, to intensify soil use, and to stress the management of natural resources and crops. Of course, these important changes take place at the expense of an increased work load, or at the expense of their productivity, the evolution of which has still to be quantified. This process generates a certain optimism about revitalizing the technical components of hillside agriculture. What diminishes the initial optimism is the economic aspect (which, of course, has to be taken into account).

Current trends, as observed through their experiments and practice, show, for example, an increased use of the planting stick (*espeque* or *chuzo)* in hillside agriculture. For many outsiders, this archaic tool should be eradicated if we want agricultural progress. Instead of disappearing, however, this instrument is making a substantial come–back in these times of acute crisis. We could almost talk of a current '*espeque*ization' though this does not mean that the farmer's experimentation discards the use of animal traction, on the contrary. '*Espeque*ization' uses a modern *espeque* technique, modern because of the work tasks that accompany its use (soil–erosion control measures, the recovery of soil fertility), and because of the combination of old and new technologies (such as the use of hybrid material). For example, when combining the use of the *espeque* with gramoxone (paraquat) and hybrid material we are talking of maize yields of 6000 kg/ha. The use of the *espeque* values the resource most available to the farmer, his manpower. In many places tractors (and sometimes animal traction) have been abandoned because of the negative effects of ploughing on soil erosion and the need to preserve stubble to produce organic material. Experimenting farmers in Central America consider the introduction of sowers using animal traction, manufactured especially to sow over cover crops, such as those built by the ingenious Brazilians of Parana and Santa Catalina States, as an option for overcoming this technical constraint and for reversing the productivity decrease of their work. In this rethinking of agriculture, the recommendations and prescriptions of the past decades (ploughing, significant doses of chemical fertilizer only, etc.) are giving way to a combination of technologies and to a technical and economic rationalization of their use and management.

Fertile symbiosis between farmer–experimenters and experts

The experience of PRIAG (*Programa Regional de Reforzamiento a la Investigación Agronómica*) in its basic grains programme offers a novel angle of attack within this general panorama. One of the programme's strategies was to strengthen the farmers' research capability, working, if possible, in groups or associations (promoter groups, local research committees, technical committees of producer associations) under the control of the community and supported by professionals. The aim was not to motivate innovating farmers to be better observers and experimenters on their own, but where possible to consolidate and strengthen their ability as creators of knowledge and technology by working in close cooperation and symbiosis with *técnicos* of whatever institutional affiliation (public sector, universities, NGOs, private sector). Placing the expertise of the professionals at the service of farmer–experimenter groups was a methodological challenge for PRIAG. Here, *técnico* is used as a generic term to refer, without differentiation, to agricultural researcher, extension worker or trainer. *Técnicos* act as facilitators.

'Scope' and 'flexibility' were the most determining words for PRIAG in its new orientation: to find a working methodology that would give sufficient scope to the technical personnel of the various work teams, and at the same time, a methodology that, apart from offering broad scope and enticing perspectives, would offer the flexibility to suit local social dynamics.

I will not mention here the numerous benefits to be gained by technical personnel from working with farmer–experimenters once they see and are convinced that *they* [the experimenting farmers] are also a part of the solution. I will, instead, limit myself to mentioning some of the contributions, with examples, of technical personnel to the process of farmer experimentation.

Helping farmers organize and communicate

The first example is associated with the initial identification of farmer–experimenters in the different geographical areas covered by PRIAG. The technical team's central goal was to organize, over a period of several days, an exchange–meeting of farmers in their zone, at which only the farmers would be allowed to speak.

The *técnicos'* starting–point for their search was their traditional clientele, the natural leaders, but they discovered that experimenting farmers and natural leadership do not necessarily coincide, and they moved rapidly on to discovering innovative farmers outside this group. Each participant was to explain his work to those invited. The rules of the game were clear: the farmer would explain and the audience would analyse the exposition, in subgroups, according to the technical, methodological and organizational aspects of the experiments, and would finally give the speaker their thoughts, comments and suggestions.

There are two ingredients for the success of such an event: the creation of a climate of trust between farmers and professionals, and the provision of a framework in which to present the innovations and ideas. Of course, technical personnel need to take some steps in advance. They must: (1) identify innovative farmers; (2) draft/edit with them a document relating to their experiments; (3) help them prepare their public talk; and (4) create methodological guidelines for the event itself. Such steps are intended not as a straitjacket but rather as a guiding instrument. The exchange–meeting is for farmer–experimenters to explain their activities and to share their practices; it is not an exercise to initiate, promote or implement a project foreign to the farmers. It starts from what farmers *do* rather than what they say. It must be stressed, however, that the meetings were conceived, promoted and organized by the technical teams, who acted on a voluntary basis and not from any feeling of obligation.

From this beginning, farmers enter into more formal experimentation. As part of their support work, the researchers taught farmers the experimental process and practised its implementation with them. The farmers renewed their traditional focus of communication and diffusion of knowledge, of knowing, doing, analysing, reflecting, planning. In the last two years, the work teams have dedicated themselves primarily to increasing farmers' knowledge and then to modifying the design of their experiments, improving the management of their trials, reinforcing the organization of experimenting groups and, only in a modest way, modifying the subjects for experimentation. Support for farmer experimentation was provided as much in circulating information as in improving experimental management techniques. This induced a change in the tasks assigned to technical staff, or as one researcher clearly pointed out in a workshop between *técnicos* and farmers:

> *Técnicos always want to make the farmers change their way of planting; it is better to change the methodology for evaluating the ways farmers experiment than to change their way of planting! Give them some seeds, let them plant the seeds their way (late or early association, in relays, etc.) and then evaluate.*

The técnicos organize days for the local dissemination of trial results to the wider community, and hold discussions at district level with farmers and *técnicos* regarding the results, or arrange an exchange of experimenting farmers between different countries in Central America.

Helping farmers' groups to experiment

Progress in organizing farmer–experimenter groups proceeds according to the rhythm, degree of progress and dynamism of the actors of each geographical area, as well as to the characteristics of each country. Of course, farmers do not usually form groups in order to experiment, they do this generally in order to obtain credit, to get better prices or sale facilities for their products, to rent land, or to guarantee social security for their families. But in several cases they did group in order to experiment. This form of grouping can help farmers achieve their objectives as producers, but it is not a cure–all.

In Baja Verapaz, Guatemala, experimenters accepted the suggestion of technicians to establish their own CIAL (*Centros de Investigación Agrícola Locales;* see Ashby 1991, and Ashby et al., this publication). There are now ten of these, with 4 to15 farmers in each. All have a formal structure (president, treasurer, secretary, spokesperson) and members are volunteers. Based on diagnoses made by their community, members draw up and design trials to tackle the problems identified, carry them out individually, and together analyse and interpret the results, and plan experiments for the following year. The *técnicos* stressed the need for more reliable data and, after negotiations, the experimenting farmers accepted this argument and increased their number of trials. For this purpose, they sought to increase the members of their CIAL. In one case, they invented a cross between CIALs of different communities; half the members of one CIAL carrying out the same experiment as half of the other. Since during a trial members of a CIAL visited all the experimental fields, this obliged them to leave their own community, which broadened the dissemination of their work. From a constraint there emerged an opportunity.

In another community, five farmer–experimenters, founders of a first–generation CIAL, rented land near their village which they named the Farmer Experimentation Centre to perform their own trials. Repetitions of each of these experiments were being carried out simultaneously by other farmers on their hillside plots. The five farmers considered themselves the consultants of the others. They lent part of the rented land to a researcher from the government research centre to carry out experiments on subjects jointly defined (best cutting date for sorghum, plant density). We observed five different levels of inter–relation; (1) among the five consultant farmer–experimenters; (2) between them and their collaborators carrying out the replications; (3) between them and the researcher; (4) between them and their neighbours, and (5) between the group and all these actors. The tasks of the *técnicos* supporting the farmer–experimenters were clear: participating in CIAL meetings, helping in the preparation of experimenters' projects, presenting the researchers' projects to CIAL members in the village itself, following the trials at the Farmer Experimentation Centre, participation in the sowing of experiments there, collaborating directly in promoting CIAL activities, and analysing results.

The difficulties encountered

The last example, below, highlights the technical content of activities and illustrates the difficulties for the *técnicos* in providing the level of support so highly demanded by the farmers. The Baja Verapaz farmers are experimenting with organic methods of fertilization, using their own farms and the land resources of the community. The diversity in the ways of dealing with organic materials is reflected in Table 3.1.

To date, the contribution of the *técnicos* has been limited to the chemical analyses of different samples of organic fertilizer. They have been unable to do more to advise the farmers on this theme. The farmers are pushing their researchers to the limit, but must largely fend for themselves, lamenting the wide gap between their technological needs and what is offered them. One would have every reason to believe that the major contribution of the experts to the experimenting farmer would be of a technical order, but here is the Central American paradox: the meeting point between experimenting farmers and *técnicos* is more in the methodological and organizational sphere than in the techno–scientific.

Table 3.1. Combinations practised by the Baja Verapaz experimenting farmers in the organic fertilization of their crops

Organic fertilizer used	Application methods	Chemical fertilizer	Crops
Manure, ash and hen droppings	applied to plants	T15 Urea	improved maize/beans native maize/native beans
Manure, ash and hen droppings	applied to furrows	T15 sulphate	native maize
Compost (processed by farmers)		T15 urea	improved and native maize
Stubble and compost (processed by farmers)	applied to plants		hybrid maize
Compost (processed by farmers)	applied to plants		improved beans
Stubble, manure, and hen droppings	applied to plants		maize/native sorghum
Compost (processed by farmers)	applied to furrows		sorghum/beans
Hen droppings, ash, lime	foliate		improved and native beans
Hen droppings, manure, ash, lime, folidol	foliate		improved and native beans

Experimentation gives strength and dynamism to farmers

The wide variety of trials being undertaken shows the extent of the farmer–experimentation universe. Trials are carried out by all age groups (12-78 years), by both sexes and under every condition: alone or in groups, against the husband, or with the support of the community. In some zones, the emergence of experimentation by women is noticeable. Experimenters often try to involve their families. Experimentation escapes the strict limits of the field to embrace many subjects, not only in agriculture but also in cattle–breeding and kitchen gardens, not only in basic cereals but also in vegetables. They want to try something different from their neighbours in order to convince them of the need for change.

The innovators acquire the conviction that they are rediscovering one of the basic functions of the farmer: to protect, create and improve their patrimony, their land. They participate in an active search to enhance the fertility of their soil, to recover the productive capacity of their fields. At a time when institutions are worried about sustainability, is this mere coincidence or a convergence of the stars?

Farmers are believing more in themselves, in their ability, in their strengths. The experiments are theirs: "Maybe the experiment is not perfect but it is mine." They have a better control of their traditional system of work. Experimenting stimulates farmers to break away from routine crop systems: "I am looking at my experiments and those of my neighbours and I am expanding my mind .... I want to leave the prison of ignorance ...", many of them say. Measuring, observing more closely, comparing, looking for the cause of a problem, sharing results with others (farmers and experts) are elements that are taking root in this critical spirit, and in farmers' decision−making. They are not waiting around for others to come and help them; they are breaking away from the chain of physical and mental dependence. Man is not developed, he develops himself. Farmers are participating in the construction of something new and feeling happy and proud to be discovering new horizons, to be broadcasting their work and teaching their neighbours (organizing their own field−days, seminars to report back results to their communities, holding training workshops), to be satisfying their thirst for knowledge. They have passed the stage of knowing, but doing little about the problems that affected their crops and their fields (erosion, decrease of fertility and yield), to a stage where they act, move and experiment. They are becoming aware that they can change and revert trends. This leap is fundamental.

Experimentation becomes a powerful tool for acquiring knowledge. Farmers recite repeatedly that learning is not only exchanging and receiving knowledge, but also putting it into practice. They do this through their experiments. Acquiring knowledge is not only receiving information about the specific technical results of the experiments. It is also reflection and analysis regarding the experimentation process: formulating a problem, implementing an action, observing the results of the action and interpreting and explaining what was observed. These two types of final products of farmer experimentation are not readily distinguishable and can sometimes appear confusing.

Combining innovation, experimentation and communication

Farmer experimentation goes beyond the field trial. Research has several stages that combine three elements: innovation, experimentation and communication. To innovate one has to be aware of technical, economic, social and organizational change not only in one's plot, but in the total production unit and even in the region. To experiment is to be aware of measuring, observing, recording, processing and analysing data, comparing, explaining and quantifying; it requires accuracy and reliability. To communicate is one of the indispensable pillars of farmer experimentation.

For a farmer, to experiment is to solve a problem. As the astonished professionals say, farmers experiment out of need (thus differentiating them from researchers, who experiment because it is their job). They are more interested in looking for solutions than in discovering how the black box works or what the agricultural inter−relationships are. They are aware that testing requires accuracy, meticulous and detailed work, more care and attention than that given to the cultivation of their commercial crops. Their dedication to experimentation entails a cost, a sacrifice in time and effort:

> *While preparing the material, I left for the field, I arrived there, I did the work. In this trial of different varieties, I spent 4 hours to plant 1/2 a* cuartilla *(quarter of a plot) ...*

> *One makes sacrifices, neglecting one's commercial crops, working the trial plots separately; cleaning, weighing, recording the beans separately, writing down the number of pods ...*

One will also hear:

> *But it is nice taking records; one can say things more clearly, learn more about the causes, the result is more efficient. Experimenting is not only toiling away. One shares the techniques and knowledge ...*

Many of these experimenters record in their log books the exact amount of additional time taken, which varies according to the nature of the experiment. These data are highly relevant; with them, the experimenter is able to separate the traditional manpower cost of a planting activity from the cost of the additional time required by an experiment. Such information is of both short- and medium-term help. In the short term it can be used to plan work for the next agricultural cycle; in the medium term, and for those farmers seeking financial support, who are anxious about the prospects and sustainability of their work, such information helps to justify the cost of this additional time, whatever the financial source (Ministry of Agriculture, NGO, development projects or contributions from their own association).

Innovation and experimentation: different but complementary

All the farmer-experimenters of any particular group carry out more than one test on their farms, and some as many as five or six, or more. They generally manage them with the whole of their production unit, consciously or unconsciously integrating in this way the diversity of their trials. In such cases experimentation quickly accelerates the innovation and change process. It is not unusual to see farms transformed by their owners in a short time (2-4 years) into mini-experimental stations or farms with a totally renovated outlook. Farmers do not spend much time on accurate experiments; they pass rapidly into the innovation stage.

Farmers' experiments vary from the simple to the most complex. For many, an experiment represents a door to innovation "the irrigation ditch is the door to the farming system". In other words, the experimenting farmers often re-digest the segmented technical messages transmitted by their neighbours, their friends and the experts, and incorporate them, modifying them where necessary, into their actual production systems.

Experimentation and communication go hand in hand

Experimenting farmers have a certain 'anxiety' or 'eagerness' to transmit the acquired knowledge to everybody: husbands, wives, sons, uncles, cousins, neighbours, their Central American friends. This desire to communicate, to involve and give account to the community, to their basic group, is a characteristic which surprises outsiders. It appears not only once the test crop has been harvested, but from the siting of the experimental plot: on the side of the road "where everybody passes", halfway up the hillside "so that people will see from the other hill when my beans ripen and become yellow before the others". These criteria stem from both communication and agriculture! Many farmers carry out experiments not for themselves but in order to convince their neighbours: "I have already verified this experiment many times, I am only doing it to show the neighbours". Others define experiments together with their community, even at the risk of not carrying out a trial that to them seems a priority.

The experimentation process not only favours the interchange of ideas and mutual support, it also stimulates, provokes and promotes ideas. The power of the exchange–meetings to share ideas among the experimenting farmers is well known and established.

> *Now that I have participated in this regional meeting, I know various types of soil conditions which are different from mine and have learned different ways to protect them. I know about the appropriate time to do things. I am more certain about what I can teach to protect our lands, to improve them. All this encourages me to return to my community with new ideas after having met with new people.*

Experimenting is closely associated with communication. When translating the concept 'farmer–experimenter' into *achi*, the local language, the Guatemalan farmers say *"Ajcha'k xuqu't ka'q naoj"*, which means 'new knowledge to be taught'. This again confirms the validity of the interweaving of these two pillars. Farmers who innovate more are generally those who travel more (inside and outside their country). The sharing of ideas accelerates the implementation and operating speed of farmer experimentation.

Limitations and risks

Experimentation involves risks. During the initial stages, it is difficult to create enthusiasm in the experimenting farmer, but easier than the same task in subsequent stages where it is important to sustain enthusiasm and interest. The sharing of ideas is one of the better ways to generate motivation; it opens up another world, allows access to other ways of thinking and locating oneself within this. It is the beginning of discovery.

In the end, the farmer does not live on enthusiasm alone, s/he is carried forward by example. Specific products and benefits are weighty arguments in favour of experimentation. That is why, once trials are underway, the experimenters must be careful of the quality of the information they spread. Divulging unreliable data is counterproductive. For example: a farmer tried 2 doses of fertilizer on his corn. The first plot with a low dosage gave him a better yield. If he had divulged this information to his neighbours he would have been making a mistake, for he had forgotten that, before planting corn on this plot, he had cultivated tobacco. Because this is a commercial crop it had received high–level fertilization, which had left a residual effect for subsequent crops. In another example, farmers planted *Mucuna* as a first crop and since they had access to a tractor they cut and turned it into the soil with a harrow. The maize planted after this gave them a good harvest. They recommended this practice to a visiting farmer who, on returning to his farm, grew *Mucuna*, then hired a tractor and harrow to turn it under. The result was disastrous. Some weeks later the plot was covered with *Cyperus rotundus*. At the time of harrowing the *Cyperus rotundus* had not been choked by the *Mucuna* and it multiplied and benefited from the nitrogen released by the *Mucuna*. The farmer who had made the recommendation did not have *Cyperus rotundus* in his *Mucuna*. To counteract the risks of spreading inaccurate information is a duty. All the necessary work for the experimentation nucleus, the explanation about the relationship between the linking of causes, problems and effect, spring from here.

Most farmers do not have enough time or interest to dedicate themselves to very meticulous work, to observe in detail and systematically all that happens each day in their test plots. They do not have the agility nor sometimes adequate means to carry this out, to record all necessary data that would permit a full understanding and explanation of the results achieved. A professional researcher looks for and is convinced by data. They are the reason for his existence. A farmer, even though s/he may be a great experimentalist, first searches and is convinced by solutions that will partially, or even better, completely solve his or her problem. Since agriculture is an inter-relation of many factors, it is frequently difficult to know the reason why a result is successful or disappointing. The method invented by scientists to arrive at possible explanations is to design experiments where only one variable is changing. Farmers often prepare their tests without taking this exactness into account, with the result that no-one can attribute the results (good or bad) to anything in particular. It turned out well this time, this year, with this amount of rain, in this plot with this type of soil, but will it be the same next year, in neighbouring plots? Many would argue that farmer-test designs are not relevant because of their methodological defects, that they represent a waste of time, and are not useful for convincing others. By inference, the valiant efforts of those who devote themselves to this meticulous work go unnoticed and get lost. The million peso question is how to find the real cause of the problem, in other words, to discover the causal links.

One risk is to put too much weight on the results attained. Not all the farmers are experimenters, nor do they want to or have the capacity to be. In Central America, few farmers are currently involved in this process and the organized groups of experimenters are not numerous in proportion to the region's 1 500 000 small producers. The most efficient way to minimize this hazard is to produce reliable results, knowledge and information. Another risk is that the experimenters will become confined, isolated, and form small islands of belligerent farmers, or become an élite, and withdraw into themselves with a consequent secrecy regarding their results, and insufficient diffusion and information. Well-managed relationships with the exterior are always enriching. The disastrous insufficiency of what professional research bodies have to offer technologically for the problems faced by the small-scale producer farming on adverse sites (hillsides or others) and with few economic resources presents a further obstacle to experimentation. In general, formal research contributes basically two elements: genetic material and information. Though important, this is not enough to encourage participation. If they want to intensify on their small farms, what technical solutions can farmers find?

Towards what future?

A quick look at a sample of these small Central American farmers reveals an unrestricted range of experimentation subjects:

* weevil control for quality of beans for the domestic July–August market
* quality of carrots to be exported to a neighbouring country
* handling of hot chilies (*Capsicum spp*) destined for the regional packing enterprise
* association of linseed (*Linaza ustratissumum*) with maize, of *Salvia hispanica* with maize, of Rosa Jamaica (*Hibiscus sabdariffa L.*) with sorghum
* control of camomile scrub
* pasture improvement to ensure good cheese production
* butterfly–breeding for export to San Diego, USA
* improved roasting of peanuts (*Arachis hypogea*)
* organic, green and cover crop fertilization, and
* domestic insecticides.

This extensive list of subjects represents the reality of their aspirations. The consolidation of a farmer experimentation process and its implementation is not about breaking through previously established frontiers. In a programme that aims at promoting food security, the farmers begin their tests with basic cereals and end them with *Xanthosoma sagittefolium*, yams, *Dioscorea L.* potato, peanuts; that is, with an ample diversification of products. We repeat: farmers experiment because of need.

Will farmer experimentation break free? Generally, those who promote or support it are part of the technical sphere. Will this process be viable? Would it not be better linked to more vital aspects? Travel towards a safer North? How can the experimentation be tied to strengthening farmer and rural economies? How can its articulation be strengthened with the creation of local employment? Through maximization of the local added value of their products, through rural agro–industry? Through the market, be it local, national or international?

What will or should the final prospects for farmer experimentation be? Conforming to a new but simple technification of information and technology? changing the actors (farmers replacing extension workers) but maintaining the same working tools? placing itself at the service of farmer movements? aiming for the long term without sacrificing the short term?

Challenges for all

For the outsiders

The farmer experimentation process questions the practices of many outside actors. But this is not to dwell on their known deficiencies, on the problems involved in national systems of technology generation and transfer. Our questioning does not seek to abolish the work methods of the researchers, *técnicos*, extension workers, trainers or planners but rather to enrich them. It seeks mutual advantage, the benefits that can be obtained by each.

For an agricultural scientist, whatever his or her expertise, the reinforcement of farmer experimentation is advantageous, because it invites him or her to participate in the renewing of, in our particular case, Central American agriculture. Farmer experimenters constitute a resource and experimental base in the field, and the more bases, the better! Is not agronomy, after all, the science of locality? Farmers ask basic agricultural questions: what bean–maize rotation should be used in a zone with 1 600 mm of rain but with very uneven distribution? what type of legumes should be planted at the end of winter to cover and protect the soil during the summer and above all at the beginning of the rainy season? and a thousand others like them, not to mention the way they carry out their work. Working with experimenting farmers results in exacting, rewarding and more efficient work.

The more that experimentation raises the level of knowledge, learning and information among farmers, the more farmers begin to need technical support and data on production and technology. Experimenting farmers can be seen as a high–voltage suction machine by researchers and *técnicos*. They make demands to the limits of their expertise and this is what professionals are really scared of, more than of losing their jobs.

For a methodologist specializing in farming systems research and development, who talks much about the need to analyse the practices of farmers, to look at their way of perceiving things, at their rationality, it is a marvelous opportunity: farmer experimentation helps to renew his or her approach; not only does it invite the methodologist to study and reinforce what the farmers say but also what they do.

For the professional it is more pleasant and stimulating to work with active and demanding people than to work with passive recipients. The subject of integrated pest and disease control illustrates this situation perfectly. Farmers know a lot about insects and insect behaviour, but even the experimenters among them do not know about the biology, reproduction and ecology. They cannot, however, carry out pest–control experiments efficiently if they do not have this knowledge. Fortunately, there are initiatives from the scientists to eliminate such deficiencies.

For the insiders

For the farmers, experimentation is a means by which they can countermand the groups, institutions and authorities that manage technological alternatives as though they were the ten commandments: thou shalt build ditches; thou shalt use device A or B; thou shalt plant in contour lines; thou shalt not burn; thou shalt plant hedges; thou shalt apply fertilizer or compost; thou shalt not use agro–chemicals; thou shalt combine with velvet beans; etc. Even though it may seem attractive to many, using a package of this type does not necessarily represent a solution to all problems, in all places, at all times, and covering all situations. It would surely be more fruitful to express the argument around the key word *if.* Table 3.2 is a guide for the professionals supporting experimenting farmers.

Table 3.2. Guidelines for the professionals

If I should be in a particular area	*results worth investigating and spreading would be*
where farmers combine agriculture with animal husbandry	the use of manure
where poultry farm are concentrated	the use of hen droppings
where population density is high	to avoid competition with basic cereals and be on the side of combining with green fertilizers
where soil is compacted	to plant legumes or plants with a 'pivoting' and penetrating root system
where *Cyperus rotundus* exists and where farmers can count on tractors with discs and who plant 2 months after the first rains	rotating cow peas, jack beans, etc.
where there is relatively deep clayey soil, and late rains or winter	to substitute crops and adequate handling of the first planting stubble

It is from hypotheses such as those in Table 2 that the usefulness of farmer experimentation arises since it stimulates the farmers' ability to observe, diagnose, carry out critical analysis, and reason. Many people are surprised when they listen to a farmer–experimenter–trainer present the results of trials using two green leguminous fertilizers (jack beans *Canavalia enciformis* and *Mucuna* in association with corn) and the corresponding data including: quantity, size of the nodes observed at the bottom of the roots in the different soil types, or the weight of its green biomass, or the yield components of corn. As they change their manner of reporting their experiments, giving less space to intentions and more to specific and demonstrable facts, farmers show their ability to be more analytical and critical. See–judge–act becomes their guiding philosophy.

It is never without value to repeat and to persist. There are no magic solutions, there is no miraculous technology which presents only benefits and no defects. Technology gives results in one situation and not in another. This is one of the many reasons for which one must test, experiment in concrete biophysical situations and engage the resources of the farmer.

This is what farmers do. They use technology from any source (they do not care which); they get it piecemeal and reincorporate it into their production systems. They do not isolate the technical component from its global management; they recombine and transform. They must, however, first test the information they receive in order to avoid unnecessary risks.

For civil society

A combination of influences is revitalizing the dynamism of farmers. They are no longer content to stand still. They are becoming involved in experimentation. They want to strengthen their groups, their associations. Acting in this way, they present a challenge to all actors who make up the civil society involved in the technological aspects of agricultural production: Is this society going to leave them to work alone or is it going to join them in their efforts and initiatives?

With good reason, the professionals ought to be concerned with this phenomenon. Whatever happens, the farmers will continue to develop their land because it is their patrimony, their means of survival. But the professionals cannot remain in their fields of expertise, in their offices, with their experiments in their laboratories, without creating something to show for it. They are after all accountable to whoever is financing them. Farmers should thus be their natural allies. These two worlds complement and need each other.

Farmer experimentation has a long road to travel. For the time being it offers an invitation to all: to the farmer to become a better farmer, to the trainer to become a better trainer, to the researcher to become a better researcher, and to each professional to become more skilled in his or her own field for the benefit of other actors in the field. In this sense, farmer experimentation is one of the best contributions of farmers to civil society, representing their adjustment, progress and adaptation to the modern world.

Acknowledgements

This chapter includes part of a document published in December 1994 in the SIMAS Christmas Records, Mesoamerican Information Service on Sustainable Agriculture, Managua, Nicaragua.

References

Arcienagas J. y P. Lacki. 1993. *La modernización de la agricultura: Los pequeños también pueden*. FAO Rural Development Series Nº 11. Santiago, Chile: FAO.

Ashby J.A. 1991. Adopters and adaptors: Farmer participation in land research. In: Tripp R (ed.) *Planned change in farming systems: Progress in on-farm research*. London, Wiley–Sage, pp 273-286.

Carsalade, H., M. Griffon et M. De Lattre. 1993. Comment définir le rôle de la recherche agronomíque publique? Propos d'étape. International Symposium. Public and Private Sector Roles in the Provision of Agricultural Support Services. IICA. World Bank, Cirad–Danida, San José, Costa Rica, May 17-19.

Chambers R., A. Pacey and L.A.Thrupp. 1989. *Farmer first: Farmer innovation and agricultural research*. London: IT Publications.

Cifuentes Y. y M.A. Rivera. 1993. Metodología para captar fuentes de conocimientos campesinos en el departamento de Baja Verapaz, Guatemala. XXXIX Reunión anual PCCMCA. 28 de marzo - 3 de abril, Guatemala.

CIRAD–SAR (ed.) *Recherches-système en agriculture et développement rural*. International Symposium, Montpelier, France, November 21-25, 1994.

CIRAN/Nuffic. 1994. *Indigenous Knowledge and Development Monitor*. Volumes 1-4. The Hague, Netherlands.

Engel P.G. 1994. *Facilitating innovation: An action-oriented approach and participatory methodology to improve innovative social practice in agriculture.* PhD Thesis, Wageningen: Agricultural University.

4. Innovative farmers in the Punjab

photo: H.S. Bajwa

H.S. Bajwa, G.S. Gill and O.P. Malhotra [1]

[1] Dr. H.S. Bajwa, (Extension Specialist) G.S. Gill and O.P. Malhotra, Punjab Agricultural University, Directorate of Extension Education, Ludhiana 141 004, India.

The Punjab Agricultural University (PAU), established in 1962, has sole responsibility for teaching, research and extension in agriculture, agricultural engineering, veterinary and home sciences to students, professionals and the farming community of the Punjab. Professionals trained at the PAU are recruited into various state departments related to horticulture, agriculture and animal husbandry to extend modern technology to farmers. The university pioneered the holding of farmer fairs in India, to which farmers thronged in large number from all parts of the state. These were held on the university campus and farmers were supplied with seeds of modern, high–yielding varieties, developed and propagated by the university's scientists on their research farms. The scientists also demonstrated and explained newly developed technologies at their research stations to visiting farmers so that the latter might adopt them in their own fields. Other Indian agricultural universities then followed this practice.

The PAU was also the first university to introduce workshops for agricultural officers. They come from the State Department of Agriculture to the university research farms for 2-3 days, where they interact with the research scientists and are introduced to the new technology being developed for dissemination to farmers. The field–staff in turn are able to discuss the problems they face in transferring new technologies to farmers' fields in their respective areas. Their observations have often helped scientists reorient their technology.

To impart the newly developed technology to the farming men and women of the state, the university has also taken a lead in introducing correspondence courses, giving lessons by post. Another PAU innovation was to introduce farmers' committees, made up of two progressive farmers from each district of the state, who meet twice a year at the main university campus. They discuss with research staff the difficulties faced in adopting modern technology on their farms and they act as agents of the university in disseminating its various new technologies. The researchers also lay on adaptive trials at the farms of these progressive farmers, using their land and labour to verify the technology developed on the research station.

At the newly established regional research stations, based on agro–climatic regions and under the auspices of the National Agricultural Research Projects (NARP), researchers have started conducting experiments based on the recommendations of the Regional Research Advisory Committees. These committees are made up of scientists posted at the stations, extension officers of the PAU and state departments, and progressive farmers of the region. *Krishi Vigyan Kendras*, financed by ICAR (Indian Centre of Agricultural Research), are also being set up in each district of the state, where male and female farmers are trained in the latest technology according to their location–specific needs.

Experiences with participatory approaches

Having read the *ILEIA Newsletter* regularly and having procured and read other related books such as *Farmer First, Let Farmers Judge,* and *Farming for the Future*, we decided to introduce some planned experiments using participatory approaches. We chose to work with an already established group with whom we had built up a great deal of confidence and trust.

The group is led by an inventive and experimenting farmer, S. Mohinder Singh Dosanjh (hereafter referred to as Mohinder Singh), and was known to us for its activities in seed production and for its experimenting nature. Something of the history of this group and of seed production in the Punjab is given here as a background to the account of our work with the group.

Local-farmer seed production

After the Green Revolution, the Punjab had a cereal-based cropping system of mainly paddy in the summer and wheat in the winter. More than 60% of the paddy and 95% of the wheat were modern high-yielding varieties. The formal seed agencies were unable to meet even 10% of the farmers' seed requirements in the state. The informal sector was and has remained the major source. Formal seed production involves only a limited number of crops and only selected varieties of these. The higher prices fixed by the seed agencies also hinder the purchase of such seed, especially by small and marginal farmers. Production is highly centralized: farmers simply receive the seed, but take no part in its production. In general, of all the components of the local production system, seeds are the most frequently exchanged elements. This reflects the important role seeds play as part of the culture of traditional sharing of varieties between farmers. As a rule, farmers select the best available produce on their farm for sowing the following year. In fact, many of the improved seeds recommended to the farmers were used and developed by the local farming communities themselves, and were only slightly modified or renamed by the station-based researchers (Fernandez 1994).

The farmer, Mohinder Singh, had established his own linkages with the PAU, various state departments and the seed-producing agencies, and he cultivated modern varieties. But he had observed that his fellow villagers were not replacing their modern variety of seeds, which slowly degenerate. A man with a strong will to serve his fellow villagers, he discussed this issue with a like-minded close friend. In 1980, on their own initiative, they opened a unit in their village which they named the Punjab Agricultural Service Centre. The centre, in addition to providing new seed for fellow farmers, also provided a forum for farmers to exchange ideas and experiences. The friends pledged to keep the service aims of the centre above the aim of profit. They employed a salesman, but he left after a year. Instead of employing a new man, they made a local grocer, Madan Lan, their partner. The partnership works on this basis: Madan Lan sits in the centre, the two farmers provide the seed, and all three share the profits equally. The centre soon established itself, but could not provide enough seed to meet farmer demand. The centre also became a meeting point, where university research scientists and field workers of the various government departments such as agriculture, horticulture, animal husbandry, and women and child development, could meet farm men and women to discuss their various problems. Mohinder Singh's wife took an active interest and participated fully in the centre's activities.

The PAU has established a voluntary organization of young farmers called the *Punjab Naujawan Kisan Sanstha* (Young Farmers Association), whose members act as agents of the university in disseminating new technology. The PAU members conduct adaptive trials at their farms. The association has units at state, district and block levels. Mohinder Singh was made the District Convenor of Jalandhar District and thus came into contact with many other farmers. His actions and decisions were not directed by any outside agency, department or individual. But to meet the high demand for seed, four more farmers joined the centre in 1986 and contributed seed. They were now a group of six, and decided among themselves which of them would grow a particular crop variety and what area they would devote to the crop. Foundation or new seed was to be supplied by the centre and 2-3 joint inspections would be made of the crop growth. The centre was to pay Rs20 a quintal (above the prevailing price for cereal crops) and Rs50 a quintal for their oilseed crops, and all would have an equal share in the profits of the centre. This arrangement worked well for three years but then the new members felt that they were contributing more produce than the others. Having developed good rapport with the nearby villages, they were also able to sell their seed directly to them and thus earn more. So they left the service centre and opened a seed shop in an adjoining village.

Faced now with a shortage of seed, the remaining members decided on a new course of action. They broadened the centre's membership: they invited farmers whom they had identified as innovative and with a commitment to work for their fellow farmers to become associate life members, at a cost of Rs100 per member. The associate members were supplied with foundation seed and the centre paid them a premium for their seed. The associate members interact among themselves, as they are from the same community and are aware of the value of sharing experiences with fellow farmers. They also act as agents for any innovations produced locally among the farmers, in this way helping to build the image of the service centre. Some members have had training in hybrid–seed production from PAU and have now started supplying locally–produced hybrid–seed to the farmers of the area. In addition to cereals, the centre also supplies seed and seedlings of crops and varieties for which seed production has not been taken up by the formal sector. For example, there is a locally–grown variety of mash (bitter gourd) intercropped in maize which is more disease resistant than the recommended variety. Farmer seed production can afford a greater diversity of varieties and thus promotes genetic stability. More farmers, irrespective of class and gender, can gain access to new varieties (Sperling et al. 1993).

Strengthening farmers' seed production and research

The university wanted to learn about the performance of farmer–to–farmer exchange and to understand the nature of farmers' experiments. Personal contact was established with the farmers and the details of their experiments discussed with them. No interview schedule was used.

The objectives and innovativeness of our project, termed Participatory Seed Production, were discussed with the Director of Extension Education of the university, who promised transport, and audiovisual and other facilities for the work. Ten farmers (five from each of two villages) from Mohinder Singh's group, and ten from another two adjoining villages about 50 km away, of comparable socio–economic level and similar type of farming and environment, were chosen. The researchers interacted informally with all of them on their farms and discussed their local seed–production problems and potentials. It was arranged that a half–acre of a rice variety of their own choice would be grown on each farm and would be compared with a half–acre of a newly recommended variety of rice seed supplied by the university.

A one−day production training programme was organized at the main campus of PAU. This permitted creative interaction between researchers, extensionists and farmers in sharing their respective knowledge, experience and information. Time was given to peasant trainer Mohinder Singh to give a lecture on his experiences not only of seed production but of his own innovative experimental work. The purpose was to sensitize the researchers and extensionists, who had come to deliver their lectures to farmers, that farmers' experiences are equally valid and that they have something valuable to contribute to the research system. The uniquenesss of this training programme was that, since it was farmer induced, attendance of participating farmers was 100% and, since a fellow farmer was given a chance to narrate his experiences and all were able to join in the discussions at the end of each lecture, it was genuinely participative. All were served tea, refreshments and lunch sponsored by KRIBHCO, a fertilizer cooperative.

A paddy nursery was sown and the transplanting was done in a way that combined researchers' recommendations and farmers' local knowledge and practice. Together with the farmers, the extensionists observed the crop growth, listening to the farmers' views of the performance of the new variety in comparison with their own chosen seed. When the crops matured and were almost ready to harvest, farmer field−days were celebrated. When a field−day was held in one village, the participating farmers from the other villages (50 km away) were provided transport by the university to attend. This enabled them to observe the performance of the same crop by farmers from other villages. We, the research and extension scientists, learnt in the cross−visits of the farmers that, since farmers are multidisciplinary experts, they not only observe the field for which they are invited but look critically at all the crops and varieties growing, the method of sowing, the implements, the animals, their sheds and their mutual interactions.

Our efforts to promote farmer−to−farmer exchange resulted not only in increased knowledge among the farmers, and sometimes even the acquisition from each other of new crops/varieties and other products, but also in a sense of self−confidence as well as curiosity in reviving farmers' abilities to solve their own problems, such as local seed production, without outside help. Demonstrations established by research and extension staff are relatively less effective in this regard. Farmers learn with more interest and more easily from fellow farmers as the latter are more credible. Farmers feel that, when one group of farmers has done something in nearby surroundings with a similar farming environment, then they also can do it themselves. All we need to do is create the conditions for the farmers to meet and to facilitate continuing discussion. Farmers communicate freely in their local language and they assume other farmers to be at the same level. As they operate with the same frame of mind, their interaction is more animated than that between researchers and farmers. Each of the participating villages organized its own field−day, and farmer−to−farmer interaction continued.

For a wider circulation of this innovative extension approach, news was given in the local newspapers, on radio, television and in the *PAU News*. Many university researchers made enquiries about participatory seed production. In this way, we gained an opportunity to explain to them the new approaches of participatory technology development (PTD) and its role in present and future agricultural development.

Participatory video

A new method of learning and teaching through participatory video has proved to be an appropriate form of recording for illiterate village people, as it makes available information in a form that people can understand. The seed-production training programme conducted at the university, at which peasant trainer Mohinder Singh shared the platform with the researchers, was video recorded. This video was shown at the field-day organized in one of the villages, which was itself video-recorded. The video operators joined us in observing how watching a video initiates discussion among farmers and inspires confidence. The content of the video message appears to be remembered for a much longer time than messages received through other media, such as lectures, radio or television. When farmer field-days are played back to the villagers, the self-image conveys the impression that their own knowledge is important and they can say and do things that previously they thought were impossible.

When a field-day was conducted in another village, our video operator was on leave. We informed the villagers that we had brought the cassette but, since we had no operator, the video would have to be shown on some other day. Since some of the villagers had participated in the training programme and knew that the cassette contained pictures of what they had talked to fellow farmers about, they arranged a television set and VCR themselves and insisted that the video be shown to them that very day. This taught us that when villagers take part in disseminating a technology, they also become involved in arranging things. By viewing the video-recording from the other village field-day, farmers were able to communicate with other farmers, and farmer relationships between distant villages were reinforced.

In another village, a confident farmer was given the video camera and asked to record what he perceived to be the most interesting events during the field-day. The farmers in attendance saw their fellow farmer handling the camera. On this particular field-day, women's participation was also ensured, as the day had been converted into a rural conference by our sponsors KRIBHCO.

Participatory video is now being used to introduce PTD approaches to a number of farmer groups and to induce them to reveal and share their own experimental activities. It has proved an excellent tool. And now, to sensitize the research and extension staff of the university and the Department of Agriculture, the first author of this chapter has incorporated the teaching of participatory approaches into the training courses on wheat production given by the Directorate of Extension Education, and uses the participatory video on seed production as a teaching aid.

Some locally developed experiments and innovations

In our interactions with farmers we have come across many examples of their inventiveness in solving problems. The following gives an account of some of these and of the extension department's intentions for future participation.

An automatic bird-scarer

The spring hybrid sunflower crop is the most important oilseed crop in the Punjab after rape-seed and mustard. It was introduced in 1990-91 by the Mahyco Seed Company, and within 2-3 years a number of other companies had also introduced hybrids. These were tested at the university and some of them were formally recommended. The university also developed its own hybrid. The area under sunflower has now increased to 90,000 ha. Small-scale and marginal farmers have also started planting the crop.

Birds, especially parrots, are a serious problem during seed development, causing a lot of damage to the flower heads. Doves, pigeons and crows also cause damage at germination stage. Small-scale farmers cannot afford automatic birds scarers, which cost around Rs1,000. To add to the problem, parrots do not accept poison bait. Research recommendations are to repel birds by dusting 5% *Malathion* dust on the outer rows of the field. Madan Lal, the partner of Mohinder Singh, keeps honeybees at his farm and he knew that these would be killed if he dusted *Malathion* on his sunflowers. He, like other small-scale farmers, could not employ a man for bird scaring, as labour costs are beyond his means. His need to solve this problem forced him to seek an alternative.

At the cigarette shop in his village, the shopkeeper keeps a rope lighted throughout the day from which the clients light cigarettes. It occurred to Madan Lal that if he put firecrackers in the rope, they would fire automatically and would scare the birds. He did not share the original idea with fellow farmers but purchased a set of firecrackers from his village grocery shop, took a rope, opened its twists and fixed firecrackers at a distance of 5-6 inches, put it on a wooden pole and lit the rope at one end. When a cracker fired, the rope stayed alight and after about half an hour the next cracker fired automatically. He was excited to see the result of his experiment. After this success, he observed that he would have to adjust the spacing of the firecrackers according to wind velocity. On a windy day he had to increase the distance and on a still day decrease it. He also deduced that the distance between the firecrackers would have to be reduced at the end of the string because it would be evening, a time when the parrot problem was greater. These firecrackers are manufactured locally in some of the nearby towns and cities, and Madan Lal observed a significant difference in the performance of various trade brands. He observed that firecrackers with the Cooker trade mark did not miss a firing and also produced more noise, creating a bigger scare for the birds than the Krishna or others brands available in his area.

Spread of local innovation. While making his experiments on bird-scaring in the sunflower crop, Madan Lal shared his observations with fellow experimenters, among them Mohinder Singh and his friend Sandhu. The latter encouraged him and were the first to follow suit. Soon other local people noticed the innovation and, since it worked well, was cheap and the materials easily available locally, they adopted it, first in the same village and slowly further afield. When an invention or innovation is worthwhile, it seems it will be adopted by farmers whether it is formally recommended or not. Farmers now use this local innovation with other crops such as maize.

Station-based researchers' observations. The station-based bird-control scientists, when contacted about Madan Lal's innovation, said that they had heard about some such farmer practice but had not observed it. They had not tested it themselves, but they assumed that it could be used in conjunction with other control measures.

Extension's future plans. We plan to take the station-based scientists to the farmers' fields to conduct experiments there with their help, and recommend formally giving due credit to the experimenting farmers for any useful results. The innovation will then be tested in other areas by actively involving farmers, including their local experimental treatments and observations, ideas and opinions. Efforts will be made to organize farmers in small groups and to facilitate the interaction of groups for farmer-to-farmer extension of the innovation.

A new use for *arhar:* a fabric twine from waste

Arhar (red gram, *Cajanus cajan*) is not a traditional grain crop of the Punjab. It is a recent introduction and has not occupied much area. With advice from PAU, the farmer Mohinder Singh grew *arhar* Al-15 in his field as grain. He noticed that it seemed to be of the same nature as the traditional leguminous crop *san* and that it grew in the same season. He conceived the idea of exploring the use of the fibre from *arhar* to see if it had the same properties as the fibre from *san.*

Earlier, while recalling the agricultural crops and practices of his father's and grandfather's time, Mohinder Singh had informed us that there were numerous crops and varieties grown by farmers in his own and adjoining villages at that time, mainly for family use. For example, every farmer used to cultivate *san* or sunhemp (*Crotolaria juncea L.*) on an area of a half to one kanal (about 1/20 ha) for making rope or twine of different thicknesses for tying produce onto carts or for attaching to the buckets used to draw water from wells. It had been used to make rope cots or beds that could easily be carried from one place to another, for instance, from home to the fields. Usually, every farming family has 4-5 of these cots in a house for common use. Nowadays, small-scale farmers either purchase fabric twine or rope from the market to make their own cots, or they purchase folding steel beds which cost around Rs500 each. Well-off farmers, like their urban counterparts, even purchase double beds made of plywood. Very few farmers now grow sunhemp themselves.

When the *arhar* was harvested, Mohinder Singh made small stakes, cut uniformly from the upper, pod-bearing, parts of the stalks using a sharp implement known as a *gandasa.* Then he made bundles of 5-6 stakes, tied the bundles with ropes at both ends and placed them in a line in the common village pond, as was the practice with *san.* This process is known as retting. Mohinder Singh then covered the bundles with dried maize stalks (*Zea mays*) or *bajra* (*Pennisetium typhoides*) and with soil from the pond itself, taking care to leave the bundles submerged but not touching the bottom. He left them in this position for 5-6 days and then checked one or two stakes to see if the fibre would peel off in long strips. When the fibre peeled off easily, he removed the bundles from the pond, laid them on the soil for a day and then stacked them vertically so they would drain and dry. He then took the bundles home. In the evening, at dinner time while sitting in the kitchen with his wife and children, he removed fibre from the *arhar* stakes as his grandfather had done with *san.*

The leftover *arhar* stalks are used as fuel. Mohinder Singh had from the beginning kept some bundles of *arhar* at home for fuel. As he was removing the fibre from the pond–dipped stakes, another experiment came to his mind. This was to see whether fibre could be removed from the stalks that had not been placed in the pond. To his excitement, he found that the fibre could be extracted in the same way as from the pond–dipped stakes. He further observed that rope made from the fibre taken from the stalks not kept in the pond was harder and stronger. He made two separate cots, one from pond–dipped fibre and one from the undipped fibre. The latter lasted longer than the former. From the experience of other crops grown he observed that, in order to have taller *arhar* plants, that would provide more fibre, he would have to increase the seed rate of the crop so that more plants per unit area would come up and they would grow higher.

Spread of local innovation. This single farmer's efforts have resulted in giving a new purpose to the *arhar* crop. It had until then been grown only for grain, but has now become a dual–purpose crop. However, although his fellow farmers observed Mohinder Singh first putting stakes into the village pond and then removing them, and some asked him what he was doing, this local innovation has remained where it originated, since *arhar* is not a main crop and is grown only by experimenting farmers with links with researchers, from whom they had obtained seed.

Station–based researchers' observations. On the formal research side, scientists in the pulse section are few, and have to deal with numerous crops. They also have less experimental land and fewer other resources as compared to the wheat and rice sections. They are concentrating on evolving varieties that give higher grain yields and are resistant to diseases and pests. None of the researchers had tried to extract fibre from *arhar*. However, if research efforts are directed towards evolving a dual–purpose variety, it might become an important crop in the Punjab. The easier production of *arhar* fibre, in comparison with that from *san*, might give rise to small–scale industry for marginal farmers and landless labourers, who would thus get local employment and could supplement their income.

Extension's future plans. We plan to conduct an informal survey among farmers to learn their opinions about developing such a dual–purpose variety of *arhar*, or whether they prefer separate varieties for grain and fibre, and what characteristics a variety should have for the different uses. We will discuss Mohinder Singh's innovative approach with them, sometimes taking him with us. Farmers' own experiences of obtaining fibre from other crops will also be evaluated and documented. We will discuss the results with station–based researchers and encourage them to include some of the farmers' ideas and problems in their agendas. Simultaneously, with the help of researchers, experiments in the farmers' fields will be evaluated and efforts made to strengthen their initiatives.

A muskmelon nursery without plastic bags

Punjab farmers and their crops face wide variations in climate. In the month of January, mean minimum temperatures are as low as 5°C and in the month of June mean maximum temperatures reach 47°C. Vegetables grown earlier or later in the season than normal fetch higher prices in the market. Various techniques are adopted to achieve this. Early muskmelon is raised in a nursery at the end of January and transplanted when about 30 days old, when the weather becomes warmer at the end of February. For the nurseries, our research recommends raising muskmelons in plastic bags of 100 gauge thickness of 15 x 10 cm in size, using a mixture of soil and farmyard manure in equal proportions. However, plastic bags of this thickness and size are readily available only in areas where many farmers grow muskmelons.

Our farmer colleague, Mohinder Singh, also grew an early crop of muskmelon. One year, however, plastic bags were not available in his area. He could not afford to waste a full day to travel 100 km to bring the bags from the nearest city where they were likely to be available. The need to solve this particular problem induced him to search for some alternative. He chose a site on his farm which faces the sun and is protected from direct cold winds by a wall. He dug a trench about 2 inches deep, 2 feet wide and 20 feet long and pressed its base well. He brought heavy soil from outside his farm, put it into this trench to form a sort of plate 1 inch thick and pressed it down gently. He sowed muskmelon seed into this soil plate, with a spacing of about 1 inch both within and between the lines of seed. The main property he looked for in this experiment was germination, observed visually. He watered the nursery daily as required.

When the nursery was about 20 days old, he and his wife removed *gachis* (earth balls) of seedlings for transplanting. He observed, however, that when the *gachis* were removed and transported to the field, some soil became loose and about 20% of the seedlings were damaged on account of this. He therefore decided that the transplanting medium should be such as to keep the muskmelon roots intact and to make it easy to carry them to the field for transplanting. The idea of testing cowdung the following year as a medium came to mind; he felt that perhaps soil did not provide sufficient nutrients. Dung would also provide the warmth needed for germination. When he discussed this idea with his wife, she corroborated that when seeds are excreted by animals in dung, a number of germinating plants can be seen in the village dung heaps and these can easily be removed. So the farmer and his wife decided to experiment by raising their muskmelon seedlings in cowdung the next year.

Experimentation by farmers is of an ongoing nature. They plan new experiments based on their previous successes and failures and on their future needs. The following year, the couple prepared plates of cowdung of the same thickness (1 inch) on the same site and sowed muskmelon seeds with the same spacing. They observed, in this cowdung medium, that germination was early and nursery growth was also better than in the previous year's experiment with a heavy–soil medium.

Unfortunately, after a few days, insects developed in the cowdung medium and up to 30% of the seedlings were damaged. This had been unforeseeable. So, again the next year, Mohinder Singh repeated this experiment with cowdung, but he took care of the insects by mixing insecticide with the dung at the time of preparing the dung plates. This further improved germination and up to 90% of the seedlings survived to transplanting time. *Gachis* of cowdung proved a good medium for holding the muskmelon roots tightly and they were easy to carry. Even so, 5-7% seedling mortality occurred in transportation from nursery site to field.

The farmer's search to improve further this method of raising a nursery continued in the following year. After mixing the insecticide with cowdung, instead of making plates, he and his wife prepared small, approximately 1 inch sized round balls and put two seeds in each cowdung ball. With this method, germination was 98% and it was even easier to carry seedlings from nursery to field. Cowdung balls become quite hard outside but remain very soft inside.

At this stage, after four years of experimentation, the farmer's search for an alternative to plastic bags was ended. Now he felt satisfied that he need not waste time and money bringing bags from the market. He also had better germination and vigorous seedlings directly from his farm–produced cowdung. Time is also saved in transporting seedlings from the nursery to the field, and he estimates that the weight of about 200 cowdung balls is equal to just 100 of the seedlings in polythene bags. The raw material for plastic bags consists of petroleum products from crude oil and natural gas, both non–renewable resources. The farmer had become aware that plastic bags are harmful, as empty bags dumped in the soil remain non–degradable for a long time and, being poisonous, are a pollution hazard. He observed that this new method of raising nurseries with cowdung balls could also be used successfully in nurseries for other cucurbits.

Spread of local innovation. During four years of experimenting, Mohinder Singh discussed his efforts, ideas, successes and failures continuously with his group and with family members. New ideas emerged from such debates, which led to further experimentation. Muskmelon is grown by few farmers in his surroundings. It has been tested, found working and appreciated by some of them. However, since these efforts of the farmers are not taken seriously by formal research and extension workers, they do not help promote its adoption by other farmers.

Station–based researchers' observations. When this innovation was discussed with research–station scientists, they agreed that muskmelon nurseries could be set up in this way. They added to our knowledge by mentioning they had also seen farmers raising muskmelon seedlings in plastic trays like those of refrigerator ice–cubes, but bigger. Unfortunately, such practices have not been tested on–station nor have they been critically examined in farmers' fields, so the formal recommendations remain: plastic bags of prescribed size and thickness for all situations.

Extension's future plans. This farmer's innovation is likely to serve as a model for inducing other farmers to narrate their experiences and to strengthen their capacities to experiment. We will prepare a video of this four–year experiment. All the types of nurseries tried in the different years will be raised in one place, and video shots taken of them separately and collectively. We will explain how the farmer, faced with the unavailability of plastic bags, started to experiment with heavy soil and ended up with the round dungballs for raising muskmelon seedlings. An informal interview with the farmer about his ideas and successes, particularly concerning this innovation but also more generally about his work, will also be recorded.

Conclusions

This has been our first attempt in the Punjab to introduce PTD approaches. We have observed that, if groups of small-scale farmers are organized to produce and distribute seeds over a cluster of villages, they will not only supplement formal seed production but will also conserve biodiversity by producing the seed of local crops. The distance between researchers and farmers in the Punjab is not great. Most of the researchers and extensionists are themselves from farming families, speak local languages and listen directly to farmers; many extensionists are also posted close to their homes. However, this participatory approach is entirely new for both researchers and extensionists. We have about 1200 station-based researchers in the Punjab who hold at least M.Sc. degrees, and the majority of them are Ph.D graduates; they are strong on the technical side of agriculture. Similarly, about 3000 persons are involved in field extension who have at least a B.Sc. Some are at M.Sc. level and a few even hold Ph.D degrees. We feel that the existing research and extension institutions have the potential to absorb participatory approaches by making certain policy changes.

On the face of it, participatory approaches appear to be what we have already been doing in the Punjab by involving farmers in *Kisan Melas* (adaptive trials), farmers' committees and training courses. But continuously and critically reading the new books and journals on farmer-first and PTD approaches has opened up entirely new vistas for development. At present, there is no in-built mechanism for involving farmers in making modifications in technology at village level. To start with, even 10% of the existing research and extension staff, identified and specially trained in a participatory approach and formed into interdisciplinary teams constituted for various agroclimatic zones, would go a long way in making worthwhile documentation and underlining the importance of farmer participation in research and extension; by changing curricula and teaching, one could influence the values and behaviour of a new generation of scientists and extensionists.

Unfortunately, the experimental nature of farming and farmers has been overlooked for too long. Now we have learnt from farmers that the high cost of inputs, the unavailability of a material or input, and the saving of drudgery and time are factors which induce small-scale and marginal farmers to innovate. Farmers have the inclination and ability to modify and adapt technologies to local conditions through experimentation (Owusu 1993). But to learn from farmers, the researchers and extensionists will have to change their attitudes, and this new approach demands time and patience. It is a means by which two bodies of knowledge can be brought together and interact so that solutions for previously non-targeted farmer groups are found over a shorter period of time. Relevant technologies can be generated through the mutual interaction of researchers, extensionists and farmers. New approaches empower farmers and extensionists to learn, adapt and do better.

PTD is a process through which conditions are created for frequent communication and discussion, thereby contributing to the strengthening of the institutional basis of local organization. It is interesting to note that some innovative farmers not only experiment at their farms with traditional and modern technologies, but have formed their own, small local groups through which they share information, open service centres and show a strong commitment to serve their fellow farmers. They have a desire to share their results with a wider audience and can publish their experimental results in regional newspapers (Mohinder Singh Dosanjh 1992) and even in a national journal of planning commission (Mohinder Singh Dosanjh 1990). Such farmers can become members of interdisciplinary teams and should be paid some sort of remuneration for taking time away from their other farmwork.

We are pleased to have become a part of a quiet revolution, which is still small–scale and scattered, by further developing, describing and disseminating farmer–first methods. A change away from the conventional transfer–of–technology approach has been intellectually and professionally exciting and satisfying. It can supplement our present system of research and extension.

References

Fernandez, P.G. 1994. Indigenous seed practices for sustainable agriculture. *Indigenous Knowledge and Development Monitor* 2: 9-12.

Mohinder Singh Dosanjh. 1990. Kheti Bari Wich mere nawen tajarbe (My new experiments in agriculture). Yogna.

Mohinder Singh Dosanjh. 1992. Kheti De Nawen Dishadian Wal March (March towards new experiments in agriculture), *Daily Ajit* (local regional newspaper) 1 August 1992.

Owusu, Y. 1993. Farm–based agroforestry: Four years of experience in Ghana. *Agroforestry Today* 5 (1): 8-10.

Sperling, L., U. Scheidegger and R. Busuchara. 1993. Designing bean seed systems for small-holders. *ILEIA Newsletter* 9 (1): 24-25.

Adding technical options

5. Village–based cassava breeding in Tanzania

Dominick de Waal,
assisted by F.R. Chinjinga, L. Johansson, F.F. Kanju and N. Nathaniels[1]

Development of new crop varieties with improved characteristics is conventionally seen as a task carried out by centralized institutes, such as research stations. The realities of limited personnel and financial resources, the physical difficulties and costs of bulking and distribution of plant material, and the immense variety of conditions and purposes which demand specifically adapted varieties have, however, made it extremely difficult for centralized crop–variety development programmes to serve the interests of the smallholder farmer.

---

[1] Dominick de Waal, F.R. Chinjinga, Lars Johansson, F.F. Kanju and N. Nathaniels, Farming Systems Research Unit, Agricultural Research Institute, Naliendele, Box 59, Mtwara, Tanzania.

Following on this assessment, researchers and scientists have begun to consider what type of alternatives might be both feasible and productive. The Naliendele Agricultural Research Institute's Farming Systems Research Unit (FSRU), after working with many independent farmers scattered across Mtwara and Lindi, has been rethinking the role of agricultural professionals. They have begun to identify tasks and approaches which show how considerable decentralization of technology generation and verification can take place. Some of the new roles for scientists, extensionists and farmers in this process are given in Table 5.1. Working in this way, outside professionals begin to see farmers as experimenters, as sources of innovation. Instead of being obstacles to development and 'laggards', farmers become research partners.

Table 5.1. Some new roles for scientists, extensionists and farmers within a participatory framework

Scientists'/extensionists' roles	*Farmers' roles*
Help farmers to seek opportunities	
Find out what farmers are currently experimenting on	Teach outside professionals about farmers' experiments
List and explain the skills and tools which scientists can offer to assist farmers' own experimentation	Learn to use scientists' skills for development of new opportunities
Offer basket of technologies	Choose what combination of technologies he or she wants to use
Suggest ideas for design of experiment	Plan trial design
Develop capacity for decentralizing the means to verify technology	Farmers work with scientists and other professionals to verify locally adapted or developed technologies
Develop methods to help farmers learn	Farmers use new methods for learning
Assist farmers as experimenters and innovators to reflect on and analyse experiments	Develop capacity to carry out detailed constructive discussion on ways to get around problems
Train village animators and facilitators	Organize themselves for joint action
Describe and illustrate the life–cycles of plants, fungi, pests and beneficial insects	Use this new knowledge, combined with experience of the local situation, to invent ways to solve problems
Give guidelines rather than recommendations	Use guidelines and knowledge to decide when and how to conduct farming operations
Provide methods which the farmers can use for self–evaluation	Assess their own group's efforts

Decentralizing some research to farmer–researchers makes a lot of sense. It is an obvious route for reducing the workload of professionals at institutes such as Naliendele, thereby reducing dependence on donor funding. Partnerships of this type, which result from the insights and knowledge of both professionals and farmers, can ensure that the benefits of the relevant work done spreads to a much wider network of collaborating yet independent farmers.

The current situation with cassava

Farmers in Mtwara Region grow many types or varieties (land races) of cassava. Informal meetings with farmers have shown that there are around 15 named types. These names vary from village to village since different varieties of cassava may be given the same name, and the same type may be given different names.

Some farmers grow cassava from seed. Cassava grown from seed (*ngogo*) is named according to how it looks and tastes, using names from the existing selection of names used in any area. This system of naming does not take into account the actual genetic origin of any particular cassava variety. In other words, new types of cassava originating from *ngogo* seed are named according to the tangible characteristics (phenotypic features) of the type, *limbanga*, for example.

Knowledge of these different, tangible, 'types' of cassava is widespread amongst farmers, vendors and town consumers. For example, all these people will know that *badi* is a very sweet type that it is available between July and September and that it is ideal as a snack food. *Sumu ya Panya* is an extremely bitter type that can be processed only by drying and pounding. The 15 or so named types of cassava can be thought of as equivalent types of tea blend, such as Earl Grey, African Pride, Green Label or English Breakfast tea. These types of cassava can be thought of as consisting of blends of characteristics which serve the various combinations of production, processing, cooking, storing and eating strategies of people in southern Tanzania.

Entry point into a village–based cassava–breeding programme

Farmer Cosmas from Msijute village (Mtwara Rural), has, like many farmers, tried on his own initiative growing cassava from seed (*ngogo*). He was surprised to find that the seeds of a sweet variety grew into both plants with bitter roots and other plants with sweet roots. He planted seed from a *Kigoma Mwanza* plant in a nursery at his farm. Later, when he transplanted the seedlings to the *shamba* (field), Cosmas marked them so he would be able to identify them amongst his other cassava plants. He told visiting researchers about his observations and experiments.

The story was followed up by specialists from the Roots and Tuber Department of the institute, assisted by the FSRU, Naliendele, and RIPS. The outside team conducted a series of conversations and observations with Mr Cosmas, much of which was recorded on film.

During the first visit to the farmer, Cosmas reported the differences between the mother and daughter plants (Table 5.2). Cosmas had learned from his own experiments that cassava grown from seed could have different characteristics from the mother plant. He did not understand, however, why this should be so. In speculating about the reasons, he thought that differences in soil types might be behind it.

Table 5.2. Differences between mother and daughter plants described by Cosmas, a farmer from Msijute

Mother plant	*Daughter plant*
Sweet	Bitter
Dark green	Light green
No black lesions on stem	Black lesions on stem
Dark stem	Light stem
Tall plant stature	Short plant stature
Many roots	One root

The challenge for scientists and extensionists was to find out what knowledge Cosmas had and what extra knowledge he needed in order to understand the biology of cassava and be more effective in his own crossing of cassava varieties. Cosmas had talks with Mr Kanju, the institute's cassava breeder, about the role of cassava growers in plant reproduction. Kanju used examples such as papaya to explain the difference between male and female flowers. This was illustrated first by showing Cosmas how to cross different varieties of cassava, followed by Cosmas trying to cross varieties himself. Exchange visits were made to Naliendele and to Msijute during the crossing season so that Cosmas and Kanju could learn the lay–out of each other's fields.

Through this learning process, the principles of cassava breeding had become clear to Cosmas. The farmer had acquired a new set of opportunities for deliberate and purposeful experimenting to develop varieties for specific uses. Using his new insights Cosmas analysed a cassava problem he had, and came up with a solution he could implement. Table 5.3 shows how the new knowledge created an opportunity for the farmer to look at a disease problem in a new way. Cosmas has seen that a blend of the resistant *Kigoma Mafia* together with the good storage qualities of *Kibaha* could possibly be both grown and marketed in his situation. Thousand of other farmers, according to the specific growing condition on their farms and the uses they have for cassava, would have their own particular requirements for particular blends of variety characteristics.

Table 5.3. Cosmas' problem analysis

Step in diagnosis		
1. Initial problem	Cassava brown streak virus *Matekenya*	
2. Ways of identifying the disease	Misshapen roots A ring of black–brown tissue when the root is cut open	
3. Resistant varieties	Possibility A *Kigoma Mafia*–sweet, very good market when fresh, especially during Ramadan	Possibility B *Sumu ya Panya*–very bitter, good for use as guard rows
4. Problems with the resistant varieties	Very low storage quality as *Makopa* because it does not have any weight when dried	Very bitter, requires careful processing, therefore not good to grow in large quantities
5. New opportunity for action	Cross *Kigoma Mafia* with *Kibaha* which is sweet and stores well because it has weight, but is not resistant to brown treak virus	Characteristics are too extreme to cross with marketable variety

It would be impractical to expect farmers such as Cosmas to undertake crossing programmes using hand pollination. Indeed, given the objective of the breeding exercise, hand pollination was thought to be unnecessary. Instead, Kanju suggested that the breeding experiment should be carried out on a plot isolated from other cassava by at least 100 metres. By planting alternate rows of *Kigoma Mafia* and *Kibaha* on staggered planting dates, and by destroying the male reproductive parts of the *Kigoma Mafia*, the chances of *Kigoma Mafia* being pollinated by *Kibaha* through insect activity becomes very high. Large numbers of seed from the cross could be collected and tested the following season. Those with promising characteristics would be vegetatively propagated by the farmer in the normal way.

Achievements and prospects

This pilot exercise achieved the following:

- it broadened the scientists' understanding of the farmers' knowledge of cassava production and reproduction
- it created an opportunity for a farmer to take the initiative in developing a new variety of cassava
- it started a process which the farmer can develop independently of the Naliendele institute's resources

- it put forward an alternative framework for the development of varieties for smallholder farmers living within highly diverse, complex and resource–poor agroecological environments, and
- it produced a video document of farmers and extensionists learning from each other. This video, called NGOGO, is available at the Mtwara Video Centre.

Conclusion

If farmers gain the knowledge Cosmas now has, then the opportunities for many of them to take the initiative and develop varieties of their own choice, using input germplasm from many sources, including research stations, are immense.

photo: Mathias Mogge

6. Extension through farmer experimentation in Sudan

*Samia Osman Ishag, Omelnisaa Hassan Al Fakie,
Mohamed Ahmed Adam, Yassir Mohamed Adam,
Khalil Waggan Bremer and Mathias Mogge[1]*

In Sudan, as in many other developing countries, government agricultural services are short
of funds and concentrated in regions where cash crops can be produced for export. Remote
areas are neglected, even though they may be important for local markets and have some

[1] Samia Osman Ishag, Khalil Waggan Bremer, Yassir Mohamed Adam, Omelnisaa Hassan Al Fakie,
Mohamed Ahmed Adam and Mathias Mogge (German Development Service), Natural Resources
Management Project (NARMAP) Kutum Province, North Darfur, c/o GTZ-PAS, PO Box 8192, Al Amarat,
Khartoum. Sudan. Mathias Mogge, Bergstr. 41, D-37139 Adelebsen, Germany.

farming potential. In the future, improving food production in these areas will be increasingly vital in order to supply food for the growing population.

In the 1980s, one such remote area, North Darfur, suffered from severe drought and food shortage. In 1989, a Sudanese–German project was set up to rehabilitate the natural resources. It encountered problems in implementing the activities planned originally, not only because the area was affected by the conflict in neighbouring Chad but also because the project was trying to cover too large an area and the staff had little experience. In 1993, the project was re–oriented, focusing on developing the agricultural potential of a smaller area around Kutum. It followed a 'Farmer First' approach (Chambers et al. 1989) of working together with local farmers to develop appropriate ways of managing natural resources.

After a brief description of the project area, an overview of the project's history and current activities is given, focusing on the process of setting up a farmer–to–farmer extension programme based on farmer experimentation.

The setting

The project lies in Kutum Province in the hot semi–arid Sahel zone of Africa. Annual rainfall ranges between 150 and 300 mm and falls from July to September; the average temperature is 23.6°C. After the rainy season, there is a relatively cool winter (October–February) and then a hot season (April–June). The landscape consists of numerous broad and narrow wadis (streams that flow only after rainfall) separated by rocky and eroded hills.

The project area covers around 2000 km² and has about 50 000 inhabitants. Most are Tunjur, Fur and Zarahwa farmers, settled in small villages close to the wadis, although some members of these groups are still semi–nomads. Women bear the main burden of work in cultivation, in addition to their child–caring and housekeeping responsibilities. Men dig wells, build huts and manage public affairs in the village. They also help their wives in rainfed cropping. Very few men work in the gardens. In the Province, some Rezegat nomads keep camels and move in a south–north pattern. According to the local Rural Council, they make up roughly 20% of the population. A few pastoral families have settled and now pursue farming as their main source of income.

The decreasing rainfall since 1960 and especially the many years of drought led to a concentration of people around Kutum town. Many men migrated to other Arabian countries or to larger Sudanese towns in order to earn money to send home to their families. In Kutum, there are few possibilities to earn cash outside farming, except for some basket–making, charcoal–making, firewood supply and trading activities.

Along the wadis where the groundwater is close to the surface, the fields are irrigated from wells. The irrigated strips vary from 200 to 500 m in width. On the gentler slopes, rainfed farming is practised, mainly with millet (*Pennisetum typhoides*). Each year, the soil cover is eroded further by water and wind. Making bunds to collect and retain rainfall is a traditional practice. Particularly the farmers in Amu, a small part of the project area, have developed a sophisticated and effective way of using stones and soil to make bunds, but this practice does not seem to have spread. Elsewhere in the project area, only a few farmers have made

Figure 6.1: Map of Sudan (Craig 1991)

very simple bunds, sometimes with stone linings or branches, but have not maintained them well. Most farmers do not apply the technique at all.

In the wadi gardens, which range in size from 1000 to 2500 m², both vegetables (tomatoes, okra, onions, carrots, beets) and fruits (mangoes, citrus, guava, dates) are grown. These gardens are important for family survival. In years of low rainfall, when little or no millet can be harvested, the families can sell the vegetables and fruits in order to buy millet. They thus depend less on external aid than in areas where only rainfed farming is practised. Nearly all the available land in the narrow alluvial area of Wadi Kutum is cultivated. Room for expan-

91

sion is limited, but there remains potential for intensifying food production by making more efficient use of resources.

History of the project

When severe drought hit North Darfur in the 1980s, the Federal Republic of Germany initially supplied food aid and then supported appraisal activities for designing a rehabilitation project. In February 1989, the Sudanese Ministry of Agricultural and Natural Resources (MOANR) and the German Agency for Technical Cooperation (GTZ) started to implement the Natural Resource Management Project (NARMAP) in Kutum Province. MOANR could not make much of a financial contribution, but it was able to second six of its staff. In addition, the two government extension officers in the Province take part in internal project workshops and farmer training courses and sometimes accompany project staff to the field.

NARMAP was originally planned as an integrated rural development project. During a two–year orientation phase (1989-91), suitable techniques and methods of natural resource management were to be identified. But by early 1990, when the Chad conflict extended to the Kutum area, project activities were slowed down considerably. The German staff had to be evacuated. The Sudanese staff continued a reduced programme, mainly building wells and schools and supplying agricultural inputs.

During this phase, we tried to work simultaneously with: the people practising irrigated and rainfed farming (planned activities included reafforestation, rainwater harvesting and the introduction of quick–maturing millet varieties); the nomads (building wells and distributing camel medicine); and the people who live mainly from making baskets (poultry farming as an additional source of income). We also planned to promote compost–making and improved stoves and to give horticultural advice. The project area was so large that we could not interact frequently enough with farmers to discuss and test innovations. Moreover, most of the staff, both Sudanese and German, were working for the first time in a multi–sectoral project. Our annual plans consistently failed to be realistic about our technical and managerial capacities. By 1992, some trees had been planted, some wells dug, a poultry shed built, some support given to local school construction, and some vegetable seeds and date palms distributed, but all far below target.

In late 1992, we started internal monitoring and evaluation of our activities. Until then, we had no clear strategy for discovering the ideas of the intended beneficiaries or for approaching them in such a way that they would develop interest in our ideas. After our evaluation, we began to develop a concept for establishing a farmer–to–farmer extension programme. In 1993, the project assumed responsibility for the government tree nursery in Kutum, with the aim of renewing the infrastructure, diversifying the fruit–tree varieties and improving nursery management to produce high–quality seedlings, but also to use the nursery for experimentation and training.

A review of project progress in early 1994 brought out clearly the previously mentioned weaknesses. At the subsequent planning workshop, the overall goal for the phase 1994-1997 was redefined as: stabilizing food production and the natural resource base in the Wadi

Kutum area through the adaptation and application of improved, resource–conserving techniques of horticulture, cropping, forestry and water management by the local people. As we realized that we did not have the capacity to work in all land–use systems, and found it especially difficult to reach the camel nomads, we focused on activities with settled farmers.

Communication between villagers and project

From the beginning in 1989, NARMAP was designed as a self–help scheme. The villagers were asked to nominate local committees of 10-14 members to act as links between village and project. Initially, four local committees were formed. They coordinated activities such as building wells and schools, and distributing forest–tree seedlings and vegetable seed which the project made available at cost price. The committees represented not just single villages but also the surrounding hamlets; as managing village infrastructure was regarded as men's responsibility, the villagers selected only men as members.

Few people were keen on being actively involved. Neither the committee members nor the villagers as a whole felt responsible for the activities proposed by the project; they were simply receivers of the services and innovations offered. If the services could improve their living conditions (schools, wells, farm inputs), they welcomed and supported them. Interest expressed initially by the committees in innovations such as compost–making, improved stoves, afforestation and poultry sheds waned quickly, possibly because their potential advantages were not clear. The committees asked NARMAP mainly for infrastructure facilities; otherwise, they simply waited to see what the project would offer next. In addition to general lack of interest, the migration of some of the members created problems.

When we started the farmer–to–farmer extension programme in 1993, the local committees were turned into Agricultural Extension Committees (AECs) which were supposed to guide the extension work in collaboration with the project. The idea was that improved horticultural techniques would be developed together with farmers selected by the committees. These farmers would serve their fellow villagers as Village Extension Agents (VEAs). They would be given training and would carry out trials in order to find appropriate solutions to problems in their areas. In monthly village meetings involving the AEC, the VEAs, project staff and all other interested people, agricultural extension activities would be planned and the joint activities of the village and project would be coordinated. An overview of the functions of the AECs within the context of the local institutions is given in Table 6.1.

By 1993, it was not easy to convince the villagers that the project policy had changed and we were now seeking their active participation in designing and implementing extension. We had to prove not only that we took their opinions seriously but also that their collaboration was essential for the sustainable development of the area. It became necessary for the project to improve communication links so that we could hear and understand the farmers' ideas.

We opened an Agricultural Information Centre at Kutum market to inform as many people as possible about project policy and activities by means of posters, leaflets and practical demonstrations, such as comparing traditional and improved three–stone stoves and showing how to make a neem solution as pesticide. Tree seedlings are also sold there. Because there are no other media such as radio, television or newspapers in the area, this shop has become an important means of communication. We also encouraged all farmers to visit the project office at any time.

A change was made in the way the monthly village meetings of the AEC, VEAs and project staff were organized: the president of the committee invites the project, instead of the latter announcing the meeting, and the AEC itself prepares the agenda.

A significant step toward improving communication between villagers and project was made when we learned to do Participatory Rural Appraisal (PRA) in July 1994. We carried out several surveys using such methods as semi−structured interviews, direct observation, group discussions, seasonal farming calendars, diagramming of daily activities by both men and women, mapping of fields and villages, matrix ranking, and staying overnight in the villages so that the evening could be spent in informal dialogue with members of farm families.

Table 6.1. The functions of village institutions involved in extension

Institutions	*Tasks and responsibilities*
Rural Councils and Town Council	• Informed by NARMAP and presidents of the PSC about activities in the villages; support ideas of NARMAP and the villages
Popular Salvation Committee (PSC)	• General supervision; integrate work of the AEC into general development policy of the village
Agricultural Extension Committee (AEC)	• Organize extension and development in a given area • Plan and manage agricultural extension and development • Supervise work of VEAs • Manage the tool bank • Distribute and account for farming inputs provided by NARMAP or bought on the market • Arrange monthly meetings of VEAs, AECs, PSC and NARMAP • Discuss and decide on expenditure of income from the tool bank • Compensate VEAs for their work according to their performance • Arrange training courses for farmers, together with the VEAs previously trained by NARMAP • Inform the PSC about problems and achievements
Village Extension Agent (VEA)	• Participate in training courses • Conduct trials in order to define improved farming practices • Train farmers • Advise farmers • Visit farmers in their fields • Exchange knowledge with farmers from other areas • Inform AEC about problems and achievements related to extension

We frequently experienced a single PRA tool opening the door to much fruitful discussion. For example, drawing a simple map led into a discussion about the tree cover and general development possibilities of the area, while matrix ranking gave a clear view of different opportunities and their relative importance (e.g. comparing different farming systems according to inputs needed, economic benefits and ecological effects) and helped both the farmers and the project to make realistic decisions. Such intensive discussions became a starting–point for joint planning. For example, it was during matrix ranking (see Table 6.2) and the lively accompanying discussion that an activity which had been in the project's plan of operations from the outset was cancelled. We had regarded the planting of forest trees as essential for regenerating natural resources in the area but, during the PRA, we discovered that the farmers were much more interested in agroforestry.

Table 6.2. Comparison and ranking of activities in Amu village

Criteria	*Forest*	*Millet*	*Agroforestry*	*Horticulture*
On which system do you depend most?	1	4	3	3
Risk	-	4	3	2
Input/output ratio	1	2	2	4
Commercialization	1	4	3	3
Impact on environment	3	1	4	2

Note: 1 = lowest; 4 = highest

Although the project had worked in the area already for five years, PRA gave us new insights and allowed us to exchange many ideas with villagers. Up to this point, we had not been able to learn of their opinions in such a way that we could react quickly. Simply posing questions had not stimulated discussion and broken the ice between project staff and villagers in the same way as was possible by applying PRA tools. With PRA we could enter frank and detailed discussions with committee members and other villagers about the way the AECs were working. This helped both sides understand the problems within the committees and between them and the project. This process of finding out about each other is still underway.

Involving women in the committees

It was after the internal evaluation in late 1992 that we started to encourage active involvement of women in the committees, as we realized that the men did not invite them to the village meetings and generally did not inform them about the results. Two female staff members were appointed to strengthen women's involvement. The villagers then formed committees consisting of both men and women. The project maintained a policy of joint meetings of all committee members; in this public setting, the women had no voice.

In the culture of North Darfur, it is expected that public decisions be taken by men. Women are not used to attending public meetings, and cultural barriers prevent them from expressing themselves (shyness in women is regarded as a sign of politeness). Most women are illiterate, and many parents still send only their sons to school. If they do pay for a daughter to go to school, she has to leave when she marries. Early marriage is very common. The family does not want to do without the domestic help of a daughter or young wife. Because many men migrate to urban areas or abroad, there is a growing number of female−headed households in the Kutum area. The domestic responsibilities of the women limit their possibilities to participate in public meetings.

Continuous discussions and negotiations were needed to lower at least some of the cultural barriers to women's participation. We managed to organize a few meetings of female committee members only and found that the women then expressed their own opinions very well. However, the men often tried to participate also in these meetings. They told us that women might not understand the point of the project and needed male help. The women generally seemed to accept that the men joined and took the lead in expressing opinions. Wherever we could, we encouraged separate meetings, forming in essence separate male and female subcommittees. Both suggested to us that they come together afterwards to summarize what they had done separately.

The men were astonished and envious when they saw how the women were organizing themselves and making their own arrangements with the project. For example, when there were only all−male committees, the distribution of seed from the project had not worked very well, as the men had kept the seed for themselves. Very often, the women never got to hear of the opportunity to obtain seed at cost price. When the subcommittees were formed, however, the women, too, had a chance to control seed distribution. One female subcommittee arranged to obtain seed on credit because the women have much more limited cash reserves than have the men. Fearing that they would not get access to the tool banks (see below) offered by the project, the women demanded full participation in the administration of these banks. These negotiation processes have greatly enhanced the self−confidence of the female subcommittees.

Of course, every village has its particularities. In one, committee members did not want separate meetings, and we did not insist on this against their will. The group continues to hold mixed meetings and appears to function quite well.

The discussions triggered off by PRA offered an excellent opportunity for the villagers to consider the importance of female involvement in planning and evaluating activities and making decisions. PRA also allowed more open communication between project staff and village women, which was of great help in encouraging the latter's active involvement in committee work. In one village, the women were very shy in discussions with both male and female project staff, even when the local men were not present. When the men were sitting close by, the women said nothing at all. We were at a loss to know what these women were thinking. During PRA in 1994, three female staff members (two of us working in horticultural extension and one newly–appointed in agroforestry) visited the village and surrounding hamlets one evening and in this very informal setting encountered completely changed women, talking eagerly and raising issues of which we had not previously heard. From then onwards, female staff have been meeting with women in this particular village only in the evening, sometimes staying overnight. It is a completely different atmosphere sitting together in the dark, not being in a hurry, not being able to see clearly the woman who is talking. The darkness dissolves the barriers to speaking out.

We have had particularly good experiences in holding planning sessions with some women's subcommittees. Each woman is given cards on which to write down her ideas. Those who cannot write ask a literate woman to do so on their behalf. The cards are pinned on a board and read out for all to see, hear and consider. By the end of the meeting, there is a board full of pinned cards expressing all the women's ideas about their problems, proposed solutions and the role of the committee in trying to achieve them. This is used as a kind of planning matrix. The same method applied with men has not been so successful, possibly because some men feel more ashamed to admit in public that they cannot write. Here, it might be better if a project staff member writes down their contributions.

The closer communication between the project and village women has led to new activities. The women are interested not only in farming but in improving family life as a whole, and they seek project support for this. At their request, we organized training courses in nutrition, family planning, primary healthcare and environmental awareness (which is being promoted by the state) at the Women's Nutrition Centre in Kutum. This centre had been inactive for several years. Also at the women's request, we conducted several village–based courses on building improved three–stone stoves. Holding one course in each village was enough to spread the idea rapidly throughout the entire village. The women are now asking for literacy classes and we are seeking the cooperation of local teachers or students in this.

Village Extension Agents

Some farmers in and around Kutum bring new techniques and experiences into the area. They are normally wealthier than average; they can travel and take risks trying out something new even if it might fail. If it proves to be successful, these farmers often keep the innovation to themselves. Resource–poor farmers and particularly women may never learn about it, or only after a considerable time–lag. Besides, the wealthier producers own pumps and enjoy better production conditions and possibilities than the average farmer.

In meetings with the village committees, project staff reflected on the rich experience of local farmers and their motivation to improve agricultural practices. We discussed the possibility of setting up a farmer–to–farmer extension programme with Village Extension Agents (VEAs) so that many farmers would have access to useful information. We suggested that the committees select average (rather than 'progressive') farmers, who represent the majority in the village area. In dialogue, the AEC and the project developed joint criteria for selecting VEAs: interest in joining the extension programme, sedentary, access to land for cultivation and, in the case of female VEAs, permission from the husband.

Training

In October 1993, four men and one woman in four village areas were selected as VEAs. Initially, they were more like contact farmers for the project and the committees, rather than extension agents. To prepare for their future role, they attended several courses about farming and communication techniques. Project staff visited these farmers once a week in their wadi gardens or fields. From time to time, meetings were held for the entire village so that everybody could become better acquainted with the work of the AECs, the VEAs and the project. These gatherings were initiated by the project but arranged by the AEC. During this quite vague initial stage with many uncertainties on the side of both the project and the villagers, our main objectives were:

- to build up mutual confidence between project and villagers
- to become better acquainted with the local farming systems
- to develop a trial programme together with the VEAs
- to discuss possible ways of disseminating information to other farmers
- to link the VEAs with the AEC and other farmers
- to define the responsibilities of the VEAs together with the AEC
- to consider ways of recompensing the work of the VEAs.

In 1994, the four villages decided to increase the number of VEAs to 16. The proportion of women rose to 60% (i.e. 10 female VEAs). This change was possible because the men had realized by then that hardly any material inputs could be obtained from the project. They were constantly seeking cement, pumps or agricultural tools, but the project offers only farming advice, seeds for on–farm trials and a concept for self–help development. The women work mainly in horticulture, and could appreciate the extension more than could the men. We feel, however, that it was necessary to start by giving men the chance to be VEAs; if we had started immediately to work with the women, the men would have been suspicious and might have put up resistance.

The Kutum Horticultural Nursery, which belongs to MOANR but is managed by the project, serves as the main training–ground for the VEAs and other farmers, and also serves as a testing–ground where new techniques and varieties can be tried out. It is the only government nursery in Northern Darfur that produces high–quality fruit seedlings. Government nurseries normally sell their products at prices too low to cover their operating costs, and staff are poorly paid. The project is trying to charge prices based on actual production costs, but still needs additional support. As it is unlikely that the Ministry can afford to give this support in the future, the project is deliberately promoting private nursery operators. They should be enabled to continue producing high–quality seedlings after the five–year period during which the project manages the government nursery. The private operators can benefit from the many new varieties being raised there and are given intensive training in fruit production.

The training given to VEAs and farmers at the nursery is practical. Courses are planned together with the farmers according to their needs and usually last 3-4 days. Most of the costs are borne by the project, but the AECs make a small contribution. In their own fields, the VEAs carry out simple trials (see below).

Payment

If village–based extension is to be sustainable, ways have to be found to recompense the VEAs for their work. There were long discussions between project and committees about how best this might be achieved: payment in kind (dates, onions), organizing a *nafir* (traditional form of communal work) in the VEA's field, or payment in cash. All the villages opted for the last–mentioned, as they regarded this to be easier than payment in kind and because there are already numerous *nafir* throughout the year. The payment begins after the VEA has received training, conducted trials and is proved to be reliable. Initially, the project made recommendations about how reliability could be assessed, but the judgement itself is made by the AECs according to written criteria; for example, the committee specifies how many times a week the VEA should visit other farmers.

In the beginning, the AEC provided one third of the cash, and the project provided the rest. The latter's share is scheduled to decrease until it becomes zero after two years. The payment for each VEA is in the range of LS (Sudanese pounds) 4000-7000 a month, depending on the decision of the AEC; for the sake of comparison, the daily labour wage is LS 500 a day. Part of the local payment is provided by the Popular Salvation Committee (see Table 6.1) of the village, using funds from the sugar tax. Another part comes from the tool bank. This means that the VEAs are paid by the village as a whole. If a VEA receives LS 7000 a month and there are, for example, 100 households in the village, each household indirectly pays LS 70. This is the equivalent of US$0.08 or one grapefruit sold. We noted that when payments started to be made, general interest in the extension programme increased on the part of both the farmers, who share the costs, and the VEAs, who take their job more seriously.

In early 1995, the project also introduced the idea of keeping a local store for agricultural tools, mainly to be used for rainwater harvesting and horticulture. By the end of that year, five villages had tool banks. We are trying to distribute the banks as widely as possible, equipping all villages that have a functioning AEC or are working with the project in rainwater harvesting, and aim to cover most of the project area by the end of 1997. Tools are lent to farmers at a daily charge: a shovel for LS 100, wheelbarrow LS 250, donkey cart LS 500. The AECs manage the accounts of these tool banks and are expected to use the income to repair old tools, buy replacement ones and, if there is still money left, pay part of the remuneration for the VEAs. To date, the tools are being lent out regularly and the payments are being made. In the longer term, however, other income–generating schemes to support the village–based extensionists will probably have to be explored.

Experimentation by VEAs

There are only two extension officers in all of Kutum Province, without a research station to support their work. In view of the economic situation and priorities of the government, there is little likelihood that the farmers will receive better agricultural services in the near future. It is therefore essential not just to transfer messages but rather to strengthen the self–help capacity of the farmers so that they can continue agricultural development on their own. If the government is able to give more support to food production at some time in the future, it will hopefully encounter farmers who can express themselves self–confidently and critically in order to demand the services they really need and who do not just wait for what is offered.

We encourage farmers to search on their own for innovations and ideas for developing better and more sustainable ways of farming. The project serves as a facilitator and supplies some basic agricultural knowledge and ideas about experimentation, so that the farmers can enhance their capacity to carry out their own trials.

Objectives

Our intention is not to show the farmers the right and the wrong way of growing fruits and vegetables but rather to encourage them to try something new and to overcome existing problems through experimentation. We offer examples of what could be done to improve farming techniques, and the VEAs choose what they want to try. Some of the innovations we have suggested are these:

- planting on ridges instead of in basins, particularly for tubers
- sowing in lines instead of broadcasting
- various forms of intercropping and crop rotation
- new rhizobium strains for leguminous crops
- using natural pesticides such as neem or garlic
- using *Cajanus cajan* as a windbreak and food crop
- pollination and maintenance of date palms
- new techniques in vegetable seed selection.

Box 6.1 gives an example of an experiment which one VEA chose to implement. It is translated from her hand–written records in Arabic.

In discussions with the VEAs, we always emphasize that we are dealing with experiments and that the results have to be awaited before knowing whether the techniques or varieties can be recommended to other farmers. In the final analysis, each farmer will have to try out the promising innovations for her/himself. The experimentation with ideas proposed by the project is meant simply as a starting–point. We do not intend to use the VEAs as channels through whom the project transfers as many innovations as possible to farmers. Our main aim is to render the farmers capable of doing their own, appropriately structured trials in the future without any help or inputs from us. This is essential to sustainability. New techniques or varieties may be momentarily appropriate, but technology must still continue to be developed after the project ends. Farmers have to be able to find solutions for future problems on their own. Hopefully, in the more distant future, there will also be some government research and extension services with which they can collaborate.

Other than seeds of new varieties, we give no other inputs in kind to the VEAs for conducting their trials. In the long term, the AECs will have to find ways of procuring such inputs for experimentation by the VEAs, using either the income from the tool bank or other sources. We hope that such a system can be set in place before the project is dismantled. Just as the payment of VEAs has increased local ownership of extension, the procurement of trial inputs by the village committees may increase local interest in the experiments.

Guidance

We encourage all farmers to try out new ideas, but we concentrate on strengthening the capacities of VEAs to conduct trials. In the beginning, we advise them how to set up a trial with a single–paired treatment design (cf. Werner 1993), often using their traditional technique in the control plot. Such simple trials, each designed with only one objective, are easy for the farmers to handle when they first embark on structured tests using new inputs. Each VEA experiments simultaneously with a broad spectrum of techniques (the number of trials varies between 3 and 10) to increase the chance that at least something will prove successful. This is important for building up a spirit of experimentation; if a trial fails, the farmers can easily be discouraged. If they see that a change in techniques is really better, they are more likely to search on their own for new ideas.

When a project staff member visits a VEA, each trial is discussed and assessed in detail. We exchange views and learn from each other; this helps to improve the trial design and generate new ideas. We ask repeatedly why a certain problem arises; for example, when a pest or disease is found in a crop, we ask what the reasons for this might be. It is not enough to propose a certain pesticide without having understood the cause of the problem.

Box 6.1. Experiment done by a female VEA

Trial 1: Onions
Seedling production (comparison between sowing in lines and broadcasting). Comparison between imported variety [authors' note: Texas early grano, resistant to pink root–rot] and local variety.

Sowing in line:	Sowing date:	15.10.1994
	Germination date:	24.10.1994
	Transplanting date:	01.01.1995
	Harvest date:	25.06.1995

Sowing in basin (broadcasting):	Sowing date:	15.10.1994
	Germination date:	24.10.1994
	Transplanting date:	01.01.1995
	Harvest date:	25.06.1995

I transplanted all my seedlings in basins. I observed that, although the seed was improved, a disease called pink root–rot appeared on the roots. Anyway, after two months, the onions were growing well. But after that, all the green parts of the onions were eaten by animals. After that, I irrigated for 3 months and the onions reached maturity. I needed a lot of time to irrigate these onions. The onions grown from improved seeds were not affected by animals, but the local onion variety did not give any yield at all. I harvested 2 sacks of the improved onion variety.

I observed some differences between sowing in lines and broadcasting: in the past I used to sow onions for seedling production by broadcasting. But now I know from the project another way by sowing in lines. It is good because it gives me vigorous seedlings and weeding is easier. I need less seed. If the line is too close, weeding is difficult.

Although encouraging experimentation is our main aim, we also offer information and training in those special skills in which farmers express interest. For example, we have held courses in the pollination of date–palms, the selection of male date–palms and the use of neem as a pesticide. During the courses, the farmers are asked to observe carefully what it is happening in their gardens. For example, a lengthy process of observation is required to find out which male palms should be used for pollination to give the best crop. The project gives advice only about how to pollinate, together with information about the relationship between selection and production. VEAs then use the knowledge they have gained about setting up trials to continue observing production and drawing conclusions. They can approach the project whenever they feel in need of help.

Similarly, VEAs are encouraged to make their own observations about what is the best concentration of neem solution to use against a certain pest. Some VEAs are, for example, testing neem against insects on tomatoes. We show them how to prepare the solution and suggest when to apply it (only when the insects appear). We explain how they could record the different concentrations tried and their observations of the effects.

It is always a good sign when VEAs take the initiative to change things suggested by the project. For example, we introduced the idea of growing crops like tomato, carrot and beetroot on ridges rather than in basins. We thought this might reduce the fungus infection in tomato and bring a higher percentage of big roots in carrots and beets. On her own initiative, one female VEA applied this technique to onions. She got good results and showed her products to all AEC presidents and other VEAs during the annual evaluation meeting (see below). Another VEA tried to sow carrots on ridges, but the result was poor: there were no carrots at all on one side of the ridges. This man started on his own to experiment by changing the direction of the ridges and covering the seeds with date–palm leaves until emergence, in order to prevent direct sunlight on one side of the ridge. He sowed deeper in the soil and somewhat closer to the bottom of the furrow. After several rounds of experimentation, he managed to obtain a more even distribution of the crop on both sides of the ridge.

Many VEAs have begun to develop their own trials, including both their and the project's ideas. During the evaluation meetings attended by all VEAs, suggestions for trials are exchanged. In one instance, a female VEA reported her experiences in planting large onions instead of the small ones of inferior quality that most farmers use for seed production. Other VEAs have taken up this idea and are comparing the use of large and small onions for seed production in their own plots.

Monitoring and evaluation

Making observations and collecting data are necessary for sound interpretation of trial results. VEAs use notebooks to record times of sowing, flowering, transplanting and harvesting, and some observations. These include qualitative descriptions, but not much quantitative information from counting or measuring (see Box 6.1). The VEAs appear to have little desire to gather measurable data. Most of them do not have a weighing scale. But is it really necessary to collect exact data? It depends on who is carrying out a trial and what one wants to know. It is easy for farmers to notice whether pollinating the date–palms had any advantage: they make qualitative assessments of the general appearance of the fruit and note the size of single fruits. For most farmers, this visual assessment is enough, and they see no point in measuring the yield.

Similarly, treatment with neem against aphids either reduces the number of aphids or it does not. It might be interesting for a scientist to know to what degree the incidence of aphids can be reduced, but for the farmers it is most important to know whether neem saves the plant from destruction or not. If the aphids remain on the plant, the farmers may increase the concentration of neem solution. They may also try out the solution against other insects on other types of plants. Close observation helps them decide what to do.

In other trials, the farmers may need to measure more exactly in order to decide whether or not a technique is useful. For example, the success of inoculating alfalfa seeds with rhizobium bacteria can be measured by comparing cutting frequencies in the trial and control plots. We encourage the recording of observations rather than just measuring. When comparing the trial and control plots, the VEAs recognize even very small changes about which we did not explicitly ask, e.g. the different size of seedlings which are sown in rows and less densely than normal practice, or the fact that carrots grown on ridges can be harvested earlier. Thus far, most VEAs make these comments orally when we visit the fields together with them, but they do not normally keep written records of these additional observations. This is an aspect of recording which we are still discussing with them. Together, we need to clarify for what purpose data are being collected. Only where the VEAs recognize information as useful for themselves and others will they commit it to paper.

All the innovations and training sessions during a year are evaluated at an annual one−day meeting at the Agricultural Information Centre at Kutum market. The presidents of the AECs and all VEAs are invited, and part of the meeting is held in a garden of a VEA. Products from the trials of other VEAs are also presented, experiences of trials exchanged, and contacts between different villages and VEAs established. Besides the informal discussions, a structured session is arranged to discuss each topic, the results of the trials and the participants' opinions about them. VEAs report on the numbers of farmers they have trained in their village areas and under what circumstances the training took place.

The project introduces new vegetable varieties and species that promise to be better than local varieties, by giving VEAs small quantities of seed for testing. The new varieties are assessed according to such parameters as taste, marketability, transportability and susceptibility to pests and diseases. The parameters are formulated by the project after discussions with the VEAs and validated by the AEC presidents and VEAs at the beginning of the session. Not all the new varieties meet with the farmers' approval. For example, one onion variety we proposed because of its resistance to a common disease was rejected because it has a white skin and lacks pungency and is therefore difficult to sell. In contrast, a tomato variety suggested by us was indeed taken up because it is firm and transports well over long distances, in contrast to the soft local varieties. In this case, at least one constraint to marketing could be removed.

We have found that the joint evaluation sessions are extremely useful for ensuring that the project staff and the villagers are thinking along the same lines. In this way, misunderstandings, mistakes and inappropriate techniques can be avoided or, at least, reduced.

Planning a trial programme

At the beginning of the 1995 vegetable–growing season, we met with the VEAs and the AEC members of each village in order to discuss for the first time a more structured trial programme. During these meetings, a rough plan for each village area was drawn up. The specific way to implement the trials was then discussed with each VEA at the trial sites. In many instances, neighbours who were curious about what is going on in the VEA's garden also joined the discussions.

During the annual evaluation meeting later in 1995, we suggested the possibility of joint planning by all VEAs in a village. This idea has already been taken up by one village without any further involvement by the project (Box 6.2). It became obvious that the whole concept of experimentation had became clear to the farmers and that it meets with their interest. Already during the evaluation session, they had started to discuss new ideas for trials, maybe because they had seen interesting results during the field visits. We asked the VEAs to bring some examples of crops grown in their trials, representing either positive or negative results. Invariably, they brought only products of the former. In the field, we had already seen

---

Box 6.2. Annual plan made by the Bowa Village Agricultural Extension Committee (VEAC)
(translated from the original Arabic)

By the name of the god
Date: 22 November 1995
Male & female VAEC Bowa
Subject: Planning of agricultural activities for 1995-96

After evaluating the needs of the agricultural season 1996, which were discussed among both male and female committees in a meeting on 21 November 1995, and after discussion with villagers, we came to the following plan:

1. Construction of bunds on 9 farms; approx. 6 feddan.
2. Wadi bank stabilization on 6 farms to protect the banks from erosion. Digging and planting of trees and Abu Salbanj grass; approx. 500 m.
3. Preparation of school garden and communal nursery.
4 Replanting forest seedlings in the communal as well as private forests.
5. Coordination of the work of male and female VEAs as follows:
    a) follow up trials of the VEAs
    b) organize training for other farmers
    c) invite villagers to the VEAs' gardens to explain the positive and negative aspects of the trials
    d) follow up farmers who were in contact with a VEA to see whether they are applying anything new
    e) each VEA should visit a minimum of 7 farmers a month
    f) each VEA should prepare a monthly report for the village AEC (female VEA for the female VEAC and male VEA for the male VEAC).

Thank you.
Achmed Omar Adam
Head of the VAEC Bowa

---

in some trials that there was no obvious difference between innovation and control, or that the control plot brought better results. But an atmosphere of constructive competition appears to be rising among the experimenting farmers, who are proud to present to the others something new which can be positive to them all.

Increasing interest of women

At the beginning, most VEAs were men, many of whom did not seem to recognize the benefits of experimentation. The whole idea of conducting structured trials was new to them, and many of the techniques we suggested appeared odd. Sometimes, a VEA with several wives was away from his garden for a long period because he was staying with a wife living elsewhere. Even the male VEAs who were not absent failed to do most of the work in the gardens. This was done by their wives according to their husbands' instructions. A few VEAs situated their trials in unsuitable places (e.g. on the border of the garden, in the shade, on poor soil), preferring to reserve the better sites to grow crops in the traditional way rather than to use them for strange experiments. After one or two years of working with the project, these VEAs began to see that others were getting better results from the very same innovations because the sites chosen were more favourable.

As the men realized that the collaboration with the project was mostly concerned with horticultural trials and brought little benefit in terms of material inputs, their interest in being VEAs gradually declined, while the women's interest increased. As more women became involved as VEAs, the work went better. The women are critical of ideas coming from the project, as they hold their traditional techniques in high esteem. They are, however, interested in trying out new methods which seem reasonable to them. Female VEAs have proved to be more motivated to conduct experiments with precision. Even those who are illiterate try to keep records by asking their children or literate female neighbours to note down the observations for them. The women carry out trials on their own initiative to the same extent as do the men. There are marked differences in how much male and female VEAs record and the importance they attach to this. When we asked all VEAs to bring their notebooks with them to the most recent evaluation session, all ten female VEAs did so but only one of the six males.

The female VEAs make up a heterogeneous group. For example, one is still at school, one is single and living with her family, one is the third wife of a rather old man. The youngest is 15 years old and the oldest about 55. All face problems with time, as they have many tasks outside their work in experimentation and extension. Some find the burden too much. One women who worked as VEA at the beginning of the project resigned because she could not find enough time; however, she remained involved as a member of the AEC. The women who continue to work as VEAs have husbands, children or other family members who are willing to take over some of the other household tasks when the women are absent, e.g. for training sessions or evaluation meetings. It is important that the women's families, indeed the entire community, understand the value of the VEAs' work and support it actively, as is happening increasingly, for example, during *nafir*. Women who hope to learn something from the VEAs are keen to join *nafir* on their plots.

Although most VEAs are women, a few male ones remain. This is important because they represent the small number of male farmers who are active in vegetable farming; moreover, taking care of fruit trees and date–palms is usually the work of men, so they are the most suitable people to be doing extension in this field.

Extension by the VEAs

VEAs give training to groups of farmers in their village areas, and also visit individual gardens. In the case of technical information such as pruning fruit trees or improving irrigation techniques, the VEA explains and demonstrates what is meant. If the topic needs verification or is controversial (e.g. line–sowing, natural plant protection, crop spacing), the VEA helps the farmers lay out small trials. During these visits, there is an intensive exchange of information between farmers. The VEAs are in a much better position than project staff to know the most suitable times and places for such meetings during different seasons of the year.

During the latest evaluation session, we learned that some VEAs gave village courses during specially convened meetings, but that training took place also during *nafir*, when one farmer invites others to help in a certain labour–intensive task and provides food in return. Numerous *nafir* are organized throughout the year, e.g. for preparing land, transplanting onions or threshing millet. Women, especially, help each other in this way. Female VEAs reported that, during *nafir* for transplanting onions in November, they showed the other women how very dense sowing results in weak seedlings which require a long time to grow big. Particularly in those rural areas where women's participation in public life is restricted, the female VEAs have difficulties in expressing themselves orally. They appear to find it easier to convey information about agricultural matters during communal activities or social celebrations. These traditional meetings are probably more effective occasions for active learning than distinct training courses in which information is conveyed in a more theoretical way.

VEAs feed back problems and questions to the AEC and to the project. During the various annual and monthly meetings, they have an opportunity to learn from each other and from project staff. The project invites specialists from universities and research stations in other areas, who conduct training courses in the nursery or visit VEAs in their villages. We take every possible opportunity to bring formal researchers and farmers together. For example, a group of researchers came recently from Khartoum with the intention of surveying the local potential for growing soft dates. Fortunately, they were willing to meet and discuss with the farmers on other topics, as well, and agreed to give some training on the spot in pollinating date–palms, separating suckers, maintaining fruit trees and recognizing virus diseases in citrus. VEAs and other interested farmers accompany project staff on trips, such as to the Jebbel Marra region, where horticulture is quite advanced. In this way, we hope to help the Kutum farmers establish useful links with institutions and farmers in other areas.

Conclusions

After two years of experience with the programme of agricultural extension through farmers' experimentation, we are already observing important changes in comparison with our earlier project work. Farmers are adapting and adopting new ideas, techniques and varieties, because they now participate in planning and evaluating experiments to address problems they have defined themselves. Besides conducting their own trials, VEAs are introducing other farmers to new agricultural techniques, like fruit–tree pruning or date–palm pollination, advising them on ways to deal with certain problems or showing them how to test the innovations themselves. Farmers are now coming to the project office proudly to display their high–quality dates from palms that had previously borne a far inferior crop. They are telling us about the better prices they are receiving for tomatoes transported to distant markets.

We are becoming more confident that the AECs will be strong enough to sustain this approach of farmers' experimentation and farmer–to–farmer extension after the project closes down in two years' time. The committees are now initiating their own meetings, often without help of project staff. Particularly encouraging is the recent initiative in one village area to set up its own development plan for fruit production. The AEC has joined with the local VEAs to check every single garden in the area in order to identify trees that are diseased or unproductive. Where such trees are found, the farmer is advised how to improve production. In this way, the VEAs are gaining a good overview of the condition of the local gardens and can contribute what they have learned in their own trials. Initiatives such as this indicate that the AEC has already developed considerable management skills as well as a keen sense of the agricultural problems in its area.

Kutum Province will remain remote. It still has little contact with agricultural developments in other parts of Sudan. Before the project closes down, we have to help the AECs open up information channels to these other areas. Through the tool banks managed by the committees, the links to private tool traders are already being established. The various committees have now begun discussing the possibility of forming a joint non–governmental organization in order to be in a stronger position to gain access to services and funds to support agricultural development in Kutum.

References

Chambers, R., A. Pacey and L.A. Thrupp (eds). 1989. *Farmer first: Farmer innovation and agricultural research.* London, IT Publications.

Craig, G.M. 1991. *The agriculture of the Sudan.* Oxford, Oxford University Press.

GFE. 1989. *Development of the wadi systems in Darfur.* Aachen, Gesellschaft für Forschung und Entwicklungsprojektierung.

Gohl, E. and G. Dorsi. 1993. *A short guide to Participatory Impact Monitoring.* Stuttgart, FAKT.

Hagmann, J. 1993. Farmer participatory research in conservation tillage: approach, methods and experiences from an adaptive on–farm trial programme in Zimbabwe. Paper presented at 4th Annual Scientific Conference of the SADC Land and Water Management Research Programme, Windhoek, Namibia, 11-14 October 1993.

Werner, J. 1993. *Participatory development of agricultural innovations.* Eschborn, GTZ.

photo: PMHE

7. Moulding our own future

Chesha Wettasinha
in collaboration with A.K. Gunaratne and Padmini Vitharana [1]

Gunaratne and Padmini originate from Angunukolapellesa in the deep south of Sri Lanka. Accustomed to the rigours of farming in that very dry region, they had long dreamed of a fertile plot of irrigated land in the Mahaweli System. Gunaratne recalls:

> *I could not believe my eyes, when I was selected to receive 1 hectare of irrigated paddy land and 0.2 hectare of rainfed highland in Mahaweli System C. A dream had come true and we didn't waste time in moving to the place which was going to be our new home, and the hope for our children.*

---

[1] Chesha Wettasinha, Promoting Multifunctional Household Environment (PMHE) Project, 20 Anniewatte road, PO Box 154, Kandy, Sri Lanka, E-mail: pmhe@slt.lk. A.K. Gunaratne, Padmini Vitharana, No.12, Veheragala Unit, Mahaweli System C, Sri Lanka.

The family thus moved into the hamlet of Ruhunupura, located in the north of System C, five years ago. Full of hope and aspirations for a bright future for themselves and their four daughters, the couple began farming in earnest. The land was new, the soil therefore relatively fertile, and water was plentiful.. The young family could hardly believe their good fortune! The first few harvests were very good, yielding almost 4.5 tons of rice per hectare.

But after about three years, or six consecutive seasons of cultivation, the yields began to fall rapidly and weed control became an ever–increasing problem. In Gunaratne's words:

> *In an effort to maintain rice yields at a profitable level, I had to apply increasing amounts of inorganic fertilizers and herbicides to my field. But the price of fertilizer and herbicides was increasing sharply, and it wasn't long before rice growing was hardly profitable. In desperation, I sought the advice of the local agricultural extensionist. He had little to offer besides prescribing more of the same medicine – fertilizers and herbicides.*

Support without handouts

It was around this time that Gunaratne and Padmini heard of a village meeting that had been summoned by a group of people who wanted to find out more about the village. They had come, so they said, to assist the villagers in solving their problems. These visitors had been walking around the village, talking to farmers, asking many questions. Though they did not promise any handouts, they seemed to be genuinely interested in what local farmers said and did. This attracted Gunaratne and Padmini to attend the meeting.

Many farmers turned up at the first meeting, as did Gunaratne and Padmini. It appeared that the visitors were from a project called 'PMHE' (which they later learned was a short form for 'Promoting Multipurpose Household Environments') which had started work in their area. This initial encounter left a positive impression and motivated Gunaratne and Padmini to continue their contact with PMHE. Padmini recollects very clearly:

> *At first we were reluctant to go, but the fact that these people didn't offer anything tickled my curiosity. What could they do if they did not bring anything to give? But all they were saying was that they were willing to help us solve our problems, and in fact that is exactly what we needed...someone to come alongside and give us a bit of support and guidance.*

Both of them joined the next two village meetings and a walk through the village with the project staff, where they, like the others, felt much more comfortable to talk openly and express their concerns. Soon they were discussing their increasing difficulties in making ends meet and the most pressing issue, the low profitability of irrigated rice. The villagers were invited to form small groups in which they could further analyse this and other problems and work together in finding solutions. Gunaratne joined a men's group, while Padmini was in the forefront of organizing a women's group. "I was so keen on making the best of this opportunity that I went from house to house encouraging other women to join the group. It has 10 members now", says Padmini.

Ways and means of improving the profitability of paddy cultivation were discussed in both groups. Reducing the cost of inputs was one of the options discussed.

> *Challenged by the project staff we tried to work out from our memories a detailed list of expenditures in rice cultivation. We were surprised to find that it costs almost Rs 20,000 just to grow one hectare of rice.*

The experiences shared by the farmers during the meetings also illustrated very clearly that there was a marked increase in the cost of fertilizers and chemicals over the years, as well as a quite obvious decrease in yields. The project staff mentioned the possibility of using straw as a means of adding nutrients to the soil and improving its structure, which would help to cut down the use of chemical fertilizer. Gunaratne says:

> *My problem was even greater due to the relatively infertile, sandy soil in our paddy field. Besides reducing chemical fertilizer inputs, I was keen on improving the fertility of my land. Therefore, straw application was a very attractive option to me – after all it seemed to provide a solution to both my problems. And what the project staff mentioned confirmed something that I had read in an article in our local farmer magazine,* Aswenna, *about the benefits of straw application in paddy fields.*

Although Gunaratne had not seen this being done, he decided to try it out. No other farmers in his village were using the technique, not even the winner of the best farmer's award. Opinion amongst the farmers was strongly against the practice, saying that straw in the field could hinder proper ploughing, by getting entangled in the plough. This explained why the farmers usually burnt the straw soon after the paddy was threshed.

Challenging 'common knowledge'

But Gunaratne was not to be stopped – he had made up his mind and would go ahead. Soon after the *Yala* (long rainy season) harvesting, he hired a man for a day, and together they carried all the straw from the threshing floor to the field and piled it in the corners of the paddies. Twenty days later land preparation for the next 1995 *Maha* (short rainy season) began. After the first round of ploughing, the straw, which by then had partially decomposed, was evenly distributed over the paddy field. The volume of straw did not suffice to cover the entire paddy field, and one section had to be left out. The second round of ploughing was done 15 days after the first, and by then the straw was well decomposed. In Gunaratne's own words:

> *At that stage I was already convinced that the rumours about straw interfering with the ploughing were baseless. The ploughing in my field was done without any trouble. The mud was very smooth and I could feel it between my fingers – the texture was much better than before.*

After broadcasting paddy, Gunaratne and Padmini observed the plants' growth and development almost daily. They were keen to find out whether the straw had had any effect on the fertility of the soil, which would show up in the growth of the paddy plants, and eventually their yield. Members of his group, as well as individuals from other groups in the village, visited the field to look for themselves and discuss their observations. During the visit Gunaratne uprooted two plants, one from the section of the field with straw, and another from the section which had been left out. He had no difficulty in explaining to his fellow farmers the differences he observed.

Observing change

> *The plant from the section with straw application looked much healthier: the leaves had a deep green colour and were rough to the touch, its roots were longer and stronger, and the plant itself had more tillers. In contrast, the plant from the other section had leaves which were much lighter in colour, its roots were weak and small, and the plant itself was tender to the touch. I think these observations made the farmers change their minds about the effects of straw application.*

Padmini took charge of record keeping in the family. She had been given some guidance by the project in her first attempt at noting down all the income and costs related to the activity. According to her records the saving in fertilizer was still quite small: 25kg less than the previous season of basal fertilizer and 25kg less of urea, which in financial terms is around Rs.500 (10US$) in total. Asked about her initial attempt at record keeping, Padmini commented:

> *At first it was a bit difficult...I had to discipline myself to write things down on time so I wouldn't forget. My husband used to keep reminding me to note things down. With some help from the project staff I soon managed to find a better system of keeping records and, for the first time, we were able to clearly see where we had spent the money and what we had got in return. And if I continue keeping records, which I am convinced I will, not only will we have a clear picture of all our expenses and income, but we will also know how much progress we have made.*

The yield, according to the records, was appreciably higher than the previous season, and Gunarante thought that straw utilization was the main factor contributing to the increase. No costs were incurred for pest control, as no pesticides at all were sprayed during the season.

> *I observed that this time the plants were able to withstand pest attacks better than in previous seasons. Here, too, the straw may have contributed to making the plants more hardy, and less vulnerable to insects.*

One clear disadvantage observed during the season was the marked increase in weeds.

I had to give two applications of weedicide during the season. Of course, this increased the cost of weed control considerably compared to the previous season. Whether this was because of the straw I was not sure. I had no data on this, but the possibility seemed very real.

Learning and improving

During group evaluation sessions at the end of the season, Gunaratne shared his findings, which were discussed intensively by the participants. Some of them found the findings valid enough to try out the practice for themselves in the next season, even with the possibility of an increased weed problem. "I had even convinced the award–winning farmer of the village to take up the practice!", he exclaimed. For Gunaratne himself, this was the beginning of a learning process in experimentation:

When I discussed these experiences with the project staff I realized that to be able to draw good conclusions, I needed to be able to compare the effects of any treatment I wanted to try. In my first effort with the rice straw, it so happened that one section of the field had to be left out for lack of straw. This turned out to be exactly what I needed for comparison. But I understood that next time I would need to plan better to be able to make such comparisons. It would also have been interesting to weigh the yields of both sections separately and then make a more accurate calculation of the increase in yield. Keeping records more accurately and without delay is another improvement that we wish to make.

This 1996 *Yala* season, Gunaratne and Padmini are continuing the process of experimentation. They are convinced about the benefits of straw application and plan to do it as a regular practice. But the issue of weeds is what they hope to address this time. Through more interaction with the project staff, they have planned and started an experiment with row seeding and mechanical weed control.

Gunaratne has finished preparing the fields for the 1996 *Yala* season. He has row seeded about 0.5 acres, and has broadcast seed in the rest of the paddies. Padmini has been maintaining prompt and accurate records so far, and Gunaratne has decided to treat both sections identically so that a good comparison can be made between the two. He intends to harvest and thresh, separately, the row–seeded section and a plot of the same size from the section that was broadcast, in order to get more accurate yield figures.

"Moulding our own future"

Both Gunaratne and Padmini are keen on continuing with the experimentation they have begun, and making it more systematic. They very much appreciate the knowledge gained so far, and are keen on going forward. Talking about their collaboration with the project and its staff, they both agreed:

It was like a breath of fresh air... the language they spoke was so simple and understandable. They did not tell us what to do, but asked us how we thought it should be done. They shared valuable agricultural knowledge with us that will be useful for all of our lives. The commitment of the staff was remarkable... they came alongside us, walked together with us and encouraged us to go forward in our own strength. We realized that we are capable of moulding our own future, slowly but steadily. We have dreams for our children... and surely we are now aware that we can make a way to realize these dreams!

Acknowledgements

The contributions of PMHE staff Ranjit Mulleriyawa in the discussions which led to this article, and Kamari Senanayeke who played a keyrole in supporting the activities documented here, are kindly acknowledged.

8. Starting with local knowledge in participatory research

photo: Sally Kent

Aresawum Mengesha and Martin Bull[1]

[1] Aresawum Mengesha, Farm Africa, FRP, PO Box 91, Arba Minch, North Omo, Ethiopia. Martin Bull, c/o 103, Purlewent Drive, Bath, Somerset, BA1 4BE England.

Many programmes of farmer participatory research still focus on getting farmers to join in research activities conceived by scientists or other outsiders. As reported by ILEIA in 1995, "cases in which the roles are really reversed, where research and development organisations support the research efforts of farmers, are relatively few".

FARM–Africa's Farmers' Research Project (FRP) was conceived from its very beginning in 1990 as a project which tries deliberately to 'follow the farmers' and build on indigenous knowledge in the local development of appropriate agricultural technologies. The overall purpose is a sustainable increase in the incomes and welfare of resource–poor rural households.

The key assumptions that underlie the project are that development and adoption of improved technology are crucial for improved productivity and incomes, and that participatory research, i.e. research in which peasant farmers play leading roles at each stage, is a cost–effective way of developing (and spreading) that technology. The project tries: to increase participation by farmers in research; to improve the links between farmers themselves, and between farmers, researchers and agricultural extensionists; to improve the capacity of governmental and non–governmental organizations to help farmers carry out research; and more generally to encourage farmers and supporting organizations to adopt the methods and principles of participatory research. The project will have achieved its ultimate success when it can leave the area confident that farmers, governmental and non–governmental organizations and research institutions can do effective research in partnership.

The project is operating in southwestern Ethiopia in the zone of North Omo, an area of about 35,000 km^2, with a human population of about three million. In some parts of the zone, population densities are very high, and land is in short supply. The average farm–holding is about 0.5 hectare. Different parts of North Omo range in altitude from over 3000 metres above sea level (masl) down to 500 masl. The total mean annual rainfall varies similarly, from 600 to 1300 mm. There is also a diversity of soil types. In short, North Omo is agroecologically extremely heterogeneous.

The FRP team has been collaborating with farmers in work on natural pest control of aphids and sweet–potato butterfly, on improving grain storage using cheap and locally available material, and on mole–rat control. This chapter focuses on the last–mentioned activity.

Appraising the problems and possible solutions

In July 1994, the FRP organized an *ad hoc* farmers' advisory committee meeting at Soddo, North Omo, in order to obtain farmers' views on research to date, to identify further research needs and possibilities of collaboration, and to select problem areas to be considered for investigation. Eight project staff members and 12 farmers from North Omo, with whom the FRP was already working and who were known in the community as experimenters, discussed many issues, with the farmers doing most of the talking. We encouraged them to give their assessment of the approach taken by the FRP in the past and to specify what they wanted the project to do in the future. The project assumed the role of arranging the meeting; providing the transport, meeting–place and facilitation; and organizing the setting up of subgroups for more intensive discussions during the meeting. We left the agenda fairly open, but felt that a skeleton framework was needed as a starting-point. When we asked the farmers to suggest topics for future partnership in on-farm trials, about 15 suggestions were made, some of them overlapping. One of them was mole-rat control.

In October of the previous year, the problem of mole rats destroying crops had been shown to FRP staff by farmers during a diagnostic survey, using Participatory/Rapid Rural Appraisal methods, in the highland area of Chencha. Also in the lower-lying Gumaide area, a survey had revealed a problem of mole-rat infestation. Similarly, during evaluation of on-farm trials, farmers in Welaita had told us that damage by porcupines and mole rats reduces the yields of root and tuber crops such as enset and sweet potato, two of their staple foods.

The farmers in these three areas had suggested that the FRP organize a seminar about controlling or eradicating mole rats on their farms. They originally had the idea that the project could bring them a high-technology solution (i.e. poisonous chemicals). The drugs recommended by the research stations were, however, either not available or too expensive for most farmers. Chemicals did not seem to be very appropriate where peasant farmers live in relatively remote and inaccessible areas and where government agricultural extension services are badly equipped. In the given situation, formal research could not offer an on-the-shelf technology suitable for testing by these farmers.

On the other hand, we had heard during the surveys that some farmers were already taking action against mole rats. Thus, there appeared to be a fair amount of indigenous technical knowledge and experience which offered avenues for exploration. During the Soddo meeting, we asked the farmers what they could suggest to motivate local research on mole-rat control. They mentioned that some farmers of Ofa Wereda (district) of North Omo were skilled in trapping mole rats and porcupines, and they suggested that the FRP might encourage such farmers to upgrade their skills and disseminate their techniques to others.

This suggestion came at a time when the FRP had been considering what type of research could be done that would give all parties involved an opportunity to acquire more experience in building on indigenous knowledge. The project was, therefore, keen to make an attempt at assessing and strengthening the local techniques of pest control. The approach we chose involved: setting up exchanges to help experienced farmers find out about each other's techniques, encouraging interested farmers to test the different possibilities and to discover the most effective methods for their own situation, and assisting them in disseminating their knowledge to others. Dissemination and cooperation is particularly important in this case, since mole rats in an infested area do not respect farm boundaries: if one farmer skilled in mole-rat control has neighbours without this skill, then he will be unable to solve the problem on his own farm.

First workshop on mole-rat control

In November 1994, the FRP held a one-day workshop involving 22 male farmers, from eleven districts in north Omo, who were known for their skills in mole-rat control, two agronomists and one Development Agent (DA) from the Bureau of Agriculture (BoA), and six FRP staff members. The objectives of the workshop were:

- to allow farmers from different parts of the zone to share local experiences in mole–rat control
- to identify control methods that are the most effective and easiest to adopt by other farmers facing similar problems, and discuss possibilities for improving these methods.

Local knowledge

The 22 farmers were asked to demonstrate and describe their methods of control. The group discussed different types of mole rats, the behaviour of the animals, the various control methods being practised in different areas, and their respective merits and demerits. The workshop discussions revealed a wealth of knowledge about the behaviour, living habits and habitats of mole rats as observed by the farmers. It was possible, through these discussions, to make a kind of inventory of indigenous knowledge, as follows:

- Mole rats are generally found in the highlands and mid–altitudes of North Omo. They do not like reddish, swampy or hard soils.
- Mole rats eat any root/tuber crops with a sweet taste.
- Male and female mole rats do not live together. When the female is in heat, she visits a male in order to mate. She then returns to her home where she will normally give birth to between 2 and 7 young mole rats.
- Mole rats travel both during the day and at night.
- Mole rats have long teeth when young but, as the animal gets older, the teeth get shorter (but are still sharp).
- The size of the hole prepared by the mole rat differs according to season: during the dry season, it makes a wider hole to remove some of the heat of the soil; in the rainy season, it makes a narrower hole.
- Mole rats sometimes close the hole to avoid exposure to the wind.
- Young mole rats are very dark in colour, but their colour changes to either light or dark grey as they get older.
- Mole rats store food for the dry season; they can even store enough food for six months.
- When food sources become scarce, the mole rat moves elsewhere in search of something to eat.
- Mole rats may evacuate their houses when there is a high accumulation of their waste products, when they are disturbed by people or when there is a shortage of food.
- During dry periods, they tend to move to moister areas; and during heavy rains, to drier areas.
- Mole rats prepare their holes using their teeth, feet and head.
- Male and female mole rats make different types of holes. Males take a larger amount of soil from the hole and leave a larger pile of soil above ground as compared with females. The tunnels formed by females are in a more zigzag design, and are narrower and deeper than those made by males. It is therefore more difficult to find holes made by females.
- Some farmers say 'mole rats are cleverer than man'.
- The farmers generally recognize two types of mole rats, differing in size and other characteristics, as shown in Table 8.1.

A great deal of information was forthcoming on where the mole rat lives, what its home looks like and how it is built. When a mole rat enters a new field it starts burrowing and throws up soil, forming molehills. It continues to form tunnels while it is living there, travelling through them in search of food. Farmers were able to draw a diagramme of the mole rat's underground home, which consists of four main compartments linked by tunnels: a sleeping area, a food–storage area, a resting area and a waste–accumulation area. Farmers call it a mole–rat 'house' and give each compartment a name as in a house for humans, such as bedroom, toilet etc. Their detailed knowledge showed how observant they are in studying their opponents, how they find out about animals' behaviour and treat them almost as though they are human (i.e. have respect for them).

Table 8.1. Characterization of the two types of mole rats

Characteristic	The large mole rat	The smaller mole rat
Body size	Larger	Smaller
Tail size	Short	Long
Colour	Grey	Red
Teeth size	Long	Short
Trapping	Easier to trap	Difficult to trap

Mole rats can dig up to three metres into the ground to prepare their home. The farmers noted that those people who lack knowledge of how these compartments are constructed believe that pouring water directly down the hole will kill the rat. The water will not, however, reach the compartment where the rats take rest, and thus cannot kill the well–prepared mole rat.

Differences of opinion were expressed during the workshop on several issues:

- regarding the issue of where mole rats come from, the notions included:
  (a) mole rats come from the sky, especially during the time of the full moon
  (b) when a mole rat become mature, it leaves its mother's home and starts to prepare its own home
  (c) mole rats are sometimes picked up by birds (their predators). In order to escape, they bite the foot of the bird, which often reacts by dropping its prey. In this way, the mole rat finds itself in a new field, where it will start a new life.

  Most of the farmers agreed with either (a) or (b). The authors believe that (c) could explain why some believe in (a) because, in the eyes of the farmers, the mole rats appear literally to come from the sky;

- on the question as to the number of offspring born, some said that females always give birth to two babies, while others believed the number could be as many as seven. The farmers debated this point at length but did not come to any agreement;
- regarding methods of mole–rat control, the farmers told each other about their practices:
  (a) closing the hole with soil and pressing hard. This is done to newly dug holes, which can readily be distinguished because the soil above ground looks fresh;
  (b) introducing ants into the hole. In areas where ants are found, farmers collect them in jars containing boiled bones as an enticement. The jars are then placed inside the hole and the ants will attack the mole rat;
  (c) using poisonous plants. Juices from plants such as sisal or *kinchib* (Amharic for finger euphorbia, *Euphorbia tirucalli)* are mixed thoroughly with mashed ginger and garlic and put into the hole. Mole rats are attracted by the smell of the ginger/garlic and eat the mixture;
  (d) using traps constructed to kill the mole rats.

Trapping

The farmers wished to concentrate their efforts on the fourth method, so discussion followed about the various kinds of traps used by the participants. The most common trap is shown in Figure 8.1. Farmers search for newly–made mole–rat holes by looking for a mound of fresh soil on the ground. They rub soil on their hands to avoid any strong trace of human smell.

Box 8.1. Proposal for on-farm-testing of mole-rat traps

Objective
Since the type of traps used in the different districts of North Omo varies somewhat, the trial is designed to test these traps under field conditions and to evaluate the strengths and weaknesses of each. The best trap(s) for future use will then be determined.

Design
The trial will be conducted by 10 farmers, largely self-selected, from areas where mole rats are a problem. They will have a meeting prior to the trial to share their experiences and to learn how the different traps are used. Each farmer will then try out the different traps on his fields.

Duration
This will be left to the farmers. The timing of the activities in the trial and of the farmer meetings will likewise be arranged to suit the farmers.

Evaluation
This will be carried out through a meeting at the end of the trial period when the different traps will be assessed and the best one selected.

Supervision
The Bureau of Agriculture of the respective wereda (district) and staff of FARM-Africa's FRP will supervise the trial.

The string is made with a noose at the tip (1) and with the other end attached to a cane of sprung bamboo (2). The noose is placed about 20 cm inside the hole and the string is covered with mud and stuck to the side of the hole so that the animals will not recognize it. The spring mechanism, made of bamboo (3) is pushed into the ground. A stick of bamboo (4) and a small piece or splinter of bamboo, which is attached to the string holding the peg (5), are balanced together with (3) to form a strong, yet delicate spring mechanism that will be tripped by the mole rat. The distance between 1 and 5 is generally the width of four fingers. This is approximately the length from the head to the neck of a mole rat. When one of the mole rats leaves its hole, it passes unknowingly through the noose and then touches the string which is attached to the peg. This disturbs and trips the spring mechanism (the bow-like structure of bamboo). As the noose is now around the animal's neck, the mechanism strangles the mole rat as it is whipped out of the hole and into the air.

The DA taking part in the workshop informed the farmers that he had seen others using this type of trap with slight modifications: the noose, or hook, that kills the rats is sometimes made of bamboo or sharp metal bits, as shown by (8) in Figure 8.3.

Proposal for on-farm trial

The workshop participants concluded that farmers in different areas use relatively similar trapping methods. There are variations in the type of material used in making the noose or hooks and some of the farmers put additional materials into the hole, such as potato or ginger, to attract the rat towards the trap. Farmers in Bolosso Sorie Wereda leave the top of the hole open but use enset (false banana) leaves to darken the inside of the hole. Although the trapping methods did not differ greatly, it was felt that there were still possibilities to experiment with slightly modified traps. Several farmers expressed an interest in testing some of the traps they had seen and discussed at the workshop. Together with the FRP, they prepared a proposal (originally written in Amharic) for a trial to evaluate these traps on their own farms (see Box 8.1).

Second workshop on mole-rat control

As the farmers asked for support with the meeting to start off the experimentation, the FRP organized a second workshop at Chencha in April 1995. Nine farmers from five districts, and four DAs from the BoA attended. One farmer came from the Konso area, where there is a problem with mole rats but no local control methods in use. The project invited him to join the Chencha workshop because he was interested in seeing, learning about and using control methods. In the morning fieldwork session, each farmer demonstrated the trap used in his area; in the afternoon classroom session, the participants discussed the pros and cons of each trap. Everyone could see the similarities and dissimilarities in the six traps demonstrated. The farmers grouped the traps into three main types. Figure 8.1 shows the most common trap, the one used by farmers from Chencha, Dita and Gofa. Figure 8.2 shows the traps used by farmers from Gerese and Boreda. Figure 8.3 shows traps that have a hook rather than a noose.

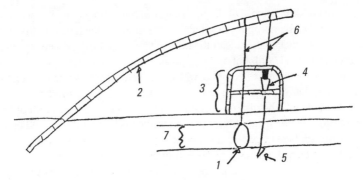

Figure 8.1. Traps used by farmers from Chencha, Dita and Gofa

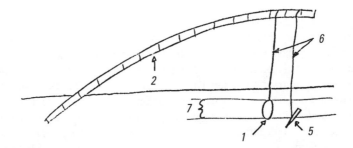

Figure 8.2. Traps used by farmers from Gerese and Boreda

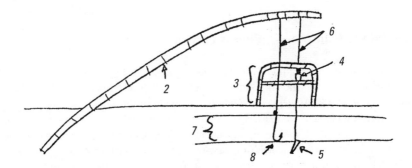

Figure 8.3. Trap with a hook (rather than a noose)

Key: 1: noose; 2: bamboo pole; 3: spring mechanism made from split bamboo; 4: piece of bamboo used to tension the spring mechanism; 5: bamboo peg used to set up the spring mechanism; 6: string; 7: mole–rat hole; 8: metal hook.

When, at the end of the workshop, the FRP facilitator asked the farmers how they wanted to proceed, they decided to test the three types of trap to see which was the most effective for their particular conditions. The three types became three treatments for the on–farm trial (OFT). The nine farmers who ultimately decided to carry out the OFT were seldom visited by project staff and did not adhere strictly to the trial design. Because they lived in different districts, they could come together only at meetings arranged by the project to discuss their results. Ultimately, what seemed to be important to the farmers was not to conduct a regimented and replicable trial but rather to gain better knowledge about how to kill more mole rats on their land. For them, it was a matter of survival, not science.

Farmer evaluation

After the Chencha workshop, the farmers set up their own criteria for evaluating the three types of traps in their informal OFT:

- length of the spring mechanism
- width of the spring mechanism
- the time taken to trap the mole rat
- simplicity
- whether or not assistance is required to do the trapping (i.e. if a person can do it on his own).

According to the farmers, if the spring mechanism is too long, it can easily be disturbed by birds and assistance is needed to set up the trap. A mechanism that is too thick does not respond well and is difficult to set up. It is particularly important that the trap can be handled by a farmer on his own.

The disadvantages and advantages of the materials used in preparing the noose and hook were also discussed during the farmers' evaluation meetings. The conclusions reached were:

- nooses made from rope
  - had material that could be obtained easily
  - stuck to the side of the hole in clay soil during the rainy season, but in the dry season might not do so and would therefore not trap the rat
  - could easily be cut by the rat;
- nooses made from wire
  - trapped better
  - had material that was difficult to obtain
  - did not last long due to rust;
- traps using a metal hook
  - were identifiable by their metallic smell; the rats would therefore run away from them to protect themselves
  - needed special care when setting up the trap

- required the ground around the hole to be dug up in order to put the hook into the hole, thus disturbing the hole
- used a material that was difficult to obtain.

The evaluation is not yet complete, as farmers in different districts are still trying out a variety of traps. Ultimately, it seems that the decision as to which trap is best is personal. To a certain degree, each farmer tries to modify the traps further to produce that best suited to his specific requirements.

Disseminating farmers' findings

Also in 1995, three of the most knowledgeable mole–rat hunters involved in the OFT came to the third annual farmers' research workshop in Soddo, organized by the project. They upstaged all the other presenters with a practical display and classroom talk about their trials on trapping methods. Most of the 80 participants were from the BoA, from non–governmental organizations, from the Institute of Agricultural Research (IAR) and from other governmental research bodies.

In the only practical display of the meeting, the hunters demonstrated two traps, explaining that the methods were derived from farmers' discussions and general knowledge in the area. One of the hunting experts told how he modified a wire hook that a DA had supplied to use in the trap: the original hook was not as effective as indigenous methods because it was too rigid and sometimes missed the mole rat or only wounded it, so he cut the hook into two sections and hinged the pieces together (see Figure 8.4). This modification makes the hook more flexible; therefore not only does it kill better (less chance of a mole rat being thrown off the hook or that the hook misses the animal completely), it is also easier to put into the ground when setting the trap. The farmer explained that he had thus been able to kill many mole rats and now teaches this method to other people.

Standard hook   *Improved (hinged) hook*

Figure 8.4. Two different types of hooks

In their classroom talk, the hunting experts described how the mole rat lives and its habits, and explained why their trapping methods were superior to other methods (e.g. trying to pour water into a mole–rat house). The only thing they didn't bring with them was a mole rat (dead or alive). Several questions were posed. One workshop participant asked whether the BoA had been informed that the hook could be modified and improved. The farmer–innovator replied, 'That's why we came here today'. The farmer–experts had an answer for every question.

Within a few months after the OFT started, these three men and the six other experimenting farmers introduced their trapping skills to 30 new farmers. Of these, nine started to use local traps themselves.

Conclusions

The work on mole–rat control continues, but some important points have already become evident:

- The farmers involved have more confidence now when conducting experiments, visiting, and sharing ideas and observations with each other.
- The farmers have been able to disseminate knowledge to other farmers in similar situations (neighbours, and people from completely different districts whom they would not normally have had the chance to meet) as well as to researchers and scientists.
- Effective indigenous technical knowledge can be spread to farmers in other areas that have a similar problem but other types of knowledge (in this case Konso), through workshops, cross–visits and meetings.
- Farmers can help themselves simply by talking to each other and taking an interest in each others' methods.
- Research–minded farmers do exist. They are interested in experimenting for themselves, and require little beyond a few small inputs and some encouragement. The FRP did hardly any prompting throughout this process and provided only logistical and organizational support, such as assistance in transport, providing a meeting–place and facilitating workshops.
- Farmers are well aware of their problems and will try their best to solve or alleviate them, with or without outside help. External organizations may, however, be able to speed up the process of local problem–solving by supporting the farmers' efforts.
- Even a very simple technology introduced by well–meaning outsiders (in this example, a metal hook) may prove to be inappropriate when tested by the farmers. If this is the case, we must accept their judgement that it is unsuitable or, as in this case, accept that they modify the idea so that it better fits their needs.

To many people in research and development, farmers' trials such as those described here may seem too simple and not sufficiently well–organized to be regarded as 'research'. The particular technologies tried and improved by the farmers are not meant to be a model for other projects, but the approach taken, of promoting the sharing and further development of the farmers' own knowledge, has worked in North Omo, and could well work elsewhere, too. The farmers with whom we worked expressed their gratitude to the FRP for helping them in a modest and sensitive way instead of taking over their experiments. Our approach rested on a 'gut feeling' we had that farmers' underlying skills in technology development can be brought out using simple and relatively *ad hoc* methods, rather than by setting up formal courses and condescendingly allowing farmers to participate in outsiders' on-farm trials that only pretend to involve them.

As an authoritarian culture still prevails in Ethiopia, simply standing in the fields and listening to the farmers can be sufficient to promote tremendous good feeling and to encourage farmers to take the initiative in discussions, trials and dissemination of their methods and results. In other cultures, other approaches may be necessary, but it is already evident to us that this approach is appropriate for Ethiopia.

Acknowledgements

This chapter is dedicated to all the farmers in North Omo with whom we have worked together to find solutions to the mole-rat problem. Without these farmers this chapter could not have been written. This is not an idle statement. It is truly the farmers who possess the knowledge on this subject. We hope that their crops will prosper in the future and that many mole rats will swing from nooses and hooks. Special praise must go to Habte Hajisso, Aweke Kaba and Wolalo Bekele, the three North Omo farmers who were presenters at the 1995 farmers' research workshop in Soddo. Many thanks are also extended to Dr Zinash Sileshi (IAR), who translated three FRP reports from Amharic into English and helped put the authors on the right path in organizing these texts. Finally we would like to thank Dr Ann Waters-Bayer for her editorial assistance and infinite patience.

Reference

ILEIA. 1995. Farmers' research in practice: Justification and call for papers. Leusden, Information Centre for Low-External-Input and Sustainable Agriculture.

9. Tillage research challenges toolmakers in Kenya

David Mellis, Harriet Skinner Matsaert and Boniface Mwaniki[1]

[1] David Mellis, Harriet Skinner Matsaert, Dryland Applied Research and Extension Project (DAREP) KARI/KEFRI/NRI, Regional Research Center, Embu, Box 27, Embu, Kenya. David Mellis, 8 Hoadly House, Union Street, London SE1 0LB, United Kingdom. Harriet Skinner Matsaert, Natural Resources Institute (NRI), Central Avenue, Chatham Maritime, Kent ME4 4TB, United Kingdom. Boniface Mwaniki, Rural Technology Development Unit (RTDU), Box 82, Siakago, Kenya.

Background

The context of change faced by farmers

Semi−arid areas such as the Lower Embu and Tharaka in Kenya present special opportunities and challenges to agriculture. Although agriculture is limited by labour rather than land, specific hindrances prevent the resource of animal power from being fully utilized. These include low population density (less than 100 persons per km^2), poor infrastructure, uncertain returns from farming and harsh technical working conditions for animals and tools (Mellis and Mwaniki 1995).

Furthermore, farmers are experiencing a period of change which is having a dramatic impact on their traditional farming system of shifting cultivation and pastoralism. Population growth and consequent land demarcation are causing weed control and soil conservation to become important management issues. There is also a high rate of migration as young men seek off−farm income and older children are away at school. Labour is thus a severe constraint and farmers are therefore interested in new tools (including animal power options) which will allow them to adapt to their changing circumstances.

Embracing a participatory approach

Participatory approaches are increasingly being used as part of the general trend towards involving the target group more in development and research activities. Participatory technology development (PTD) has recently been much advocated for the types of farming found in semi−arid and similar areas. Three types of agricultural systems have been identified in recent literature on agricultural development: industrial or commercial; Green Revolution; and a third type, characterized by resource−poor, complex and risk−prone farming (Scoones and Thompson 1994). In the first two types agricultural research has traditionally been top−down, with the assumption that technology can be transferred directly from research institute to farmer. In the third type of agriculture, however, this has not worked, since researchers are unable to replicate the complex and marginal physical and socio−economic environment in which these farmers live. An alternative approach has therefore been sought for such areas. It has been variously labeled PTD, farmer back to farmer, farmer first, farmer participatory development (Hudson and Cheatle 1993), but, in general, the aim has been to increase the involvement of the beneficiaries in the research and development process.

The semi−arid agriculture found in the Dryland Agriculture Research and Extension Project (DAREP) mandate area falls within the third type of farming system. Attempts have been made by the project to develop a participatory methodology for agricultural research with farmers, artisans, traders, extension workers, researchers and non−governmental organizations. The project has embraced a PTD approach with the aim of empowering the participants by increasing the confidence of the artisans and farmers in their own knowledge and in their capacity to innovate, experiment and cope with change.

This chapter draws on our experience of PTD in a pilot programme with *jua kali* (small−scale workshops in local towns) metal workers, and with farmers in the semi−arid Lower Embu and Tharaka areas. Institutional issues are explored through the involvement of non−government organizations (Farm Implements and Tools, FIT), a government applied−

research and extension project (DAREP), government extension staff (from the Rural Technology Development Unit, RTDU) and local commercial traders. The opportunities and obstacles within PTD specific to animal traction are explored and options for meeting the challenges are suggested. Among the obstacles, the role of international projects is highlighted, especially in terms of the difficulties they face in fostering sustainable social organization for innovation among different stakeholders.

The PTD Process

Institutional approaches

Traditionally farmers in the area have used tools such as axes and the *miro* (a digging stick with a metal blade at the end), made by local blacksmiths. Recent changes include the importation of tools and materials to the area. Blacksmiths still smelt their own iron to manufacture tools, but they mostly forge tools from scrap metal and repair tools. The main source of technological change has been external travel by the local population and inward migration. For example, in Tharaka victory ploughs came into the area from their Akamba neighbours to the south in the 1940s, and more recently from locals working off–farm in towns such as Embu, Chuka and Meru to the north (Skinner and Mwaniki 1994). An ICRA study in 1984 found 23% of farmers owning ploughs, while in 1993 DAREP found the figure had increased to 44%. Mobile traders have also brought in new technology, such as *jembes* (Dutch hoes) and forked *jembes* to local markets. Hand tools are sold in many weekly markets, but larger items such as ploughs and wheelbarrows are available only from large towns, necessitating expensive travel and transportation.

It would seem that agencies promoting improved technologies have had little impact on technological change in the area. From 1982 to 1988 the Embu, Meru and Isiolo (EMI) project gave free tools to groups of farmers to carry out soil conservation. From 1989 DAREP offered some shop–bought and locally–made tools such as wheelbarrows and weeders to farmers, at cost price, displaying them at nine sites throughout the region. These tools were tested extensively with farmers, but there was no adoption. This may have been due to the fact that DAREP was not able to respond to farmers' comments, nor to deal with related issues of credit and supply and, for their part, the farmers had become used to being lent or given free tools.

As project designers became aware of the need to develop technology with farmers rather than for them, the Dryland Agricultural Research and Extension Project, DAREP, was conceived. It was to adopt a more participative methodology. The main objective was to develop and evaluate sustainable agricultural technologies and participatory research methodologies. The project operates within a decentralized research infrastructure and is a collaborative project between the Kenya Agriculture Research Institute (KARI), the Kenya Forestry Research Institute (KEFRI), the Ministry of Agriculture, Livestock Development and Marketing and the Natural Resources Institute (NRI). Research scientists work as an interdisciplinary team, and technology components include cropping systems, soil and water management, livestock and agroforestry.

DAREP's work on tools was carried out within the soil and water management programme, which looks at the constraints facing farmers in tillage generally, and this has led to research on tillage tools, land husbandry and water harvesting (Skinner and Mwaniki 1994).

Getting started: PRA

Although the context of change faced by farmers is complex, labour is one of the most severe constraints. Hence, as an entry point, the project took an early focus on improvements in tools and tillage to try to tackle the problem. Although broader diagnosis of the constraints in the local farming system followed later, including livestock, agroforestry and agronomy aspects, not much change was needed to get the tools and tillage component started. This was partly due to the obvious nature of the constraint and the thorough reviews of other work in this and similar areas, but also to the participatory nature of the approach used, whereby farmers were able to set and re-set the research agenda at many stages during the process (see Table 9.1).

The entry activity for the soil and water management programme was a focused participatory rural appraisal which included stratified samples and group meetings (Skinner and Micheni 1993). The PRA exercise made use of wealth ranking, household interviews, group and individual interviews for triangulation and verification of information, and flash cards of tools to stimulate discussion. In terms of tools, farmers claimed that production was constrained by a shortage of ploughs at the optimum time for land preparation, a lack of transport for carrying manure to the fields, a lack of labour for weeding, and a lack of tools for building soil conservation structures. The lack of tools was a result of their high cost, the lack of credit, poor returns from farming, and high transport costs to purchase them.

Possible remedies identified during the PRA were to strengthen supply networks, credit support, and the training of local blacksmiths. In the discussions between researchers, farmers and extensionists, the participants concluded that research should be carried out on low-cost tools which could be made or repaired locally. The PRA entered local markets, established sources of supply and repair, and identified some of the linkages between farmers, blacksmiths, traders and manufacturers.

Finding what to try: farmer groups

Following the PRA with farmers, the researchers carried out a literature and project review of potential technology and means to alleviate tool supply and tillage constraints.

To keep farmers involved in the process, the results of the PRA were publicized at the nine DAREP field stations during open days and farmers were invited to participate. At this point the researchers decided to work from only two field stations in order to enable a more in-depth involvement with farmers while keeping within their resources. Farmers were selected on the basis of their interest, wealth rank and gender. This enabled two enthusiastic groups of about ten farmers to be formed which represented the resources and tillage systems of the local community.

DAREP was initially concerned about the group composition. It was thought that perhaps the differences in wealth within the focus groups would make their interests too divergent to allow them to work together on technology development. Needs identification was based on

Table 9.1. Constraints on farming: the view of the farmers. September 1993 at Mutuobare and Kajiampau Farmer Focus Research Group (FFRG) meeting

Constraint	Source	Ranked as important by farmers	Farmers' Comments
Late planting is a constraint to crop production	DAREP survey	Yes	Danger of squirrel damage for early planted crops. Wehome and Diasina from Mutuobare suggest pre–soaking seeds.
Hard soils prevent early land preparation	DAREP survey		
Lack of labour and suitable tools constrains timely land preparation, planting, weeding	DAREP survey	Yes	Farmers at Kajiampau said they would buy tools if credit was available. They felt that the investment would be worth-while (when asked if the loan wouldn't be better spent on something else).
Unreliable rainfall constrains production and makes investment in farming risky	DAREP survey		
Soils are low in fertility	DAREP survey	Yes	Most of the farmers in Kajiampau apply manure. Esther and Francis do not because the shamba is too far from the homestead and they have no wheelbar-rows to transport manure.
Lack of soil and water conservation measures	DAREP survey	Yes	Farmers at Kaji said there was a problem of animals destroying terraces and also a lack of tools and labour to build them. Stone lines, tree and grass planting and mulching were thought to be possible solutions to the soil conservation question.
Pests and diseases constrain production	Farmers	Yes	
Lack of markets reduces price for produce	Farmers		
Lack of certified seed constrains yields	Extension		
Lack of drinking water	Extension		
Farmers' lack of planning constrains production	Extension		
Lack of extension	Farmers		

Source: Minutes of FFRG meeting by Matsaert.

a survey carried out in two areas of Mbeera and Tharaka districts. Wealth ranking was followed by interviews with different types of farming households: plough owners, plough renters and hand–tool users. However, it was later found that hand cultivators may occasionally hire a plough, or aspire to plough ownership, and plough owners often cultivate some of their land by hand. Furthermore, although representation by women was low at first (in view of the fact that they do most of the farm work in this area), over subsequent seasons more women replaced their husbands and the groups are now balanced. However, it was recognized that efforts were needed to ensure that meetings were scheduled at the most convenient times for women to attend (e.g. when older children are back from school and can manage the farm). The tools project tried working with the women's groups that had been used for some initial tool evaluations, but found they were more interested in gaining access to inputs than in research and technology development. Many of the women's groups have farms but these tend to be cared for only after their own farms are in order, so they are not very suitable for research purposes.

The group meetings were extremely useful. Both women and men were able to debate and reach consensus on the selection of technologies and evaluation of trials, and the groups also took responsibility for presenting the results to the wider community on project open days. Focus groups chose to test tools for land preparation (Bukura and Mutomo ploughs), planting (rotary injection and jab planters) and weeding (chief's cultivator, *emivator* and *pye* hoe). An ard plough was rejected as appearing to be too weak for their hard soils (it broke during demonstration).

It should be noted that tools were only one element in a range of technologies for soil conservation and weed control tested by farmers. They are also investigating *zai* pits, contour furrows, tied ridges, water harvesting and manure placement. The broad range of technologies available has been important in sustaining the PTD process, as will be seen below.

Trying out: farmers' testing

Technologies selected for adaptive research were taken from promising technologies and management practices identified during the surveys, literature and regional review of technologies used in similar farming conditions, and from tools developed by an earlier FAO project for small farmers in Kenya. The screening of proposed technologies was carried out by farmers. First the constraints identified during PRA, together with some additions from the extensionists present, were reflected back to the farmers who were asked whether this was a true analysis of their situation. Farmers were encouraged to add or withdraw constraints and rank them (see Table 9.1). During the ensuing discussion, existing or suggested solutions were explored and recorded. The researchers and extensionists then added some solutions of their own from their experience and reviews. Some tools were demonstrated during the meeting (e.g. the ard plough borrowed from the university) and others were presented in pictures and photos. Finally, farmers were asked if they would like to try any of the techniques and tools shown. Some technologies were rejected at the initial screening; the reasons for this were noted, allowing researchers to rethink the basis for selecting a particular technology. One technology, water harvesting, which was initially rejected by most farmer research group members, was later re–presented as an option. During an officers' study tour to another dryland area, researchers had been impressed by the performance of water–harvesting structures on farms. From this experience a farmers' tour from the DAREP area was organized and the members of the focus groups all changed their attitude to water harvesting. All of the farmers who had travelled wanted to try one or more of the techniques of tied ridges, cambered beds, road–water harvesting and earth basins.

Some basic principles of research design were discussed at research planning meetings. However, once farmers had selected the technology they wanted to test, they were encouraged to decide for themselves on design parameters such as size and location. Farmers were also encouraged to adapt the technology if they so wished, such as the size of the planting pits used or the amount of manure applied. The aim of this was to allow farmers initially to experiment with the potential of a technology and to use their own knowledge and experience to adapt it to their own farming conditions. Once the group had decided which technologies looked promising, more formal testing could be carried out to attempt to quantify benefits. In the second season participants decided to standardize parameters within the group in order to permit useful comparisons and conclusions to be drawn. Focus group meetings were held to search for and screen the available options, initiate the research, monitor the progress and results with farmer–to–farmer visits and evaluate the group's experiences at the end of the season.

Trials were designed and implemented by farmers in their own fields. They selected the criteria for monitoring their trials, collecting both quantitative and qualitative data. Criteria for assessing technologies were decided jointly by the researchers and members of the farmer research group. Monitoring was carried out by farmers using monitoring notebooks and by researchers making regular visits and collecting qualitative data such as durability and ease of use.

Farmers in the groups particularly liked the farmer–to–farmer monitoring visits and, as a result, farmers continue to try new technologies which had previously not appealed to them. After experimenting with new technologies in the first season, farmers had suggestions for further developing them. For example, one farmer suggested developing the *zai* pits first presented, into furrows which would be easier to make with a plough, or by hand. Farmers were also concerned about issues concerning the supply and maintenance of the tools that they had been testing.

Improving and innovating: *jua kali,* the 'small–scale workshop' groups

In order to respond to farmer evaluations and concerns with new agricultural tools, it was necessary to work closely with tool designers and manufacturers. During the first season of trials DAREP attempted to involve local blacksmiths, *jua kali* tool manufacturers, large–scale tool manufacturers, Ministry of Agriculture extensionists, and researchers from the University of Nairobi. *Jua kali* tool manufacturers from larger towns such as Kivaa and Embu responded rapidly and enthusiastically to farmers' evaluations with only a small amount of external input. Engineers from the local government Regional Technology Development Unit (RTDU) were involved in the process, and had their doubts about the durability and efficiency of some of the implements but it was difficult for them to respond practically to the farmers' needs due to the lack of tools and equipment at their workshops and to limitations on transport. The university was also involved, but was unable to respond rapidly to farmers' requests or *jua kali* needs within their existing academic programme.

Having no experience or expertise in working with small manufacturing businesses, DAREP collaborated with a Nairobi–based NGO, Farm Implements and Tools (FIT), and a local Peace Corps worker, in order to link the farmer focus groups to a number of *jua kalis* working in Embu district. FIT made a survey of metal workers to assess their capabilities and skills and then invited them to join farmer focus groups at one of the field stations. During this meeting farmers were able to communicate their agricultural implement needs very effectively, and the *jua kalis* were invited to respond. At meetings between *jua kalis* and farmers, local inventions, such as the cultivator designed by a local chief, and a wooden plough made for use with a single donkey, were displayed, and gave inspiration for further tool development.

At this point the *jua kalis* decided to form an agricultural tools group. To achieve this the provincial officer for applied technical training was invaluable in liaising with the umbrella Embu Jua Kali Association, and he was able to smooth over the suspicions of the association's officials. This agricultural tools group was then able to share raw materials, equipment and ideas to meet farmers' demands. One member procured most of the scrap material, enabling buying in bulk, and another did most of the forging work due to his skill and equipment in that area.

With a small grant for working capital (about $10-$20, provided by FIT), and some ideas for tool design from books (*Tools For Agriculture* 1992) and drawings (from a local artist), the *jua kalis* quickly made some new and modified tools based on farmers' recommendations. These included an improved version of the Mutomo wooden–beamed plough, a light one–handled plough, two adapted versions of the chief's drag hoe, two spray pumps and an improved jab planter. The artisans were thus able to incorporate farmers' existing knowledge, external knowledge from the book on tools, and their own expertise in metal–working processes. The tools were then presented to farmers by the *jua kalis* at a tools show before the next season. A panel of farmers (four women and four men) judged the tools and awarded a prize to the best according to the following criteria (Tanburn and van Bussel 1995):

- type of materials and quality of work
- function (flexibility and efficiency)
- durability
- number of operators required
- applicability to different soil types
- portability.

FIT suggested an additional two criteria:

- originality/innovation
- suitability for use by women in particular.

The prize was awarded to a wooden plough which was light to use, could be used by women and older people, had very good penetration, could be used for wet or dry ploughing and for weeding, and which looked easy to repair (Tanburn and van Bussel 1995)

Sustainability: marketing and quality control

During the meeting farmers agreed to invite the *jua kalis* to the DAREP open days where they could display and sell their tools. DAREP held field–days attended by some 200-300 people at each site, where promising technologies, as evaluated by the farmer research groups, were presented to the wider community. Since the relationship between *jua kalis* and farmers now seemed established and the groups had arranged to communicate, no more funds were given to the process in order to see how sustainable it might be. Back in Embu, the artisans sold some of the prototypes (including the wooden plough) and obtained orders from farmers in the neighbouring high–potential areas.

The following season the artisans received invitations to the open days at Mutuobare and Kajiampau, but sold no tools, nor did they receive any orders from farmers in the drylands. As a woman farmer who often rented a plough and weeded with a panga claimed: "Some implements were expensive, others seemed poorly made, others were complicated and we did not understand them and therefore could not buy" And from a male plough owner who weeds with oxen: "The items were a bit expensive. We had given our contribution on how others [the prototypes] could be modified, but the changes had not been made as we suggested". Others were viewed as unsatisfactory and so were not purchased (Mwaniki 1995).

Thus, although the prototypes had been enthusiastically received, the production models were less well made or satisfactory (ploughshare angles were wrong, giving poor penetration; plough handles were too high; finishing was of poor quality), showing up the difficulty of copying what was now the third generation tool. However, agreements were made that farmers would order tools either directly from the artisans or by writing letters through DAREP. By this method artisans were also invited by the farming community to display their tools at three other DAREP stations in July 1995, and some drag hoes were bought, but only by extension or project staff. Since then, some of the Mutuobare farmers have visited *jua kali* workshops in Embu, and a plough, wheeled hoe and drag hoe have been bought by farmers from semi–arid areas. Tools continue to be sold to farmers in the higher–potential area around Embu.

The seeming lack of demand from dryland farmer groups has not dampened their interest in research, however. They either want to save enough money to buy the tools they like, or to see improvements in *jua kali* tools. The fact that they feel an identity as a group has encouraged them to seek solutions to problems from their own resources. One group has formed a savings group and meets every month for this purpose. Members have used the money for buying *jembes* and *pangas* or paying school fees. Both groups continue to research methods for improving water and soil conservation using animal traction and hand–tillage methods. These include post–plant ridging with a plough, plough weeding, *zai* pitting, tied ridging and water harvesting, Having contact with the DAREP multidisciplinary team has meant that the same farmers are trying out other technologies as well, such as new crops and crop varieties, water harvesting for trees and crops, and cultural pest control methods. The diversity of technological options has kept the farmers' interest high and maintained the momentum of the PTD process even though one option (access to tools) has been delayed by the artisans.

A follow–up evaluation of the progress so far was sponsored by FIT and carried out by engineers from the RTDU (Mwaniki 1995). They found that some tools made by *jua kalis*, such as manure forks and water sprinklers, were performing well and were appreciated by their buyers, while a wheeled hoe and drag hoe were not functional due to poor manufacture. The RTDU continue to observe problems of design quality with other tools circulating around Embu. Ploughs bought by local NGOs and stockists have wrong share positions, weak beams, poor adjustment mechanisms and wrong mould–board shapes. It appears that, even if producers know how to make good tools, the customers are not able to get the quality they need.

However, both farmers and artisans claimed that they had benefited from the process. Typical comments were: "It was good, near to the farmers", Jennifer Kiura (Farmer Research Group). "Farmers were able to tell producers their problems. I gained in knowledge and would like to participate in future", Andrew Gatiti (Chairman, Farmer Research Group). "I have new customers, new marketing ideas and have gained knowledge in manufacturing the jab planter. In the future I would like to have jigs and fixtures put in place", David Kamau (artisan). "[I] have learnt new marketing skills and have more confidence", Gerald Ngugi, (blacksmith from Mwaniki). Farmers have been exposed to a number of new tools and new sources of tool supply. Both women and men have learnt to evaluate tools on their own farms and at open days. They have learnt that they can communicate their needs effectively to tool makers and now know where these artisans are to be found.

Jua kalis have gained confidence in adapting and inventing tools, increasing their skills and product range. They have become more aware of the farmer market and of methods to gain market information and advertise their wares. They also say that they are now more aware of the importance of standardized production and of the use of jigs and fixtures. As already mentioned, one group has formed a merry–go–round savings group. This is a common form of savings group in the area, but it is unusual for it to be focused on tools. Most other groups are single–sex groups for general fund raising without any guidelines on how the money should be spent.

The organizations involved in supporting the artisans have met with them twice recently in Embu, and progress has been made in identifying the limitations and opportunities that now face the PTD process. The first meeting highlighted constraints of credit, marketing, group development and quality control. The meetings suggested several ways to overcome obstacles, and to identify solutions that would require little outside support and which would build on the achievements so far. Examples include working more closely with stockists or 'middle men' to obtain raw materials on credit and improve the marketing channels; exchange visits and training to help directly in improving design and production skills while also improving group identity. Design and quality of tools could be improved through more field–testing by farmers, artisans and engineers. In summary, the artisans felt that the methods used so far should be repeated, with a few extra linkages, in order to develop the products further.

Following these suggestions, FIT organized and sponsored a meeting between *jua kalis* and local stockists using a small business advisor as facilitator. A good relationship was started between these two groups, and interest was shown in *jua kali* products by the stockists.

Discussions continue to be held by all stakeholders as to how tool quality can be improved in a sustainable manner. Recently FIT introduced an idea pioneered by Volunteer Services Overseas (VSO) in Mombasa. Product information useful to artisans was put on a single A4 sheet of paper and the printing costs were paid for by advertising on the reverse side. In the Embu tool development process, plough design information could be printed on such 'fact sheets'. This may enable artisans to be more aware of the critical parameters in making a plough (share angle, mould−board shape, handle height etc.), and customers would know what characteristics to look for and demand in good quality tools.

Conclusion

Lessons learnt

The use of more participatory methods has several distinct advantages over a more conventional research approach, which might start with on−station research and then perhaps later extend into on−farm research. A number of useful lessons have been learnt from the Embu PTD experience.

- Developing animal traction technology, especially in semi−arid areas, is a complex activity, involving as it does linkages between farmers, artisans, engineers, business advisers etc. This makes its development particularly suited to a PTD approach.
- The main external inputs required are in helping group selection, identifying ideas to try, supplying small grants of working capital, less than US$200 in total (Tanburn and van Bussel 1995), and facilitating communication between the users, sellers and producers of technology. The PTD approach encourages researchers, engineers and farmers to interact, since the technical staff go to the field, talk with and respond to farmers. This is important to enable synthesis of local and external knowledge.
- The development of organizational structures such as farmer and artisan groups is an important part of the PTD process. These structures increase the self−confidence of participants and allow them to address associated issues of supply, credit and sharing resources. While tool prototype development through the Kenya Agricultural Research Institute was relatively successful, problems occurred when the project moved beyond the prototype stage to production and marketing. The problem here is that agricultural tool prototype development needs different and additional skills and resources, such as those in small enterprise development, which is the required subsequent step. Unless supporting agencies (in this case KARI/ODA/NRI/research agencies) are prepared to get involved in issues of marketing, quality management, credit, raw material supply and mobilization and training, then prototype development will get no further.
- Tools are best developed as part of an integrated and problem−oriented approach, rather than as a separate enterprise. This is especially important where there are different, inter-

dependent groups. Thus if one solution or group fails or stalls, the other group can still continue developing solutions without losing momentum.

- PTD improves the effectiveness of technology selection and screening, as local experience and knowledge is involved from the early stages.
- The quality of trial management, monitoring and evaluation is high when farmers are involved in designing their own research activities. Farmer groups were able to make very specific recommendations for technology evaluated on farm type, soil conditions and on the detailed instructions for its use. Farmer–to–farmer dissemination of technology is correspondingly powerful.
- PTD is an iterative activity, involving constant learning and re–planning. Flexibility, creativity, as well as regular monitoring and evaluation by all stakeholders are important parts of the process. The process must allow time to learn from mistakes and to be flexible to respond to changing circumstances.

It is too early to say how successful the process will be. The important issue in withdrawing external support is that the participants be first given the opportunity to build on what has been achieved. Hence, PTD, just like PRA, involves responsibility on the part of the outsiders to follow through what is started. If long–term commitment is not possible or institutional support is inadequate, it may be better not to start. In Embu PTD there are many challenges still to be met but the progress to date is encouraging.

References

Hudson, N. and R.J. Cheatle (eds). 1993. *Working with farmers for better land husbandry.* London, IT Publications.

ITDG, 1992. *Tools for Agriculture.* London, IT Publications.

Mellis, D. and B.M. Mwaniki. 1995. Challenges to draught animal technology in semi–arid areas: Experiences from Lower Embu and Tharaka. Paper presented by DAREP and RTDU, Siakago to the Second KENDAT National Workshop on Meeting the Challenges to Draught Animal Technologies and Use in Kenya, Ngong, Nairobi, Kenya, March 1995.

Mwaniki, B. 1995. *Evaluation of Jua kali Agricultural Tools Programme.* FIT Programme Report, FIT/ILO, 4 Route des Morillons, CH-1211 Geneva 22, Switzerland.

Scoones, I. and J. Thompson. 1994. *Beyond farmer first.* London, IT Publications.

Skinner, H. and A.N. Micheni. 1993. Tools and tillage survey of Lower Embu and Tharaka-Nithi. DAREP, Box 27, Embu, Kenya.

Skinner H. and B.M. Mwaniki. 1994. DAREP/RTDU: Tools and tillage on–farm research, September 1993-August 1994 technical report. DAREP, Box 27, Embu, Kenya.

Tanburn, J. and P. van Bussel. 1995. The potential for development of improved agricultural equipment by *jua kali* metal–workers: A case study in Embu, Kenya. Paper presented by the FIT Programme to the Second KENDAT National Workshop on Meeting the Challenges to Draught Animal Technologies and Use in Kenya, Ngong, Nairobi, Kenya, March 1995.

10. Farmer–research brigades in Zaire

Sylvain Mapatano Mulume[1]

In the 1980s, in an effort to help alleviate rural poverty, several non–governmental organizations (NGOs) were formed in the Bushi area of eastern Zaire, bordering Rwanda. The vastness of the territory and the complexity of the problems have made their work extremely difficult. Nevertheless, as a result of their activities, numerous small village organizations have emerged with a keen awareness of the problems in their environment.

Local farmers cannot count on formal scientific research to find solutions for them. The content of such research in Zaire, as in other countries, is defined largely by the international structures with which it is linked. The research organizations have neither the money nor the staff to concern themselves with all the areas in which the farmers face problems. Farmers are therefore obliged to resort to self–help.

[1] Sylvain Mapatano Mulume (Ing. Agronome) Actions pour le Development Integre (ADI-Kivu), c/o PREFED, BP 3446 Bujumbura, Burundi. *Because Mapatono's country is involved in a civil war, his address is for the time being) PREFED Kigali, BP1897, Kigali, Rwanda*

The agricultural technicians of one of these NGOs, Action for Rural Development in Kivu (ADI–Kivu), first held a series of meetings with farmers and then organized a workshop in 1990 to analyse jointly the land–use problems in Bushi. The participants suggested the creation of local research units, to be called farmer brigades (*brigades paysannes)*, which could serve the farming communities directly. A brigade would study a problem and share any useful findings with other farmers and, on this condition, would receive support from ADI–Kivu. In this chapter, a brief description of the research by the different brigades is given, but the emphasis is on the way these groups share the results of their work with other farmers.

Wide variety of research topics

Each farmer brigade focuses on a technical theme, with sometimes two or more brigades working on the same one. The topics include potato growing, rearing of small ruminants, storage of beans, controlling pests in cassava, and growing coffee.

Potato growing

Three groups have focused on potato research:

- the Farmer Research Brigade in Bugobe (17 persons)
- the Ngaba Kuguma Brigade in Kamisimbi (12 persons)
- the MUPROSSAN (*Mutuelle pour la Promotion Sociale et Sanitaire de Numbi*) Brigade in Katana (21 persons).

The *Farmer Research Brigade* in Bugobe was formed in 1991 to discover the secrets of growing potatoes, a relatively new crop in which many Bugobe farmers were interested. The potato is being promoted by ADI–Kivu as a food crop addition to the local staples of cassava and plantain. The research group was given impetus by several farmer leaders. The members come from 17 peasant associations (4 female and 13 mixed), 12 of whom had already tried growing potatoes and 5 of whom intended to. The aim was to master the techniques of potato production from planting to post–harvest. Since its formation, the group has accomplished the following:

- participation in technical training workshops requested by the brigade and organized either by ADI–Kivu or other researchers, e.g. on potato pests
- visits to potato producers in other areas
- conducting various trials in potato agronomy and plant health
- on–farm meetings with scientific researchers
- planning the above activities
- negotiating with local authorities (including the *Mwami*, the traditional chief) to obtain collective fields
- multiplying seed for distribution to other farmers
- setting up potato–storage facilities.

This brigade has developed a system of rotating collective fields for their research. A member loans a plot to the group for one season in accord with certain conditions (e.g. the group gives part of the harvest to the field owner). The next season, the group uses the field of another member, observing the rules of crop rotation for that site. In collaboration with researchers, the brigade has also developed ways of staggering their sweet-potato harvest to reduce problems of storage. The group's experiments of putting ash and charcoal in the planting holes for potatoes have proved effective in reducing the incidence of bacterial disease in lower-lying areas, providing they are not too swampy.

The *Ngaba Kuguma Brigade* was formed after problems arose with potato seed. As one member put it: "We have been growing potatoes for a long time, but very few people can plant large areas because there's not enough seed. Diseases often attack the plants early in the season, sometimes endangering the entire crop." Younger than the first brigade, this one formed in 1993, but with a clearer orientation: seed production. This also requires knowledge of cultivation and pest control in the field and in storage. The brigade did various trials in seed multiplication: e.g. using the berries and removing the sprouts from germinated potatoes.

This is the only group that has ventured into action research in potato-seed marketing. It has investigated who else grows potatoes, how much they grow of which varieties, and when. The research is done by all group members, using the links each has with people in other potato-growing areas. Some members also sought information from INERA (*Institut National pour l'Étude et la Recherche Agronomique*) and from other NGOs; for example, to find out the cost of long-distance transport (such as the 200 km route from Bukavu to Goma), they sought approximate data from people in contact with the distant areas.

Within their own group, members are currently trying to organize staggered schedules of planting and harvesting so that they are not all trying to sell on the same day; they have observed that this pushes down the price. The group meets once a week to work together, make observations and exchange the information collected by individual members. They have agreed that anyone who is absent twice without a good excuse is excluded from the brigade.

The *MUPROSSAN Brigade* is a dynamic group of young people who have revolutionized their village by promoting work of communal interest and by demanding farmers' rights from the local authorities (both traditional and state). Potatoes were first grown in their area in 1992, and farmers quickly became enthusiastic about the new crop. The brigade decided to produce seed for other groups, starting with a small nucleus of seed received from ADI-Kivu. Their first attempts were not very satisfactory. Realizing that they needed to know more about cultivation and especially about dealing with plant diseases, members asked ADI-Kivu to help them visit a research centre dealing with potatoes. After a visit to INERA at Mulungu, researchers came to visit brigade members in their fields, helping them analyse their problems and suggesting possible solutions to test. Over time, and continuing on their own without any direct intervention from researchers, the brigade has acquired enough knowledge and experience to produce good potato seed.

Rearing of small ruminants

Two further research groups focus on the rearing of small ruminants (Mapatano 1994):

* the Koler'Olubaga ('working for the people') Brigade in Ikoma
* the COLUMAPHAR (*Comité de Lutte contre les Maladies par Pharmacopée*, Committee for Fighting Disease with Medicines) Brigade in Katana, 60 km from Ikoma.

The *Koler'Olubaga Brigade* was formed in 1991, after a joint appraisal by villagers and ADI−Kivu staff on the rearing of small ruminants, which fulfil important social and economic functions in the area (Mapatano et al. 1995). This appraisal was initiated by ADI−Kivu after the local development committee had requested support to obtain veterinary drugs for goats. Initially, the farmers gave priority to treating animal diseases, but after the joint appraisal they began to think about why the diseases occur. The brigade members (17 men and 4 women) were given a mandate by the community to look into questions not only of animal disease but also of feeding, housing, breeding and optimal manure production.

In cooperation with ADI−Kivu, an animal scientist and a veterinarian from the *Centre de Recherche en Sciences Naturelles* (CRSN) in Lwiro, the brigade accumulated enough knowledge to share with other farmers concerning the prevention and treatment of diseases in small ruminants, the opportunities and limitations of crop−livestock integration, and genetic improvement through controlled crossbreeding. It obtained the information by meeting and discussing with researchers and with resource persons in neighbouring villages, by organizing an agricultural fair at Ikoma, and through their own experimentation.

The *COLUMPAHAR Brigade* focuses on the use of medicines for treating illnesses in general, with one section (13 men) looking at animal diseases. This brigade unites people who want to make their own and other local people's knowledge available to the whole community. Members have compiled information about common animal diseases and local ways of treating them. They invest a great deal of time in amassing information from elderly people in their community. In collaboration with specialists from CRSN−Lwiro, they are also working on ways to conserve herbal medicines. ADI−Kivu assists the brigade in this work and, where necessary, makes available small materials, such as jars for storing dried herbs (Mapatano and Chifundera 1993).

Storage of beans

The *Katanga Young Farmers Brigade* is looking into techniques of bean storage. Members have collected information about how different farmers store beans in Katanga and other areas, and about alternatives suggested by development agents. They have made comparative tests of these techniques: e.g. mixing leaves of *Eucalyptus maideni, Iboza riparia* and various other local plants with the beans; coating the beans with palm oil, kaolin or ash from bean residues; mixing in a powder made from small peppers (*Capsicum frutescens*); using hermetically−sealed calabashes; and the traditional method of vessels coated with cow dung. They sought methods which would allow them to conserve beans between two growing seasons, not only to have seed but also to be able to sell beans at a better price or to eat during periods of shortage. The traditional ways of storing beans are no longer suitable: because of population growth, there is less arable land per family and therefore less harvest, so storage losses have to kept as low as possible; also beans can no longer be stored in the field, for fear of theft.

Experiments were carried out over six months, taking samples every week to see how many beans were damaged by insects in the different treatments. The brigade repeated the experiment for another six months to check the results. These showed that the best method for the area was to coat the beans with palm oil (one tomato tin of oil per kg of beans) and store them in a tightly closed vessel. The group also tested germination and cooking to find out how long the beans could be stored for seed and food.

Controlling ladybirds in cassava

Throughout Rwanda, Burundi and Zaire, researchers have been concerned with the problem of ladybird attacks in cassava, but have still not found efficient methods of control. Farmers, meanwhile, have also been looking into the question.

The *Agricultural Research Brigade* in Katana experimented with using local plants to control the pest. They ground *Tephrosia vogelii*, *Vernonia amygdalin* and *Iboza riparia*, extracted the juice, and sprayed this over the cassava plants. The parasite population was obviously less in the plants which were treated every week. The farmers discovered that the result depended also on other factors such as the cassava clone used or the soil type. While doing this research, they gained knowledge about the insect's life−cycle and the conditions favouring its development, and they considered ways of treating infested plants at different stages of the evolution of the pest.

ADI−Kivu helped the brigade understand the life−cycle of the insect by undertaking literature research, and encouraged the farmers to make regular observations and to quantify how they were preparing the sprays so that they could share this information with other farmers. ADI−Kivu also assisted them in making contacts with researchers at INERA−Mulungu, to whom the brigade members put precise questions and then reflected on how to continue their work. The researchers also came to see the brigade's experiments in the field.

The farmers started with a priority problem: a pest in cassava. Through their observations and experiments, they began to realize the role played by fertilization, varietal resistance, the cropping calendar and relations between farmers of adjoining fields. The analysis showed that the ladybird moved from one field to the next, so the neighbours had to cooperate to control the insect. By analysing the specific problem of a crop pest, the brigade developed a systematic approach to investigating other farming problems: going beyond the initially observed symptoms and looking more closely at causes and how these could be tackled.

Growing coffee

The *Brigade Café* was formed in Kavumu, where coffee is the main cash crop for smallholders, who face numerous problems, notably:

- selling the produce; the coffee growers have to sell illegally and at high risk in Rwanda, as there has been no local marketing organization in eastern Zaire for several years

- uncertain prices; the price paid to the producers fluctuates greatly, and the buyers take advantage of times when the farmers are in dire need of money (e.g. to pay school fees)
- difficulties in improving cultivation practices where agricultural extension services do not exist.

The brigade comprises 45 members, representing the interests of 500 coffee–growers, and is divided into three subgroups: agronomy, marketing and credit. As cash crops are primarily the concern of men, and food crops the concern of women, there are only seven women in this group. The brigade seeks solutions by investigating promising practices of other local coffee farmers (e.g. ways of combating ants, use of local products against coffee diseases, preventing premature dropping of the fruits). The subgroups also investigate ways to organize the marketing of their produce and to make credit available to producers.

Chemical products for coffee cultivation are available on all markets and are widely used. However, the farmers found that some of the products they bought were not effective because they had been mixed with other things like cassava flour. The chemicals are also expensive. Many coffee–growers are interested in finding effective alternatives to the chemicals. A group of farmers with a good understanding of the local situation needs to work together on this.

Disseminating the results

The farmer–researchers have a mandate from their communities and must therefore report back their findings. Most farmers agree that one cannot be happy on one's own in a village. As one farmer expressed it: "If you alone have a good harvest, you will have all the village on your back". It is for the common good that innovations must be shared, not only the successes but also the failures, so that everybody in the community can learn what does and does not work. Sharing between experimenting farmers is facilitated by virtue of the fact that they belong to an organized group: the research brigade. The results of their research are spread also to farmers who are not members, via workshops, fairs, exchange visits, village activities organized by the brigades, and by informal means.

Workshops

Workshops are often organized on the initiative of village groups so that they can talk with others about practical issues. Depending on the level of group organization and the capacity of the leaders, the workshop facilitators are farmer–leaders, ADI–Kivu staff or an external facilitator. Farmers researching on the theme of the workshop are invited to report their findings. If topics are included which are not the object of systematic research by farmers, members of the brigade approach NGO staff or research scientists to contribute any information they may have on the subject. As research by individual farmers often predates structured investigations by a brigade, these knowledgeable farmers are asked to participate in the workshop; after such a workshop, a new brigade is sometimes formed.

Fairs

Each year, ADI–Kivu organizes an agricultural fair to create a forum for exchanging and disseminating the research findings. Each fair is normally focused on a specific topic (e.g. goats or potatoes) and is held for 5 to 7 days in the village which, according to ADI–Kivu's monitoring, is the most advanced in research on that topic. One larger fair was also held, which covered all the research themes of the brigades, so that ideas about methods could be exchanged.

The topics of the fairs to date have been proposed by ADI–Kivu: usually issues on which farmers outside the brigades have been requesting information. The fairs are designed:

- to allow all participants to appreciate the achievements of farmers' research in the area
- to give brigade members an opportunity to enrich each other's research by making constructive criticism
- to make the village and its researchers a centre of attraction and in this way give value to farmers' research.

Participants include individuals or group representatives with interesting information to offer on the subject (farmer brigades, other farmer–researchers, scientists from the national agricultural research institute, NGO staff) and interested farmers. The brigades participate actively in planning and implementing the fairs, but their capacities to organize such fairs themselves still need to be strengthened.

Because of financial constraints, generally only a few delegates designated by each brigade can take part. However, everyone in the host village can join in: men and women, young and old, not only the farmer–researchers in that village. This permits a wider dissemination of results. In addition to the roughly 80 people who actively participate in such a fair, another 100 or more stop by to see what is happening.

It is difficult to quantify how many people benefit. The information from the fairs travels quickly and widely by word of mouth. For example, an evaluation of the impact on rearing small ruminants was made six months after a fair in 1992. ADI–Kivu staff visited the delegates to see if they were applying anything they had learned during the fair. This gave them an opportunity to 'read' from the land the 'proceedings' of the fair. Other local farmers were visited to find out what they had learned from the delegates; for example, of 112 farmers visited within a 50 km radius of the fair, 73 (about 65%) said that they had learned from their delegates how to build goat–houses and had already started constructing their own.

Exchange visits

During the research, support organizations like ADI–Kivu play an important role in linking farmers facing a particular problem with other farmers investigating the same problem. ADI–Kivu checks first which farmer brigade has already gained relevant experience, perhaps a technical solution they have tested or a methodology they use in their own trials.

Some exchange visits take place without the intervention of ADI–Kivu. If farmers know that a brigade has made progress in an area of particular interest to them, they organize a visit themselves. They may have heard about the brigade's work via extension workers, or a farmer–researcher may have been encountered by a villager who was travelling or attending a fair.

Village activities of the brigades

Each research brigade has influence on farmers in the area immediately around the village, generally by informal contacts between members and other villagers. As local development groups, the brigades organize activities to share their findings. For example, the Koler'Olubaga Brigade working on small ruminants held a reception during the festivities in Ikoma to celebrate the end of 1993, and invited other development associations, agricultural technicians, local leaders and administrators. This gave the brigade an opportunity to publicize and, by slaughtering a buck, also to celebrate its research.

The groups researching potatoes in Bugobe and Katana each set up a system of seed credit in order to provide quality seed to members of development associations in their respective communities. The association receiving the seed agreed to pay it back in kind with 100% interest. To ensure that seed of equal quality is repaid, brigade members check regularly to see that the borrowers are cultivating according to their norms (disease–free soil, necessary precautions during cultivation and harvest, seed selection etc.). In this way, the local development associations can benefit from the guidance and knowledge of the farmer–researchers during all stages of production.

Models as communication tools

Three–dimensional models have proved to be a very useful communication tool in the workshops and fairs. Models are constructed by groups of 10 to 15 people, who may include male and female villagers, research scientists and ADI–Kivu staff. They depict what the group has seen, such as erosion–control measures, or what they would like to see, such as how goats could be kept. The villagers use materials that are close at hand and give a miniature representation of reality (or their vision of a possible reality) that can be seen and understood by everybody, whether literate or not. Constructing models allows farmers with little or no formal training to express themselves easily (Hahn 1991).

Modelling gives space for debate, as all participants try to build in their own ideas, based on what they know or have observed when visiting farmer–researchers or when doing research themselves. What is not agreed upon by all is rejected. The model that emerges from these discussions is thus a consensus, but also a more or less complete representation of the research outcome, having been added to or corrected by each person involved in building the model.

The public character of modelling facilitates dissemination of the farmers' research findings. The model, built and presented openly in the middle of the village, is seen by many people, even if it is the work of only a few. The democratic process of building and presenting such a model in public is important for areas such as ours, where democracy is just beginning to be cultivated.

The value of models as a communication tool becomes evident when farmers who were at a workshop or fair return to their villages and report to fellow farmers. They use exactly the same tool, rarely forgetting anything that was in the models they had built or seen at the event.

From research to development action

Research continuously gives rise to further questions for investigation; nevertheless, results gained along the way can be put to use. In the Bushi area, dissemination of the results of farmers' research has sometimes led to the design of specific development projects. For example, during an agricultural fair in December 1992, information obtained by the Koler'Olubaga brigade working on small ruminants was disseminated. In groups of 10 to 15 persons, the farmer–delegates and development agents from government services and from ADI–Kivu visited both members and non–members of the brigade to see the situation for themselves. To be sure, the brigade had gained much experience in improving goat–keeping, but had by no means solved all the problems. The small study groups reported their observations back to a gathering of all the groups. Several problems were identified and discussed:

• animal nutrition
• housing of goats and sheep
• diseases in goats and sheep
• genetic improvement
• husbandry (buck service, weaning, culling etc.)
• crop–livestock integration.

During the exchanges and debates, it became obvious to all that there were still gaps needing further research. The brigade collaborated with ADI–Kivu and two research institutes (INERA–Mulungu and CRSN–Lwiro) to draw up a 'Support Project for Goat–keeping Systems in Bushi'.

Likewise, the Potato Forum, held in Bugobe in July 1994, not only helped spread research findings about potato growing but also led to the design of a development programme. The participants decided to meet again three months later to consider how research scientists could support the farmer–researchers concerned with seed multiplication. Plans are also being made to set up a platform which will bring together all support services for potato growers in the area. This was possible only after the government services had become aware of the farmer–researchers' activities.

Role of support organizations

Support organizations like ADI–Kivu facilitate the dissemination of farmers' research findings in the following ways:

• by giving organizational support to smallholder communities
• by providing technical support in analysing problems and designing research activities
• by making available useful documents and other technical information to the farmer–researchers
• by linking farmer–researchers with resource persons and specialized institutions (e.g. experienced farmers, research scientists)

- by providing advisory support in organizing fairs to exchange information
- by providing material support (e.g. small equipment such as weighing–scales).

The support organization is not there to protect innovations and to see that they are widely applied. Our approach is to work together with the farmers to analyse what is happening and why. We endorse the view of Robert Chambers (quoted in Haverkort et al. 1989) that "The outsiders as development workers should abandon the role of missionary who transfers exogenous technology, and should rather adopt the role of convenor, catalyst, colleague and consultant. The outsider convenes discussions and analysis by farm families and speeds up reactions." Of course, if techniques from elsewhere do exist which might help solve local problems, we inform the farmers of them. The farmers' own experimentation will help them decide whether or not to incorporate an innovation or to modify it to suit their circumstances. This contrasts with past practice when extensionists were expected to transfer new techniques from research stations to farmers and to ensure that the latter followed the scientists' instructions.

For example, when a group of farmers from Bushi made a study trip to Rwanda in 1990 and saw the contour ridges and trenches, sometimes reinforced with plants covering the hills, they came home keen to combat the erosion menacing their own hills. They found it very difficult, however, to implement what they had seen in Rwanda. During a meeting called by ADI–Kivu to review the situation, the farmers explained: "We haven't succeeded in doing it like the Rwandans because we are limited by many things: our tools are not suitable for this type of work, and making the anti–erosion trenches is tedious and requires the contribution of many men. But many men have left the village to look for gold in the forest. Besides, we live from day to day: because of the difficulties to survive, it is difficult for us to invest such effort with no benefits in the short or medium term."

This analysis obliged ADI–Kivu and the farmers to spend several months trying to gain a joint understanding of why and how erosion occurs and to find integrated methods of fighting it through a combination of different cultural practices, such as cultivation ridges, mulching, mixed cropping and live fencing. As the yields on the research plots improved, other farmers became interested in visiting the erosion–control sites and learning from their peers. ADI–Kivu continues to encourage such study trips, but it is up to the visiting farmers to judge for themselves the feasibility of the innovations for their own situation, and to adopt, adapt or reject them.

Social effects

The events for publicizing farmers' research findings fulfil an important social function by giving value to farmers and their achievements. The exchange fora or workshops (co-)animated by farmer–researchers bring together different actors (farmers from other zones, researchers and development agents from public and private organisations, political–administrative authorities etc.) and gradually efface the social barriers between them. These events also give farmers an opportunity to complain, make demands and negotiate to remove hindrances to development highlighted by their research findings (e.g. land–tenure problems).

The sharing of farmers' findings leads to a kind of immortalization of indigenous knowledge and encourages an emulation not only of the techniques but also of creativity and of sharing. This is a value which is in danger of disappearing in our society.

After the results obtained by the brigades had been made public on several occasions, the farmers realized that better organization would allow them to make greater use of the strength they had gained through methodological research. The experience thus far has proved that:

- farmer organizations are capable of coordinating their activities and choosing partners who respond best to their aspirations and needs
- as relations between farmers and the development–support organization turn into a true partnership, the importance of negotiation grows
- the patience required by a researcher in order to gain useful results gradually becomes a way of thinking that guides all farming activities and promises greater sustainability
- in order to find adequate means of communication (and thus dissemination), the farmers have to nurture human contacts through which they not only learn what others are doing but also strengthen their social network.

Limits

It would be illusory to believe that farmers' findings can be spread with no problems whatsoever. The flow of information tends to be slow, especially when there are limited means to bring farmers together. Initially, only the immediate neighbours notice the improvements in the fields or animals of brigade members; farmers living further away hear about or see the results later, often by chance. The more appropriate the innovation for a wide spectrum of farmers, however, the quicker news of it seems to spread from person to person. Examples are the various ways of inducing oestrus (heat) in goats, and the local plants that are effective in the treatment of animal diseases. Dissemination of results is also favoured by the fact that the farmer–researchers are working on problems considered urgent by many of their peers.

The only way in which the findings of the local researchers are currently being spread is by direct meetings of the brigades with other farmers and support services. This means that word is spread within only a small area where the same language is spoken, encompassing about 300 000 households, and where support organizations can help in providing transport facilities.

Other communication tools, such as the rural press or radio, are being considered by ADI–Kivu as a means of disseminating the research findings more widely. These would allow farmers to follow the progress of the research they have seen in the field during the workshops and fairs. Rural radio is operating in the Bushi area, but farmer–researchers need to be trained in its use. Producing technical brochures in the local language is also being considered as part of training in functional literacy. This would help farmers learn to read and write, and at the same time spread the news about farmers' research.

Towards an association of farmers and technicians

Different attitudes

Two attitudes are observed among villagers confronted with this approach to agricultural development through supporting farmers' research. Some think it is too slow; they would prefer to be given ready–made solutions which can be applied directly: what use is an agricultural technician if he does not bring his baggage of technology to solve the problems? During evaluations of workshops or fairs, these farmers never fail to say: "We have the impression that the technicians have brought us nothing; they have only profited from our own knowledge." The technicians' contributions recognized by these farmers are simply the raw materials and techniques. For a specific animal disease, they want the precise name of the product to buy. If they are in a position to buy it, then why re–invent the wheel?

There are also development agents who come from this same school of thought. In their eyes, the approach does not easily produce results that can be presented to external evaluators or project funders. Objectively verifiable indicators are not easily found in this game of trial–and–error. They do not trust the results of farmers' research.

Farmers who are fans of the approach have, however, become its greatest defenders. They say that, as they are being taught to fish, they will have fish every day, as nature is full of resources still to be developed; besides, they do not have the means to adopt the 'modern' agricultural techniques and buy the inputs. During each event to publicize results, the farmer–researchers take care to invite different actual or potential collaborators. Technicians who have come to appreciate this approach are included. Beyond these exchange fora, some technicians remain in touch with the farmer–researchers working on a topic of mutual interest; likewise, some farmers later visit a particular technician in order to discuss ideas, if they think he or she has knowledge relevant to their own research.

Farmers' research networks

The brigade members and technicians involved in the research are, of course, involved in other activities, as well, and their time for research is limited. They have started recently to reflect on the possibilities of setting up a research network made up of those with proven competence in topics of interest to farmers. They hope that this will allow some division of labour in their research, avoid duplication of efforts, and give a better chance to everyone to learn from the methods and findings of the others.

This network would provide a framework for larger–scale farmer organization. The farmer–researchers would like to see their brigades well–rooted in the community, and are likewise concerned that other local development associations gain autonomy from support organizations (NGOs, state structures or private extension agencies). Moreover, the farmers' research methods could be applied not only to improving crop and animal husbandry, but also to improving other aspects of rural life. A subnetwork is already beginning to form around the topic of potatoes: it involves brigades in Bugobe, Kamisimbi and Katana and the tuber programme of INERA–Mulungu; likewise, the brigades in Ikoma and Katana researching small ruminants have started to work more closely together so that they can make more rapid progress. Another type of subnetwork is forming around coffee, a crop of great importance to many farmers over a wide area.

All these networks of brigades involved in thematic research belong, in turn, to a much wider farmers' research network, as yet still very informal. Even though technicians may be advising on specific topics, the overall management of the network is the concern of the farmers. Forms of support, whether material, advisory or financial, are negotiated by them with the various specialized services in the area. It is important that the farmers do not depend on a single support mechanism but can collaborate as partners with several different structures.

Conclusion

The experiences described above indicate the efforts being made by farmers to undertake research and let others know about it. Some inherent difficulties and perspectives for improvement have been highlighted. Farmer-researchers, farmers not directly involved in the research, and technicians in governmental and private support structures all have their roles to play. Useful results concern not only technical innovations but also methodological approaches which open up opportunities for farmers to profit from the human and material resources around them. The research has not only a technical but also a social purpose: the results obtained become a focus of attention and a reason for celebration.

These experiences also show that difficult political and economic conditions do not inhibit initiatives by farmers, quite the contrary; the critical situation prevailing in Zaire as a whole, and particularly the situation of great need in the Bushi area bordering Rwanda, seem even to have stimulated the inventiveness of farmers, both in their own research and in publicizing their findings.

References

Hahn, A. 1991. *Apprendre avec les yeux, s'exprimer avec les mains: Des paysans se forment à la gestion du terroir.* Langenbruck, AGRECOL.

Haverkort, B., W. Hiemstra, C. Reijntjes and S. Essers 1989. Renforcer la capacité des paysans en matière de développement de technologie. *ILEIA Bulletin*, Edition spéciale, janvier 1989, pp 3-8.

Mapatano, M. 1994. Fair to share farmers' findings. *ILEIA Newsletter* 10 (1):15.

Mapatano, M. and K. Chifundera, 1993. Dynamique paysanne et usage de la pharmacologie dans l'élevage au Bushi. Unpublished manuscript.

Mapatano, M. et al. 1995. L'élevage de petits ruminants au Bushi: Une démarche et des actions participatives. *Capricorne* 8 (2): 11-16.

11. *Kuturaya:* participatory research, innovation and extension

Jürgen Hagmann, Edward Chuma and Kudakwashe Murwira [1]

[1] Jürgen Hagmann, (Consultant) Talstrasse 129, D-79194 Gundelfingen, Germany. E-mail: jhagmann@ aol.com. Edward Chuma, Institute of Environment Studies, University of Zimbabwe, PO Box MP 167, Harare, Zimbabwe. E-mail: erudo@esanet.zw. Kudakwashe Murwira, ITDG Chivi Food Security Project, PO Box 1744, Harare, Zimbabwe. E-mail: itdg@harare.iafrica.com.

Out of a need to reduce the severity of soil erosion on smallholder farms in the Communal Areas of Zimbabwe, the agricultural extension service AGRITEX initiated, in 1988, a research project on conservation tillage supported by the German Agency for Technical Cooperation (GTZ). Research was carried out on two research stations until 1990, and afterwards an on–farm trial programme was added. The original goal was to test and develop conservation tillage in order to formulate a technical package that the extension service could promote among farmers. As work progressed, however, the project went through an iterative learning process which led to a dramatic change in emphasis away from the traditional trans-fer–of–technology model, towards farmer–centred research and extension, an approach which became symbolized by the word *kuturaya*. When Shona farmers were asked to provide a word for research, this was the word they came up with. *Kuturaya* gradually took on a broader meaning. It became synonymous for 'spirit of *kuturaya*' or experimentation, and 'school of *kuturaya*', which stood for learning and improving through experimentation. It grew to symbolize a specific approach.

The objective of this chapter is to describe this approach and how it developed in the conservation tillage project, working in close cooperation with the Chivi Food Security Project. The latter is supported by the UK–based NGO Intermediate Technology Development Group (ITDG) and is aimed at increasing food security among peasant farmers. The development of the *kuturaya* approach was a slow process, but a learning one that led AGRITEX to reorient its efforts from a top–down approach towards a flexible stance of farmer–led participatory research and extension.

The chapter opens with a general discussion of the approaches and framework used in the conservation tillage and food security projects. It then gives some of the background to extension in Zimbabwe, and describes and analyses the different phases of the projects. Finally, it summarizes the preliminary findings, which it is hoped can offer some lessons for others wishing to develop and support farmer–centred research and extension.

Reviving knowledge and confidence through experimentation

The *kuturaya* approach is geared to the sustainable management of natural resources and food security in smallholder farming, in this case, in areas of Zimbabwe. It aims to develop and spread sustainable farming practices and enable rural communities to handle their problems in a self–reliant way. The philosophical and developmental framework is based on participatory technology development (PTD) techniques (Waters–Bayer 1989, Haverkort et al., 1991) and the wider ideas of Training for Transformation (TFT). This training programme was developed in Kenya in 1974 and adapted to Zimbabwean conditions by Hope and Timmel (1984). It originates in the work of the Brazilian pedagogue Paolo Freire (1973) and builds on conscientization through participatory education, where learning is based on the experiences of the living world of the social actor. Teaching consists of dialogue via problem posing, facilitating a process to help groups discover for themselves the root causes and solutions to their problems, rather than imposing external solutions and realities. The TFT programme developed some concrete methods and tools for implementing Freire's approach. It stresses the importance of participation and cooperation in organizational development in order to build institutions that enable people to become self–reliant and aims to strengthen people's confidence with messages such as "nobody knows everything, and everybody knows something" (Hope and Timmel 1984).

Freire's key principles form a philosophical framework relevant for any individual and applicable in almost all situations in life. The link between TFT and farmer experimentation, in our case, was created through the principle that problems can be solved only through the testing of ideas and the developing of innovations, not through ready–made recipes.

The process is not linked exclusively to agricultural research and extension but is part of a broader, open–ended development process where research and extension are support agencies and, ideally, participate in people's programmes and not vice versa. Strict adherence to soil and water conservation, for example, would automatically have excluded a considerable number of villagers who did not view it as a priority. If non–agricultural problems are prioritized, then the respective support agency has to be willing to provide the know–how to help people find their own solutions. This might mean that conservation activities can be introduced only in the second or third year, after the other problems have been tackled. This requires flexibility in programming on the part of the implementing agencies. It likewise requires considerable investment in awareness–raising in order to help farmers understand the impact of land degradation on agriculture and the relative importance of soil and water conservation.

Our conceptual model for participatory research and innovation included techniques to encourage farmers to experiment with ideas and methods arising both from their own and others' experience. The aim is to stimulate farmers' re–evaluation and appreciation of traditional knowledge, its combination with new techniques, and a synthesis of the two. This should also develop their ability to choose the best among several options, and to develop and adapt solutions appropriate to the conditions and circumstances in which they find themselves. Problems identified during the experimentation process form the basis for a research agenda and resulting on–farm trials, in which emphasis is then placed on quantitative data to support the earlier findings. If the technical processes and results are not fully understood, farmers' ideas can be taken to the research station for further research under controlled conditions. Figure 11.1 is a diagrammatic way of representing the *kuturaya* model. The central column of the figure can be considered the main process of learning and development through experimentation. Further details on how to implement this model are given in Hagmann, Murwira and Chuma (1996).

A crucial task in stimulating *kuturaya* is to find effective ways of spreading farmer innovations. One way of doing this is through field–days where farmer–to–farmer extension can take place, and through workshops which strengthen in various ways the self–organizing capacities of individuals, their rural communities and institutions. Extension has a crucial role to play in helping to create an environment where people feel free to talk and share their skills and experiences with all members of the community. Once this level of communication flow is reached, a vigorous dynamic in farmer–to–farmer extension can result. The *kuturaya* concept as described in Figure 11.1 is a result of an action–learning process over three years. More details about this process are given in the following sections.

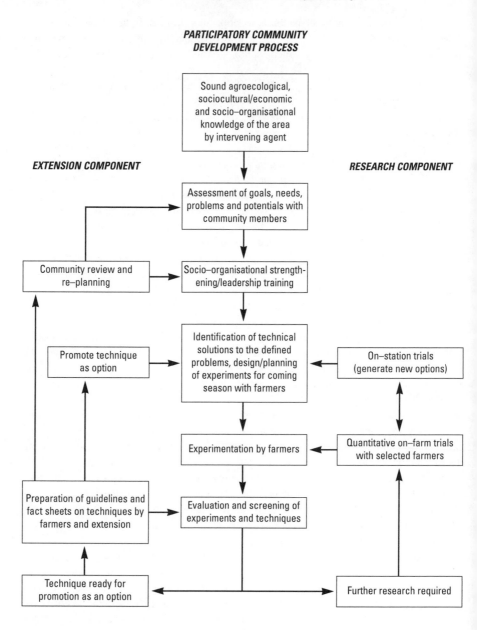

Figure 11.1. Conceptual model for participatory research, innovation and extension

Indigenous knowledge, research and extension

Zimbabwe has a long record of intervention in smallholder production which stretches well into its colonial past. Agricultural extension was started in the 1930s by an American missionary (E. Alvord) whose goal was to replace "premature African agriculture which wastes and destroys" (Alvord 1926) with a "civilized" Western technology–based cash economy. This entailed the introduction of plough–based agriculture ('the gospel of the plough') with maize as the main crop, together with monocropping and the clearing and levelling of fields. This practice has been pursued assiduously over the past three or four decades (Madondo 1995) and has largely replaced traditional agriculture (Rukuni 1990). It proved so successful that the indigenous farming system was modified to such an extent that annual ploughing is nowadays regarded as the traditional system, but it has contributed substantially to unsustainable farming practices and soil erosion, which, in turn, had to be fought by imposing and enforcing mechanical conservation works.

During this period a great deal of indigenous technical knowledge was lost and its state can now be classified as poor. The superiority of the Western model of agricultural production and its accompanying technology has been internalized by Zimbabwe's peasant farmers, who have consequently become reliant on the government extension service to guide their production strategies.

Indigenous agricultural knowledge tends to be considered backward and inferior by all players. Formal research and technology development is viewed by government agents and farmers alike as the exclusive domain of research institutions, which generally follow the conventional model of technology generation and transfer. Experimentation and technology development by farmers themselves, where it does occur, is ridiculed as being primitive or as, at best, an amusing diversion. As a result the one–directional flow of agricultural information from researcher through extension to the farmers remains prevalent. Extension packages are formulated by researchers and are based mainly on formal trials conducted on national research stations. They are promoted through extension workers as rigid, blanket recommendations. As they do not take into account the variability of sites, soils, farmers' skills or resources, they fail in many situations; as a result, adoption rates are disappointingly low. Adaptation of packages is not encouraged. The government's Master Farmer Programme, for example, insists that recommendations are followed 'properly'. This discourages farmers from experimenting, and Master Farmers, with their certificates awarded after the programme, more so than most.

If farmers are to be encouraged to innovate and develop, new approaches must gain institutional support. Many of the extensionists working with the Conservation Tillage and Food Security Projects became convinced of the benefits of a change in orientation. An opportunity to begin a more general process of institutional change began in 1994, when AGRITEX made several key policy decisions which led to new perspectives in the extension services and much greater emphasis on promoting and supporting farmer participation in research and extension (Makhado 1994).

The Conservation Tillage Project: evolution and learning

An iterative process of implementation, evaluation and replanning took place over the various phases of the Conservation Tillage Project from its inception in 1990/91, when trials were initiated in one area of Masvingo Province, to its final phase beginning 1994/95. The description of the phases is deliberate in its detail allowing us to obtain an insightful and honest picture of the successes and failures, development and change brought about over this period.

Phase 1 (1991-1992): adaptive on–farm trials

The procedure. At the start of the on–farm research programme in 1991, extension workers from four different Communal Lands in Masvingo Province were requested to select clusters of 8 to 10 farmers (according to mixed gender and class, preferably with access to animal draught power) from each area who would like to collaborate with researchers and carry out trials on conservation tillage. Various farmers were chosen, men and women, but the majority were members of the Master Farmer Clubs, government–supported groups of progressive farmers.

These farmers were invited to the research station and asked about their main problems, the most significant of which turned out to be the lack of water. The farmers were then exposed to different soil and water conservation techniques (mainly conservation tillage) that would protect the moisture in the soil. After discussions they decided to test a technique called no–till tied ridging (Elwell and Norton 1988). This was the technique the researchers had in mind, but did not admit to until after the farmers had made their choice. Procedures for using the technique were explained, and the farmers were told that they should manage the trials themselves, and modify and improve the technique. A simple paired design was the major tool in the experiment, allowing a continuous qualitative assessment of the innovative ideas in comparison to the conventional technique, side by side in one field. This would help the farmers to understand the factors which contributed to the differences, which in turn would enable them to improve on these factors in future (learning by experimenting). They agreed eagerly, until they heard that fertilizers and seeds would not be provided. Previous experience with trials executed by research and fertilizer companies had led them to expect this. Nevertheless, after lunch at the research station and further discussion, the farmers decided to join the programme, not yet really convinced that there would be no fertilizer.

The process and the lessons learnt. The first surprise came when we visited farmers to discuss their choice of field for running the trials. One originally enthusiastic farmer could not be found. During a second visit, neighbours told us that he was hiding because his wives refused to do the work on his behalf, as he had demanded, and he was unable to carry out the trials himself. Another husband was out, and his wife knew nothing about either the visit to the research station or the trials. With most of the other farmers things worked out well, but the women were not enthusiastic about the joint venture. So the first lesson learnt was that extension workers should ask the farmers to bring along their wives. Communication in the household appeared to be weak and the family as a productive unit would have to be addressed. The involvement of women was crucial to success.

Although farmers had been told that they should feel free to modify and experiment with tied ridges, they had changed hardly anything. In some cases they were waiting for us to tell them how to begin. Whenever farmers were asked what they thought about the technique, they praised it, even when it was obvious that the crops were doing worse under it. Some extension workers had been telling farmers surreptitiously that they must follow, to the letter, the recommendations given. Through the intensive (weekly) dialogue, over time trust was built up and some openness developed, although many women still appeared uninterested. This revealed that farmer participation is not a method but a process which develops slowly. Top−down communication had become a very strong culture which could not be reversed simply by asking farmers their opinions and trying to involve them in our programme. Farmers have to gain confidence in their own experimental capacities before they feel free to experiment.

Tied ridging proved to be a good entry point for overcoming these handicaps. During the first year of the programme, we were able to collect much formal and informal data which enabled us to understand more of the farming system, the farmers' rural livelihoods with their potentials and constraints, and the extension system. This led us to develop tools to increase farmer participation in the following season and to make the process far more farmer−led. The paired design worked well for collecting quantitative research data, and the detailed monitoring and intensive interaction with farmers provided a good base for analysing the effects of the improved technique.

Phase 2 (1992-1994): farmer participatory research

Training for Transformation as framework for introducing kuturaya. Workshops with farmers, researchers and extension workers were organized before the start of the next growing season. The goals were to catalyse participation and the spirit of experimentation, and to gain a greater understanding of farmers' problems and priorities. Viewing participation as a process, it was decided that what was needed was a way of stimulating the farmers' confidence in their own capacities and encouraging a change in the existing hierarchical roles of researchers, farmers and extension workers. Training for Transformation (TFT) as described in the introduction was the approach chosen. The workshop was one of the tools of this approach which was used to particularly good effect.

Workshops to catalyse participation and experimentation. A number of three−day workshops with farmers (husbands and wives), extension workers and researchers were organized at a local training centre, and moderated by a local community facilitator trained in TFT. A maximum of 40 participants were invited to attend. Project staff designed an agenda and agreed with the facilitator on the implementation of the programme. The facilitator encouraged the process of group dynamics and, except for a few technical sessions, ran the workshops. All participants took part as equals.

The workshops were held during September 1992, at the end of the worst drought for a century. In some areas farmers had lost all their animals and were demoralized. Farmers were invited to a training centre for the three–day period so they would be free to concentrate on the issues at hand. The programme consisted of the following four steps:

Step 1: *A warm–up to catalyse participation.* After the objectives and the expectations of the workshops had been clarified, participants were familiarized with key elements of TFT: communication, perception, feedback/criticism and transformation. The objective was to break down social barriers in communication, increase confidence and self–awareness, encourage openness and indicate the role individuals should play in personal and community development;

Step 2: *Farmers' goals, problem analysis and solutions.* A combination of different methods was utilized to obtain a deeper insight into farmers' perceptions and understanding of their sociocultural environment and of the farming system: definition of a common goal or vision (adapted from Savory 1991), problem analysis and elaboration of solutions (both elements of the objectives–oriented project planning methodology, GTZ 1987) and problem ranking (adapted from Crouch 1991). Participants went into small work groups for discussions and presented their visualized results in a plenary session;

Step 3: *Clarification and evaluation of the concept of research and experimentation.* The objective of this phase was to create a link between the problems and potential solutions identified in the previous phase and the need for experimentation to find concrete answers to overcome some of the problems. Examples of farmers' own earlier experiments were discussed as practical examples of how local solutions can be developed instead of waiting for external input. The trial programme was introduced into this context, and the research concept and the roles of farmers, researchers and extension workers in adaptive research were clarified. Basic principles of small–scale experimentation were explained, activities of the previous season were evaluated and a research agenda for the following season was agreed;

Step 4: *Closure of workshop with participants' evaluation and field demonstrations.* Field demonstrations were carried out to stimulate farmers' ideas and link the theoretical discussions with practical issues.

The methodology used in the workshops consisted of group discussions, role plays, codes (for example, pictures which symbolize real–life situations and are used to deduce important points in discussions), poems, exercises on perception, proverbs and songs, all of which could be adapted to different situations. Some components were utilized in joint evaluation tours and informal discussions. A more detailed description of the methodology is given in Hagmann (1993).

Lessons from the workshops: the social crisis and implications for innovation. The workshops were most instructive in what they revealed of socio-organizational and cultural problems. It was particularly surprising that farmers perceived social problems as more severe and more constraining than technical ones. The elaborated problem tree on non-technical problems, as prepared in one of the workshops (Figure 11.2), illustrates this well. In a ranking exercise, the problem of highest priority was the lack of cooperation among people. The major underlying cause of the social problems was identified as sociocultural change, which has split rural society into those who want to follow a 'modern' life, mostly the younger people, and those who accuse this group of not sticking to traditional norms and values, mostly the older members of the community. According to the farmers, this generational conflict, and increasing individualism and monetarization of society, has created an atmosphere of mistrust, jealousy and discouragement, and has weakened traditional leadership structures (Nyagumbo 1995).

New leadership structures capable of integrating the various social streams and buffering conflicts have not developed strongly and are easily undermined by the individualized and hierarchical communication structures. A solution to this leadership and cooperation crisis would require community members to identify a common vision and a shared philosophy.

In terms of innovations, the tense social atmosphere was given as a reason for the prevailing fear of new things. Despite farmers' recognition of a need for innovation to cope with social and ecological change, the fear of being laughed at in the case of a failed experiment or innovation is stronger. Given this negative attitude, people prefer to prove that things do not work rather than try to make them succeed. A general apathy and reluctance to experiment is the result.

Another constraint to the development of innovations and knowledge transfer is the weak communication structure within local institutions. Such comments as "people with ideas should talk to the chairman" or "leaders should respect the members" or "we should have rights in the groups" indicated the existence of an authoritarian approach which created frustration and was said to result in lack of will and commitment. People do not feel represented by their leaders. A permanent power struggle between traditional and modern political elites aggravates the situation. Such an atmosphere does not encourage a joint learning process, nor does it help to solve the crisis of communally-managed lands. It was apparent that socio-organizational issues had to be addressed in any attempt at technological development and that social innovation had to be an integral part of the process.

The workshops were successful in encouraging farmers to talk about their real problems and attitudes without fear of being criticized. Their analyses placed us in a better position to understand some of the events of the first year, for example, when a rather successful farmer had his trial field 'accidentally' grazed by a neighbour's cow, although he guarded the field almost day and night. We began to appreciate the constraints of extension based on a few Master Farmers. Most of these certified farmers (the exemplars and 'carriers of farming knowledge') did not want others to adopt the innovations they used, as they feared that this would result in lost prestige.

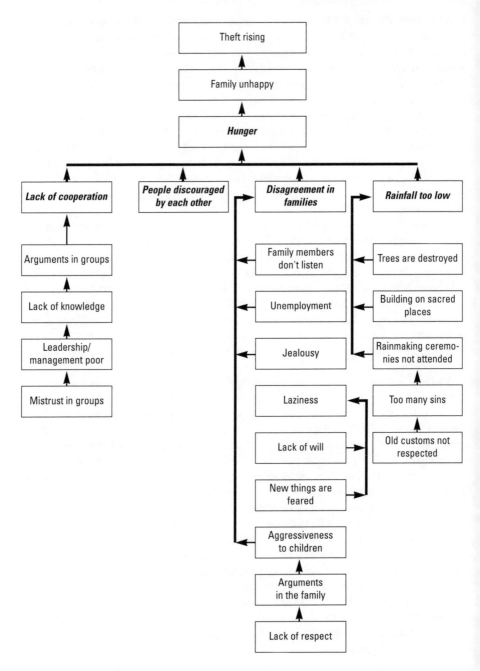

Figure 11.2. Problem tree (non-technical problems only) as put by farmers from Zaka/Chivi Communal Lands

Continuation of trials and expansion towards innovation in 1992/1993. The trial programme (testing tied ridges) continued after the workshops, but the focus moved to include other farmer–initiated experiments which addressed many farming problems not related to the initial programme. Farmers were actively encouraged to experiment with techniques and ideas from whatever source. Mid–season evaluation tours were organized jointly with farmers, where all the participating farmers went to see the experiments in the fields, and the owners explained what they had done and found out. The in–field discussions were open and lively, and the farmers' level of understanding of processes showed that *kuturaya* (learning by experimenting) was proving highly successful.

Details of the techniques used in their experimentation are presented in Table 11.1 (Hagmann 1996; Hagmann and Murwira 1996; Chuma and Hagmann 1995). Farmers also gained an obvious pride and their confidence rose due to the presentation and valuation of their knowledge. This manifested itself later in field–days initiated and organized by farmers in almost all communities. At one such day, more than 220 people were invited, and research and extension workers were guests, a role which was hard to accept for some of them. In some cases we heard about such field–days only afterwards, when farmers proudly reported them to us. It seemed that the experimenting farmers had managed to inspire their communities and had overcome some of the social constraints described during the workshops.

Extension as research focus 1993/94. Before the onset of the 1993/94 season, another workshop was held where the activities of the previous season were evaluated and feedback given on the quantitative research results. Forthcoming research activities were planned, and a field visit to the research station was organized where farmers could comment on the on–station research. We realized that to spread such positive developments we had to focus more on extension, while continuing with the technology research process as it developed.

An analysis of the teaching, learning and knowledge of the different social actors was undertaken. The role of agricultural extension had to be focused predominantly on facilitation of the process, especially in the initial years, until farmer–leaders were trained and experienced enough to take over that role themselves. Facilitation involves introducing the methodology for the process, enabling communication and information flow, and providing technical back–up and options. As the project got underway, extension staff began more to guide and support the process without making unilateral decisions or dominating farmers. Documentation of farmer knowledge and experiences, as well as production of guidelines and fact sheets with and, most importantly, for farmers, was started.

A field–day programme was developed for the research station, which served as an inspiration for farmers and visiting extension workers. More than 20 technical options in soil and water conservation and animal–draught power (many of them farmers' ideas brought to the research station for further testing and demonstration) were shown to farmers, who were encouraged to try, adapt and improve them. Visual learning tools and simulation models were developed to help in understanding the ecological processes which make techniques succeed or fail. These aids played a major role in creating awareness for conservation and for *kuturaya*. For example, different treatments (e.g. mulch, tied ridges and conventional ploughing) are simulated as demonstrations in small trays (0.5 m x 0.3 m) that are moistened with a watering can and have an outlet to collect surface run–off in glass jars. This has a spectacular effect on farmers' awareness for soil erosion under ploughing. An example of linking the effect of soil erosion through the reduction of soil depth to drought is demonstrated by using two glass boxes with one soil column of 15 cm and another of 30 cm depth. After pouring the same amount of water in each, farmers can observe how the shallow soil loses most water to deep drainage, while the deeper soil is able to make the water available to plants. Farmers manage extremely well to link these processes to their environmental reality. Farmers' interest in environmental issues indicated that extension should generally be refocused from a purely yield–based orientation to one with a broader emphasis.

Table 11.1. Experimentation on techniques by farmers: ideas, source and state of development by mid–1995

Innovation/Experiment	Source of idea	State of devt
Implements:		
• animal–drawn disc ridger	ConTill Project	on the market
• donkey–drawn toolbar (multiple purpose)	farmers	on the market
• ripper tine mounted on plough beam	ConTill Project	on the market
• planting device mounted on plough beam	farmers	on the market
• animal–drawn weed roller	ConTill Project	under testing
Soil and water conservation techniques:		
• tied ridges/furrows	ConTill/Chiredzi*	promotable
• basin tillage (widely spaced ridges/semi–circular bunds)	ConTill/Chiredzi/farmer	promotable
• vetiver applications	ConTill/CARD	test & promote
• methods for rill reclamation	farmers/ConTill	promotable
• the modified fanja–juu	ConTill/farmers	promotable
• infiltration pits	farmers	promotable
• stone bunds	farmers	under testing
• subsurface irrigation for gardens	Chiredzi	promotable
• inverted bottles for irrigation in gardens	farmers	promotable
• plastic sheet to prevent rapid drainage (gardens)	farmers	test & promote
• mulching in gardens	farmers	promotable
• mulching in fields	ConTill Project	test & promote
Other organic and biological soil management methods:		
• innovative planting techniques	farmers	promotable
• various planting dates (various crops)	farmers	under testing
• various methods of making compost	ConTill/farmers	test & promote
• spreading of termitaria as fertilizer	farmers	test & promote
• various manure and fertilizer applications	farmers	under testing
• green manure and *Crotalaria* sp.	farmers	under testing
• planting and use of hedgerows	ConTill/ CARD	under testing
• a relay–cropping system	farmers	test & promote
• various intercropping combinations	farmers	under testing
• natural pesticides	farmers	test & promote
• raising of indigenous trees	farmers	under testing
• chicken manure as top dressing	farmers	under testing

* Chiredzi Research Station

These field days were meant to be a starting–point to initiate farmer experimentation, but they became so popular that several farmer groups who had heard about them organized their own visits to the station, covering all transport and food costs themselves. By 1995, the Zimbabwe Farmers Union made a request to take more than 1000 farmers to the station. The effective link between on–farm experimentation and the research station had transformed the latter into an options think–tank for the duration of the research programme.

Lessons learnt

About participation

When asked to assess the new approach and compare it with previous extension activities, farmers mentioned equal partnership as one of its strongest points. Workshops enabled farmers and researchers partly to overcome social constraints. TFT in particular helped stimulate communication and initiate role changes, self–reliant development and participation. The relationship between the researchers and farmers developed into a form of partnership in which feedback and criticism were voiced openly and without fear.

Following the workshops, experimenting farmers showed their strengthened commitment by digging tied ridges, even by hoe; some worked in groups. A major reason for this dedication was that women had begun to identify with the trials. In the formal assessment of the impact, they expressed satisfaction at having been included in the process. Their initial suspicion and scepticism gave way to enthusiasm and interest following the workshops and in some cases women have become the driving force behind the success of *kuturaya*. During the weekly visits to the farms, they appeared to feel competent and were active in discussions, even in the presence of their husbands.

The approach had an impact on community activities and on the awareness of the need to cooperate. Asked about the activities they had undertaken as a result of the first workshops, out of 27 farmers who were interviewed eight months later, 8 said that they had initiated a club (garden, bakery, broiler, building) with other members of the community; 25 farmers had discussed the workshop with other members in the community; and in 10 cases other members had asked to join the trial programme. This growing interest became evident during the weekly visits to the farms, when we were approached regularly by people who wanted to join the programme. Table 11.2 summarizes the farmers' assessment of the differences between the old and new approaches and can be taken as an indication of the impact of the latter.

Competitions were introduced among all the farmers in a community for the best ideas (not only for soil and water conservation) and among neighbouring communities for the highest number of farmers participating in trials. These stimulated the process of experimentation and the revival of farmer knowledge. Competitions between individuals brought with them a high risk of victimization for the innovators. This was lessened, however, if these were combined with contests between communities, since success then linked directly with experimentation. In this situation, experimenting farmers were respected and appreciated even in the event of losing the contest. For organising and judging the competitions, farmers were encouraged to form or elect a committee comprised of individuals whose leadership qualities they defined in the first workshop. These activities encouraged farmers to exchange ideas with members of their communities and to motivate them. Within the groups, cooperation improved greatly, as was shown in one group when an uncooperative member, who had not worked in the fields of the others even though they had worked in her field, felt ashamed and rejoined the group. The impact on the communities indicates that TFT has considerable potential for community development.

Table 11.2. Differences between the old and new approaches according to farmers (results of evaluation workshops with farmers)

Old approach:
- Forceful methods were used
- Only a few people could benefit (e.g. literate)
- Intercropping was forbidden
- Failed to address soil and water conservation (SWC) convincingly
- We were told to do things without questioning
- Usefulness of conservation works was never explained
- No dialogue between farmers and extensionists
- Little cooperation among farmers
- Extension agents treated our fields as theirs

New/participatory approach:
- Everyone benefits as all are now free to attend meetings
- There is dialogue
- Process is well explained (teaching by example)
- Farmers are the drivers now
- Intercropping is encouraged to boost yields
- Farmers are being treated as partners and equals
- No discrimination against poor or rich, educated or uneducated
- We are given a choice of options
- They pay attention to us and take time to find solutions to our problems
- We are being encouraged to try out new things

The most important aspects of the new approach:
- It helps farmers to work cooperatively
- Farmers now practise SWC with the knowledge of why they should do it
- Learning from others through exchange visits/learning through sharing
- It helps farmers to develop the ability to encourage each other in farm activities
- Encouragement to practise SWC through various options
- It is capable of mobilizing large numbers of people with satisfaction
- The approach brings about desirable SWC techniques through participation
- Farmers are free to ask for advice
- Yields have increased through SWC techniques
- The dedication of modern extension agents/researchers
- It has brought development into the area
- It is very effective in the conservation of trees, soil and water

---

To conclude, the methods which were applied in the TFT workshops to encourage farmer participation were highly effective and had a marked effect on the implementation of the trials. Participation was generated, however, not only through the workshops, but through the farmers' full involvement in the choice of technology and in the planning and evaluation of the trials, and through the frequent visits of the researchers to the farms where a stimulating exchange of ideas took place.

During the first three years, it was realized that participation is not a method but a gradual process, which has to be learned and developed slowly by all the stakeholders (researchers, farmers and extension workers). A relationship based on mutual trust is the starting point of all of these efforts.

The success of a participatory approach depends largely on the personalities of the researchers and extension workers and their personal attitudes towards farmers and to participating with them. Researchers and extensionists need an ability to empathize, a commitment to share a part of farmers' lives and a willingness to accept farmers as equals. In a society where small-scale farming is considered the very last resort for people who cannot find a better job, this is a real constraint for a researcher who enjoys high social standing. Building confidence and revaluing indigenous knowledge are crucial elements in strengthening participation for all involved.

About experimentation and research

Similar to the experiences relating to participation, learning about farmer experimentation also proved to be a gradual process. Several factors were crucial as catalysts. One was clarifying the difference between trials and demonstrations. In contrast to well-established demonstrations (where farmers are requested to follow precise recommendations), adaptive trials require the farmers' own experimentation, and can imply failure as well as success. These were new concepts to both farmers and extension staff. Master Farmers in particular tend to be less innovative, as they depend too much on the extension worker's recommendations. Before initiating their own experiments, farmers needed

- to gain self-confidence
- a high level of participation to overcome social/hierarchical constraints
- initial stimulation of ideas
- basic knowledge of methods of small-scale experimentation (same treatment for new and traditional technique, e.g. planting date, fertilization etc.) to obtain reasonable comparisons between the two.

Once the fear of new things had decreased, all participating farmers started their own trials independently of the project, and presented them proudly during joint evaluation tours. In one area, a total of 36 self-initiated trials on 16 farms were counted at the end of the 1992/93 season. Several innovations (e.g. on the use of implements, planting methods, relay cropping etc.) were generated. The number of farmer-initiated trials increased steadily, once farmers had gained confidence and become more familiar with the approach. In the third season each of the farmers had at least 3, some even up to 12 different trials in their fields, derived mainly from their own knowledge. The fear of new things has been replaced by an experimenting spirit. A major factor in the spread of farmer experimentation was the exchange of ideas among farmers during the workshops and joint evaluations. Farmers' own experiments are reviving the indigenous knowledge system as they become confident enough to talk about traditional knowledge and share it with fellow farmers and extensionists without fear of being classified as backward. The generally competitive spirit among farmers has supported this process, as everybody tries to be innovative. The way farmers presented their findings proved that the new spirit has raised their morale and strengthened their identity as farmers, which has in turn helped reduce the apathy and resignation often observed amongst them.

It was possible, by means of frequent interaction and observations to match the adaptive research component to quantitative research. The paired–treatment design with only one variable proved appropriate, and enabled farmers to compare the performance of new techniques and researchers to obtain quantitative data. The quality of that data improved with the strengthening of the farmers' experimental capacities. Variability in soil and fertility was so high that reasonable results were obtainable only when closely–spaced, paired check–plots were used by the researchers. Where farmers have fully understand the basics of small–scale experimentation and where there are sufficient observations during critical times (e.g. planting, harvesting) by researchers, check–plots can provide data which will satisfy scientific standards. Data quality in trials managed and implemented by farmers, without frequent contact with researchers, proved to be more questionable. The same is true of farmers' records, which were of good quality (for researchers) only if the researcher showed strong interest and requested them on a weekly basis.

The informal collection of socio–economic data and the analysis of problems by the farmers were indispensable complements to formal surveys. Intensive long–term observations of experimenting farmers (case studies) and the farmers' analyses of problems provided the basis for understanding rural dynamics and decision–making patterns influential in the adoption or rejection of technologies.

About extension and the institutional context

Although it seemed at first that farmer–to–farmer extension as begun in the self–initiated field–days would animate other farmers to adopt and adapt the locally developed innovations, the results were not what we expected. Farmers appeared to think that there was an exclusive club, which they had to join, or that the new techniques were for Master Farmers only. We concluded that there is no alternative but to involve the whole community right from the start and to give attention to institution–building through more active leadership training, an approach that had already been started by the ITDG Food Security Project (Murwira 1991).

In the agricultural extension service the participatory approach was favoured and supported by most officers. However, field staff (older extension workers and extension supervisors in particular) were more sceptical, as they tended to follow a rigid, top–down approach. Situations arose where the project team members were busy encouraging farmer experimentation, while the extension supervisor was busy ordering farmers to experiment only with the approval of the extension worker. In other cases, during evaluation tours, it became obvious that the farmers' practical knowledge exceeded the (mostly theoretical) knowledge of some extension workers. Such incidents made some extension workers insecure and they interpreted this active farmer participation as a loss of respect and power. For better–trained staff it was easier to admit to not knowing everything, as their background provided them with greater respect and authority.

The clash of the two approaches created reservations on the part of extension workers, as they could see that *kuturaya* required a change in authoritarian structures. Where field staff felt unable or unwilling to hand over some of their power to farmers, it was difficult to integrate them fully into the process. This dilemma was later specifically addressed through organizational support to AGRITEX.

Another general handicap for farmer initiatives are the aid policies of certain external support agencies. Extensive discussions and observations revealed that farmers tended to hand over responsibility for their lives to other authorities. Whenever serious problems arose, government or donors were expected to help. These expectations were often met through direct subsidies in the form of free external agricultural inputs such as seeds and fertilizers, food–for–work and other gifts. The ability of local people consequently to maintain or revitalize their self–reliant community structures was undermined. A telling example is food aid. On several occasions farmers reported that, in the past, traditional headmen (local chiefs) had more land than their people, but were obliged to lend food to those kraal members who were unable to produce enough for themselves. Since the appearance of food relief, however, headmen and even entire communities no longer feel the need to maintain these traditional distribution and production systems. The social safety nets have disappeared. One farmer expressed this predicament succinctly: "Now Mugabe [the president] is our chief". Grosser and Moyo (1993: 22) even found an attitude where *not* sustaining local livelihoods was the goal of some people. Local leaders deduced that "the earlier the kraal area [village] is made desert, the better; government will then be obliged to resettle us on better and bigger holdings".

Participation in self–reliant development and associated experimentation is difficult when the experimenting farmers receive free hand–outs from other organizations. This happened several times where farmers were offered a 'better deal', and we almost lost through donor competition. Such disturbances always required discussions to convince farmers of the necessity of self–reliance. Some farmers were proud of not getting donations from us; they once explained to others that they only got 'brain donations'. Other farmers still did not believe, after three years, that they would not obtain donations from us in the future. An old man was once so disappointed that he stated seriously: "If only I could have my own donor, things would work out well for me."

Promotion of farmer experimentation

The following conditions are required if successful farmer experimentation is to be promoted:

- An input to make the social environment more conducive is often necessary. This requires a philosophy, strategies and tools to improve communication with and between farmers, and which contribute to strengthening local institutions and capacities without imposing Western models and values. A focus on technology alone is too limited to achieve successful innovation development and spread.

- Intervention should be geared towards community activities in order to avoid victimization of experimenting individuals and increase acceptance of the process. A high level of participation (in terms of numbers of people involved and quality) is necessary to overcome social/hierarchical constraints.

- Activities should address the households in communities as key units of decision-making, but make special efforts to address intra-household relations (especially gender relations) related to access and control of resources.

- Support of the institutional environment (extension and research) must be gained through active involvement. All players must be fully involved right from the start and be willing to 'let it happen'.

- A gradual approach, with an entry point (e.g. adaptive trials, visits of innovative farmers to research stations, workshops), is needed to build trust between researchers, extensionists and farmers.

- Initial stimulation of ideas for experimentation is required and farmers' self-confidence in their abilities to experiment has to be built up.

- Basic knowledge of methods of small-scale experimentation (same technical treatment for new and traditional technique) must be understood by farmers in order to obtain good comparisons between techniques.

At the end of Phase 2 we agreed that we had to refocus our activities and build the insights, lessons and conclusions from the first two phases into a more integrated approach, where research/innovation development and extension based on farmer experimentation are embedded within a participatory process. The testing of this new approach (described at the beginning of this chapter) began in 1994/95 with the launch of Phase 3. The main elements were to be: two-way communication, farmer experimentation and strengthening the self-organizational capacities of rural communities.

The close collaboration with ITDG's Food Security Project contributed to this shift in focus. ITDG had been following a very similar approach focused on extension of soil and water conservation techniques since 1991. Through our close collaboration we were able to have considerable impact on the extension department, but a fully-fledged concept which the extension service can follow had not developed before the start of Phase 3. Then, we combined the best elements of both approaches in order to devise one concept which still allows for flexibility and diversity (see Fig. 11.1). To do this, ITDG drew on its extensive experience with local institution-building, while we used our knowledge of technology development and research. The synthesized approach is not meant to be a blueprint for any given situation. It needs to be modified and adapted to each local context, but the impact to date is encouraging. As demonstrated in Table 11.1, the number of experiments that farmers are undertaking is impressive, as is the spread of various soil and water conservation technologies (see Table 11.3). Strides have also been taken in strengthening cooperation and communication among farmers and between farmers and the research and extension institutions.

Table 11.3. Adoption of SWC techniques in Chivi (Ward 21) in 1992/93, 93/94 and 94/95

Technique	adopted as options by number of farmers		
	92/93	93/94	94/95
Cropped fields			
Tied ridges/furrows	28	>100	>500
Infiltration pits	20	289	>800
Fanja–juu	0	4	n.d
Mulching	2	3	n.d
Intercropping	≈50	>450	n.d
Spreading of termitaria	78	>128	n.d
Tillage implements	0	96	n.d
Gardens			
Sub–surface irrigation	≈50	68	n.d
Plastics/inverted bottles	1	>200	n.d
Compost	4	14 *	n.d
Mulching	85	>300	n.d

* groups out of a total of 37

Conclusion and outlook

From the perspective of conventional agricultural research and extension, the task of developing improved tillage techniques appeared straightforward. Our close interaction with farmers, however, has shown us that the conventional way of doing things is inadequate and can act as a constraint to experimentation. New ways of developing and spreading innovations had to be found, which led us far from our initial technical objectives.

The *kuturaya* model for participatory innovation development and extension has shown great potential. It increases self–confidence and the farmers' ability to develop, test and modify both external and indigenous technologies. The pilot activities have demonstrated to the formal research and extension services that it is possible to increase the number, variety and quality of farmers' innovations and accelerate significantly the spread of the farmer–developed and –tested techniques.

The scope for institutionalizing this approach now appears favourable in Masvingo Province. Before it can be scaled up and incorporated into the organizational culture of the Department of Agriculture, however, much work needs to be done to change the attitudes of the stakeholders. This will require more intensive training and follow–up exercises, as attitudinal change is a long–term process.

In our case, through close cooperation and networking between our two projects, one governmental and research–oriented and one nongovernmental and extension–oriented, we managed to have a real impact on the AGRITEX extension department. To introduce a bottom–up approach in a highly bureaucratic system is a complex process and raises as many

171

challenges as it offers solutions. It highlights, in particular, key policy and planning issues which need support and commitment from the top.

At present, the concept of *kuturaya* is geared towards innovation, development and extension on individual arable lands. To achieve the sustainable management of common property resources, however, the concept will need to be integrated into a wider concept for community–resource or watershed management. This presents another challenge for the future.

Acknowledgements

We would like to thank Mr O. Gundani, Mr M. Diza and Mrs M. Tamirepi for their valuable and dedicated fieldwork. Without their good interaction with farmers our work would have been impossible. We would also like to thank the participating farmers for their hospitality and the inspiration they provided.

References

Alvord, E.D. 1926. The great hunger: The story of how an African chieftaincy improved its farming methods under European guidance. *Native Affairs Department Annual*, Salisbury (now Harare).

Chuma, E. and J. Hagmann. 1995. Summary of results and experiences from on–station and on–farm testing and development of conservation tillage systems in semi–arid Masvingo. In: Twomlow S., J. Ellis–Jones, J. Hagmann and H. Loos (eds), *Soil and water conservation for smallholder farmers in semi–arid Zimbabwe*. Proceedings of a technical workshop, 3-7 April 1995, Masvingo, Belmont Press.

Crouch, B.R. 1991. The problem census: Farmer–centred problem identification. In: Haverkort, B. et al. (eds), *Joining farmers' experiments*, London, IT Publications, pp 171-182.

Elwell, H.A. and A.J. Norton. 1988. No–till tied–ridging: Recommended sustained crop production system. Harare, Institute of Agricultural Engineering.

Freire, P. 1973. *Pädagogik der Unterdrückten*. Hamburg, Rowohlt

Grosser, E. and E. Moyo. 1993. Initiating self–help development at village level in communal areas in Masvingo Province, Zimbabwe. Masvingo, Coordinated Agricultural and Rural Development Programme (CARD).

GTZ. 1987. *ZOPP, Zielorientiertes Planen von Programmen der technischen Zusammenarbeit: Einführung in die Grundlagen der Methode*. Eschborn, German Agency for Technical Cooperation (GTZ).

Hagmann, J. 1993. Farmer participatory research in conservation tillage: Approach, methods and experiences from an adaptive on–farm trial programme in Zimbabwe. In: Kronen, M. (ed.), *Proceedings of the Third Annual Scientific Conference*, 5-7 October 1993. Gabarone, SADC Land Water Management Research Programme, SACCAR, pp. 319-330.

Hagmann, J. 1996. Farmer–driven development of a single–donkey–pulled toolframe for weeding, ridge–tying and opening planting furrows. In: Starkey, P. (ed.), *Animal power for weed control*. Proceedings of a workshop of the Animal Traction Network for Eastern and Southern Africa (ATNESA), 1-5 November 1993, Tanga, Tanzania.

Hagmann, J. and K. Murwira. 1996. *Indigenous soil and water conservation in Southern Zimbabwe: A study of techniques, historical changes and recent developments under participatory research and extension.* IIED Drylands Programme Issues Paper 62. London, IIED.

Hagmann, J., K. Murwira and E. Chuma. 1996. Learning together: Development and extension of soil and water conservation in Zimbabwe. *Quarterly Journal of International Agriculture* 35 (2): 142-162.

Haverkort, B., J.v.d. Kamp and A. Waters−Bayer (eds). 1991. *Joining farmers' experiments: Experiences in Participatory Technology Development.* London, IT Publications.

Hope, A. and S. Timmel. 1984. *Training for Transformation: A handbook for community workers.* Gweru, Mambo Press.

Madondo, B.B.S. 1995. Agricultural transfer systems of the past and present.. In: Twomlow, S., J. Ellis−Jones, J. Hagmann and H. Loos (eds), *Soil and water conservation for smallholder farmers in semi−arid Zimbabwe.* Proceedings of a technical workshop, 3-7 April 1995, Masvingo, Belmont Press.

Makhado, J. 1994. Introductory remarks by the director at the Annual Technical Conference held 21-25 February 1994 in Harare. Harare, AGRITEX.

Murwira, K. 1991. Report on institutional survey in Ward 21 (Chomuruvati Area) in Chivi District, Masvingo Province, Zimbabwe. Harare, ITDG.

Nyagumbo, I. 1995. Socio−cultural constraints to development projects in communal areas of Zimbabwe: A review of experiences from farmer participatory research in conservation tillage. Conservation Tillage Project Research Report 14.. Harare, Institute of Agricultural Engineering.

Rukuni, M. 1990. The development of Zimbabwe's agriculture 1890-1990. Department of Agricultural Economics and Extension, Working Paper AEE 7/90. Harare, Faculty of Agriculture, University of Zimbabwe.

Savory, A. 1991. *Holistic resource management.* Harare, Gilmour Publishing.

Theis, J. and H.M. Grady. 1991. *Participatory Rapid Appraisal for community development: A training manual based on experiences in the Middle East and North Africa.* London, IIED.

Waters−Bayer, A. 1989. *Participatory technology development in ecologically−oriented agriculture: Some approaches and tools.* Agricultural Administration Unit Network Paper 7. London, Overseas Development Institute.

Improving experimental design

photo: Henri Schmitz

12. Why do farmers experiment with animal traction in Amazonia?

Henri Schmitz, Aquiles Simões and Christian Casellanet[1]

Why should researchers interested in ecologically–oriented agriculture get involved in a project clearing tropical rainforest with bulldozers? The answer lies in their desire to support farmer–led research and experimentation. This is a story of learning and negotiation by various actors in a process of participatory technology development (PTD): researchers, technical advisers, local administrators, politicians, smallholder farmers and their organizations, all with their own particular knowledge and interests.

[1] Henri Schmitz and Aquiles Simões Universidade Federal do Pará, (UFPA/LAET), Cx Postal 101, 66017-970 Belém, Brazil. Christian Casellanet, (LAET/UFPA/GRET) Laboratório Agro–Ecológico da Transamazônica, Cx.Postal 231, 68370-190 Altamira, Brazil.

The process of learning and negotiation grew in the course of involvement in research by members of the *Laboratório Agro-Ecológico da Transamazônica* (LAET), situated in Altamira, Pará State, Brazil. They were asked to monitor a project on mechanization in Altamira, the largest municipality in Transamazonia, although they had had no influence on its planning and implementation. A parallel study of existing practices of agricultural mechanization in Transamazonia was carried out by LAET in Uruará, some 200 km west of Altamira. This latter study was followed by action research at the request of the farmers. The projects and the research took place in overlapping stages between 1993 and the present, and still continues. The overall aim of the research was to investigate the economic and ecological consequences of mechanization and intensification of annual cropping in Transamazonia, that is, increasing the output per unit of land by means of a higher input of labour and capital.

This chapter examines the results of these various pieces of research. It looks at the motivations of the experimenting farmers and supporting researchers, and describes how the various actors involved tried to ensure that their own interests and convictions were given due consideration.

The partners in research

Researchers of LAET work within a programme of research, training and development which began in 1989 with the establishment of the CAT (*Centro Agro-Ambiental do Tocantins*) in Marabá. The programme expanded in 1991 with the establishment of a specialization course on Family Farming and Agroecological Development in Amazonia, which was later transformed into a Masters course on Agricultures of Amazonia, coordinated by NEAP (*Núcleo de Estudos Integrados sobre Agriculturas Familiar*) of the Federal University of Pará (UFPA) in Belém. LAET is also linked with EMBRAPA–CPATU, the Agroforestry Research Centre of Eastern Amazonia, a branch of the Brazilian National Agricultural Research Institute EMBRAPA. LAET operates along roughly 500 km of the Transamazonian highway in Pará State. Its aims are to promote family farms and ecologically-oriented agriculture.

The farming partners in the research are the smallholder settlers along the Transamazonian highway, which stretches from northeast Brazil deep into the rainforest of the Amazon Valley. The highway was built in the 1970s as a means of opening up the rainforest for colonization. It was meant to solve land shortage problems (and avoid land reform) in other parts of Brazil by giving 'land without people' to 'people without land'. The settlers are 'refugees' from large-scale agricultural modernization schemes in south and southeast Brazil and from recurrent droughts and land scarcity in northeast Brazil. The original colonization plan foresaw allotments (*lotes*) of 100 hectares, and the farmers settled on roads running at right angles to the main highway, every 5 km to the north and south for as far as 50 km inland. However, after the economic crisis of the early 1980s, state support for colonizing Amazonia shrank, and services such as health, education, agricultural research and extension, and road maintenance deteriorated rapidly.

Today, the Transamazonian highway is a poor dirt road, often cut by fallen bridges, mud and pot-holes. The western half of the highway is impassable. In reaction to this, the Movement for Survival in Transamazonia (MPST), a coalition of local people's organizations, came into being in 1989. The strongest are the farmers' unions and the associations of smallholder settlers, but the movement also includes groups of women and black people and unions of teachers and health workers. In total, 25 farmer associations, 4 cooperatives and 8 smallholder unions belong to the MPST, making it the largest non-governmental organisation in the region. It has the organizational form of a foundation, with the motto 'To Live, to Produce, to Preserve' and pursues political and social goals: strengthening the smallholder economy, improving local living conditions, protecting the environment, and making demands on the state.

The MPST operates in the same geographical area as LAET and is its major partner in participatory research and development. In regularly held seminars, farmers and representatives of smallholder associations and the multidisciplinary team of researchers from LAET plan joint activities of development-oriented research. The overall Agroecological Programme of Transamazônica has several lines of research: intensification of agriculture, mechanization and fertility management, administration of smallholder farms, commercialization, credit, pasture management, cattle keeping, the use of wood, agroforestry systems, and the representativeness and functioning of smallholder organizations. The LAET team is composed of researchers from UFPA, EMBRAPA, GRET (*Groupe de Recherche et d'Echanges Technologiques, Paris, France)* and CIRAD (*Centro de Coopération Internationale en Recherche Agronomique pour le Développement, Montpellier, France*), who either live or work in Altamira in Transamazonia as permanent members, or as associate members, working there temporarily on specific topics.

Most of the farmers in Transamazonia practise shifting cultivation and rotate the cropping area inside the farm. This farming system is economical in terms of labour, and ecological in terms of maintaining soil fertility as long as the fallow periods are sufficiently long. Shifting cultivation and the associated land clearing by burning are often criticized as environmentally destructive. Alternatives are being proposed by local government institutions and representatives of smallholder organizations in order to limit further deforestation and to intensify agriculture to produce higher yields from less land. Social and economic reasons are also given for promoting more intensive farming. The colonization model (of 100-ha family farms) has resulted in settlements far from the main road, with a low human population density. According to Hamelin (1994), the average is two families per kilometre on the roads that lead off from the main highway, and the farmers now face considerable transport problems in marketing their products and gaining access to the few remaining services for health, education and extension. In the course of decentralization, the national government has pushed the responsibility for road maintenance onto the local municipalities, who do not have the resources to take on this burden. There have therefore been suggestions by, for example, the Foundation for Sustainable Development of Uruará, and by Hamelin, that the farmers give up their original large lots and move to smaller and more intensively worked *chácaras* of some 25 ha, closer to the main road. A further 25 ha (officially 50% of the farm has to be preserved as a forest reserve) could be transferred to an area further from the road and be worked communally. This would allow a more dense settlement of farmers closer to the municipal centres and the Transamazonian highway. Studies by LAET have indicated that farmers with 10 ha, located near the main road, obtain, on average, the same income as farmers with 100 ha located far away (Schmitz and Castellanet 1995).

Initiating joint research

The farmer organizations in the Transamazonian region were keen to have joint research on mechanization to make more intensive agriculture possible. This was made clear at a workshop in August 1993 when LAET researchers and the farmer organizations in the MPST first worked out their programme of development–oriented research. The need was again stressed in October 1993, when the Altamira Department of Agriculture presented its programme for basic food production. Under this programme the municipality, the government extension service EMATER and the smallholder union of Altamira decided to introduce mechanization by draught animals to an intended 50 farms. The programme was formulated without the participation of LAET. LAET researchers reacted to the farmers' suggestions on research into mechanization with reservations, as they feared that ploughing the soil of tropical rainforests by machine, even if animal–drawn, could lead to considerable ecological problems and to high costs.

However, as LAET had the philosophy of regarding the farmers as partners, and orienting its research to farmer demand, it agreed to monitor the farmers wanting to gain experience in mechanized cultivation in Altamira, and, in parallel, to study the experiences of farmers along the Transamazonian highway who had already used mechanized cultivation. Refusing to collaborate in this research would have weakened LAET's relationship with farmers. By getting involved and following the farmers' experiences, LAET would be in a position to help them adapt the technology or, if mechanization failed, to help them draw conclusions and find alternatives for developing smallholder farming in the region.

Monitoring farmers wanting to mechanize in Altamira

The mechanization programme in Altamira began in November 1993 with the participation of 22 farmers situated directly beside the Transamazonia highway. Most of these were selected by EMATER and were not members of the farmers' associations or smallholder unions. As already stated, despite its reservations and the fact that it had played no part in the planning, LAET agreed to monitor the project and to help judge whether mechanization was an economically and ecologically appropriate technique for intensification of annual cropping in Transamazonia. The farmers and initiating institutions, however, did not appear to be clear about LAET's role. In their eyes, LAET shared the responsibility for the success or failure of the project. This view led to friction and made it difficult for LAET to continue its work in a constructive way. LAET monitored 17 of the 22 farms involved in the Altamira project. Data were collected on the history of the area cultivated, on crop rotation, labour inputs, crop yields and the costs of preparing the land for mechanized cultivation. Soil samples were taken on three of the farms in order to monitor changes in soil fertility.

The Altamira project involved clearing all the roots and stumps from approximately five hectares of land for each farm, with a bulldozer provided by the municipality, and preparing seedbeds by tractor–drawn disc harrow. The cost of this exercise (destumping and seedbed preparation) was at least US$ 2000 for 5 hectares, without counting the cost of the manual labour. Weeding in that year and both ploughing and weeding in subsequent years were supposed to done with draught animals and equipment.

In the two growing seasons monitored so far, none of the 17 farmers used animal traction to plough their field, although 8 used it for ridging and weeding. Four used the animal–traction equipment (simple scarifiers, but not ploughs) made available to them free of charge by the Altamira Department of Agriculture. The others already owned the equipment before the project began. No–one bought equipment on account of the project. In 8 cases, ploughing was done by tractor (7 of these used municipal or hired tractor services). The land was prepared by hand on 3 farms. One farmer had already used a tractor for ploughing and transport before the project began.

In the second growing season, 11 farmers continued to grow annual crops on the cleared land, 3 sowed pasture (2 of them on part of the area only), one planted permanent crops on a part of the area and one let the land go to fallow. Of 13 farmers interviewed at the beginning of the third growing season (1995/96), 10 will continue growing annual crops, but 2 of these on part of the area only. In one of the cropped areas the maize is already being interplanted with grass for pasture improvement. Two of the cleared areas have now been completely transformed into pasture, and one lies fallow. The differing number of farmers interviewed is due to the fact that 2 farmers died and 2 moved.

The results are difficult to interpret and to generalize from for several reasons:

- The municipal services of destumping with a bulldozer and seedbed preparation with a disc harrow, which were supposed to be paid back in kind, have remained largely free of charge: of 16 cases in which the land was prepared by bulldozer and tractor, only 6 repaid, in amounts that varied greatly. The municipality has made no further claims.
- Most of the farms have unusually favourable soils: *terra roxa estruturada eutrófica* (*alfisol* according to American soil taxonomy), which are among the most fertile of tropical soils, and found in only 10% of the area through which the Transamazonia highway was built (Falesi 1972, 1986); but if the soils up to 50 km inland from the highway are also included, then only about 5% are *terra roxa*, according to estimates by LAET.
- The farmers used animal traction for weeding and ridging only a few times.
- As there have not yet been any extension activities (on farmer training, credit for acquiring equipment, information about adequate quantities and composition of mineral fertilizers), the project could end the moment the municipal subsidies are dropped. The subsidies were already greatly reduced at the start of the third growing season.

Assessment of the yields of the mechanically–cultivated areas is not yet completed, and the planned evaluation by farmers has not yet taken place. However, as most of the farmers are cultivating *terra roxa* soils and paid little or nothing for the services for destumping and seedbed preparation, the results of the assessment will be of limited value in answering the original research question. Nevertheless, the farmers demonstrated great interest in cultivating annual crops over a longer period than has been usual until now. Some farmers have even had their fields destumped and the soil cultivated at their own cost, independent of the municipality. LAET is now seeking closer links with these farmers.

Study of experiences with mechanized cultivation

The aim of this study was to find out under what conditions mechanized cultivation was already being practised by farmers. As most experience with animal traction or tractors in Transamazonia had been gained further west in Uruará, it was decided to select this municipality for the study. The study team was composed of two researchers from LAET and an agricultural technician from EMBRAPA working in Uruará. Thus, the most important partner of LAET, MPST, was involved in the work, and this facilitated contact with farmers. The team conducted a survey and used Rapid Rural Appraisal techniques: direct observation, mapping, seasonal labour calendars, wealth ranking and some techniques of semi−structured interviews, with many open questions permitting the formulation of questions during the interviews (structured open−ended interviews). This type of interview tries to combine the advantages of structured with those of semi−structured interviews, avoiding some of the problems associated with the latter. For example, the researcher is less likely to miss asking pertinent questions during a conversation with the farmer, as can occur when using only a checklist. Finally it ensures a high proportion of answers for each question. The wording of many questions is already formulated in the questionnaire, but can be expressed in a different way if the farmer does not understand. The interview can then better lead on to the sensitive issues and the interviewer has less difficulty taking notes. The farmer is free to speak his mind in his own language and categorize and mention facts that had not previously occurred to the researchers. Discussion partners were mainly male household heads; only occasionally did women and adult sons also take part.

There are at least 3000 farms in Uruará (our own conservative calculation based on Léna and Silveira 1993, and Castellanet et al. 1994). With the assistance of the local technicians from MPST and the national extension and research institutes, as well as the local smallholder union, only 9 farmers could be found who had had experience with mechanization in Transamazonia. Although these farmers had access to much larger areas (310 ha on average), they used on average only 5.5 ha for sowing annual crops. One farmer with an unusually large family cultivated 18 ha. Most of the farmers used the tractor or draught animals only for transport. Mechanical soil cultivation and weeding was done on only 3 farms, and only rarely on one of them. On 2 farms, the use of machines had been totally abandoned. Of 7 tractors, 3 were idle or had broken down and one was very rarely used.

The main reasons given by the farmers for their low use of machines to clear and cultivate their land were:

- They had other crops (54 ha per farm, on average) that did not need mechanization: perennial crops such as cocoa, *feijão-de-abafado* (bean–growing with a technique requiring only manual labour) or pasture; only in the case of pepper would there be any sense in using animal traction for weed control.
- They had problems with soil fertility; some farmers observed that production levels fell if the land was not burned; others observed that production fell greatly in the second year; still others found that after 3-4 years, it was no longer possible to grow annual crops without applying fertilizer.

They have still enough land to maintain soil fertility by fallowing: On average, 68% of the farm is forest and fallow land (often forest fallow, called *capoeira*) and 13% pasture. One farmer, the only one who works with animal traction for soil preparation, is experimenting with mineral fertilizer. He is also the only one to leave his cattle in the corral to obtain animal dung. Another farmer is using animal dung in the plantation of pepper.

Researchers' and farmers' knowledge about mechanization

According to the literature on farming or agrarian systems (Ruthenberg 1980, Boserup 1972, Pingali et al. 1987), there is no reason for farmers in Transamazonia to be interested in mechanization. In the traditional system of shifting cultivation a forest area is cleared, the organic matter is burned, the area is planted with annual crops for 1-2 years, and is then left fallow. As the human population grows and land–use intensity increases, the fallow period is shortened. This leads to a reduction in soil fertility and an infestation of weeds, so that more labour is needed to grow the same amount of food. One way to prevent further decline in labour productivity is to mechanize. This transition is generally made at population densities and land–use intensities much higher than those in Transamazonia, where in the rural parts of Uruará, for example, there are only two persons per square kilometre (Hamelin 1994).

One of the main problems in the transition from shifting to permanent cultivation is maintaining soil fertility (replacing nutrients, regulating pH), achieved by burning and fallowing in the traditional system (Sanchez 1976, Martins et al. 1991). This problem is particularly severe where soils are inherently low in fertility, as is the case in most of Transamazonia. Solutions to this problem are either labour–intensive (organic manuring) or costly (mineral fertilizer).

As mechanization is closely linked with the transition from shifting to permanent cultivation, it cannot be introduced at any arbitrary point in time. If the time is not ripe for animal traction in terms of the ratio between labour demands in the existing system and the demands of mechanization, then mechanization will reduce rather than increase labour productivity (Schmitz et al. 1991). Adopting animal traction entails costs to the farmers in terms of their own learning time, training and caring for the animals, removing tree stumps and establishing and maintaining pasture for the animals.

The knowledge expressed by farmers in interviews and reflected in their practices confirmed this 'scientific logic'. The farmers in Uruará stated that the problem of soil fertility is a decisive constraint to permanent cropping and thus to mechanization. In view of the low prices for annual crops, they find that using mineral fertilizer is unprofitable. Fallowing therefore continues to be the predominant method of maintaining soil fertility. Most farmers have sufficient land reserves to continue with shifting cultivation, so mechanization would not increase labour productivity.

The study in Uruará also revealed that farmers were carrying out their own experiments with alternatives to the traditional slash—and—burn system. For example, one tried to cultivate without burning. He laid out small trial plots where he tested different methods of fertilizing, comparing these with non—fertilized areas. He came to the conclusion that, without burning, yields could be maintained only by using fertilizer. This confirmed earlier observations that a cleared area which did not burn well because of continuous rainfall did not bring good crop yields.

In the individual interviews and group discussions, farmers reported their experiences with land—clearing by bulldozer, and suggested less costly alternatives. In a process which farmers call 'taming the soil', after hand—felling the trees, the stumps and roots rot under the cover of secondary vegetation. After the third year of this decomposition process, the land can be worked by draught animals, which work around the larger stumps. After some years the stumps are easier to remove.

The LAET researchers found that the type of draught equipment already being used by the farmers (e.g. the *fuçador*) differs from that being recommended by the technicians, and is particularly suitable for the very difficult conditions in Transamazonia (existence of stumps, roots and large quantities of organic matter). The *fuçador* (described in Schmitz et al. 1991) is an implement for soil preparation which loosens and mixes the soil but does not turn it, consisting of a wooden drawbar which is fastened to the yoke of the draught animals (oxen), a leg and a shovel—like plough body. Most of the implements could be produced locally, as was already being done by some farmers.

With the *fuçador* it is possible to work in areas where the fallow vegetation has only recently been cleared and burned, as long as most of the tree stumps are not too thick. With this implement, animal traction can also be used in the shifting cultivation system, as the soil can be worked with the *fuçador* right up to the stumps. In order to speed up the process of decomposition of the trunks, they are sometimes buried in a furrow opened up with the *fuçador*.

In discussions with farmers experienced in mechanization, other problems associated with it came to light. Farmers were particularly concerned about the problem of the fungus disease *mela* (caused by *Rhizoctonia microesclerotia*) in beans (*Phaseolus vulgaris*). They stressed that the problem is greater on uncovered soils. They therefore normally sow the beans into year—old bush fallow which is cut only after the beans have germinated. The cut branches are left to cover the soil and prevent raindrops from splashing soil onto the leaves and thus spreading the fungus. This bean—growing technique (*feijão-de-abafado*) requires labour only for sowing, chopping the bush and harvesting. With mechanization, the fungus cannot be controlled so easily. Alternative solutions were discussed.

Reactions to the findings

The preliminary results of monitoring the mechanization project in Altamira and of study-ing experiences with mechanization in Uruará were presented in July 1994 to local exten-sionists and farmers at seminars in both municipalities. Farmers from elsewhere also attended. The main thrust of the findings presented by the LAET researchers was that:

- mechanization is not at all widespread in Transamazonia
- most farmers who had experience with mechanization elsewhere did not apply the tech-nology in Transamazonia
- most farmers who had already tried mechanization in Transamazonia and even owned equipment, no longer applied this technology
- the cost of mechanization (destumping, clearing the area, and seedbed preparation if made with a tractor) is high in relation to the price of food crops.

As a basis for discussion about the appropriateness of mechanization for Transamazonia, the views of the LAET researchers on the economics of animal traction, local knowledge and techniques of the farmers, and the results of farmers' own informal experimentation were presented at the seminars.

The reactions to these findings were contradictory. Many seminar participants seemed to be dissatisfied. They would have preferred something more positive, presenting mechaniza-tion with animal traction and tractors as a solution which could be introduced without hes-itation. Various associations had already included the acquisition of a tractor in the fund-ing proposals for their projects. On the other hand, when asked directly in public, few farm-ers expressed an interest in investing their own money in mechanization.

But despite this, and much to the LAET researchers' surprise, several groups of farmers from different municipalities expressed an interest in starting experiments with animal trac-tion. These farmers did not want to wait 3-4 years for the results of further scientific research before starting to gain experience of their own. An important argument in favour of action research was that confidence in a technology does not grow out of several years of scientif-ic research but rather out of joint on−farm activities. The farmers in Uruará, who were already well organized in a local smallholder union and the farmer association APRUR, requested that the LAET researchers support their experimentation. LAET responded by entering into action research with 20 farmers selected by the union and APRUR.

The aim of this action research is to monitor closely the key factors which determine the economic and ecological sustainability of mechanization over a lengthy period, so that the farmers will have reliable results on which to base their decisions. This approach also allows consideration to be given to the positive experiences farmers have had, especially of those few who practise mechanized farming and can be regarded as examples by others. At the same time, the statements of the farmers can be compared with their actions, particu-larly with respect to measures for maintaining soil fertility.

Action research in Uruará

The action research began with several meetings of the interested farmers, their organizations, extensionists and LAET researchers, to specify aims and procedures. One of the farmers had also participated in the study of experiences with mechanization. It was jointly decided to collect economic data and to study changes in soil fertility and labour productivity associated with mechanization. It was agreed that soil samples would be analysed to assess fertility, and that the farmers would record precipitation using rainfall gauges. To keep track of labour inputs, income and expenditure, as well as movement of products (harvest, consumption, sales), a management notebook was designed to be filled in by the farmer, his wife or another family member. Once a month a LAET researcher goes through the records together with the farmer and checks how the measurements are made. The results from the machine−cultivated areas are compared with plots worked in the traditional way, to allow both the LAET researchers and the farmers to assess the differences. LAET was given the task of analysing the data for presentation to and discussion with the experimenting farmers.

During these meetings, the farmers laid out and agreed upon the rules of the game which all would follow during the research: a one−hectare test area, with rice, maize and beans as the crops used in the rotation. Consensus on the varieties for each crop was reached by voting. The farmers would cultivate at least three years in the same area. It was further agreed that each would be free to choose the type of land (secondary forest, bush fallow etc.) and whether to use burning or not for clearing; whether to use bulldozer, winch, or to remove tree stumps by hand; and to do so at their own expense through payment in kind (rice, which has the most stable price) to be fixed at the time of clearing, to be paid within three years via the smallholder union. The use of the winch was proposed by LAET based on experiences of other regions of Pará State (Gazel P. and Martins P.F.S., pers. comm.), although it was not known to farmers at the time of the research. The attempt by LAET researchers to set a uniform seeding rate was not accepted by the farmers, as each had his own working rhythm with the manual sower, the *matraca*.

The first step in the research using the open−ended interview technique determined the need for equipment, animals and training. The areas to be worked by animal traction were visited with the farmer, and the soil type and land history recorded. The standing vegetation was noted in order to assess the difficulty and costs of preparing the land for mechanized farming. The LAET researchers also recording additional information to help identify the socio−economic profile of farmers wanting to intensify their land use, and to confirm or disprove hypotheses about the economics of transition from shifting to permanent cropping.

Initial data confirm previous results about mechanization by smallholders. The farms have, on average, an area of 110 ha with approximate 3 ha cropping area, 2.5 ha permanent cropping (cacao, pepper) and 25 ha pasture. Most of the area is primary forest and fallow land (*capoeira*). Fourteen of the 19 participants in the research were found to have experience with mechanization (2 of them with tractor), but only 3 had gained this experience in Transamazonia. The others had practised mechanized farming only in the areas from which they had migrated, i.e. under completely different conditions. Three farmers were still using machines, but only for transport (two with animals, one with tractor). Despite existing experience, no-one was using machines for soil cultivation. Thus, the number of farmers found in Uruará who had experience with mechanization in Transamazonia rose to eleven.

To obtain realistic results from action research, the main principle was to give nothing to the farmers without payment. Only in the case of risk or necessity resulting from research conditions was the possibility of compensation provided. The farmers acquired the equipment, carts, draught animals, corral material and a manure shed on credit from the local agricultural bank via APRUR. The seed for the trials was provided by LAET, in order to ensure the same starting conditions for all and to help decrease the risks taken by the farmers. LAET also procured a hand-winch in order to offer an alternative to destumping by bulldozer.

The interested farmers were given training in animal traction by three experienced farmers (questioned in the study of experiences with mechanization, one of whom is participating in the action research), who made available their own animals and equipment because funds for acquiring them had not yet been authorized. Groups of trainees practised with different animal species (oxen, horses, mules) and equipment on both 'clean' fields, and a field that had just been cleared and burned after four years of fallow. The training also addressed questions of soil fertility and animal husbandry, and the winch for destumping was tested. At the end of the training, each participant explained how he intended to work his field (clearing, burning, soil cultivation, weed control, and animals and equipment he intended to use).

A technical team was formed of people from LAET, EMATER, the cocoa research institute CEPLAC and EMBRAPA-CPATU. To support the action research and the diffusion of results to other parts of Transamazonia, a group was set up by MPST to be responsible for the circulation of information (GCI).

A written contract was elaborated to specify the responsibilities of each partner (LAET, extensionists, union, association and experimenting farmers) during the course of the research:

- The LAET researchers were responsible for soil sampling, setting up rain gauges, monthly checking of management notebooks, giving farmers guidance in recording and analysing data, preserving the anonymity of records, and organizing meetings with experimenting farmers (also attended by the GCI) to discuss possible technical alternatives which could be tested during the action research. LAET also assumed responsibility for the risks of lower than average production on account of the research.
- The farmers assumed responsibility for all the work and related costs, including hired labour arising in connection with manual destumping (e.g. by winch), soil cultivation, weed control, harvesting or processing. They agreed to keep careful records in the notebooks and in other forms (e.g. rainfall records), to comply with the decisions reached as a group (e.g. related to rotating crops, growing annual crops on the trial plots for at least three years), to save part of the certified rice seed for the next sowing, to maintain the winch in collaboration with APRUR, and to pay the costs of destumping within three years. Each farmer was individually responsible for his credit; APRUR monitors only the repayment.

- The local government institutions (EMATER, CEPLAC, EMBRAPA–CPATU) and the municipality are responsible for drawing up applications to the bank for credit, informing farmers about conditions for credit, giving guidance in the use of the winch and, in the case of the municipality, destumping by bulldozer. LAET was given the task by local government institutions of negotiating the formal agreement with their respective superiors in the capital, Belém.
- The task of the farmers' organizations was to mobilize farmers, manage the winch, monitor the farmers' financial obligations and exert any necessary pressure on local institutions and LAET researchers.

Further agreements between the local institutions and LAET related to participation in the action research (each institution at least three days per month), to information about problems and effects of the programme, to reports and publications, scientific seminars, organizing meetings of the technical team and the GCI, and to disseminating experiences. Changes in the research programme could be made only with the agreement of all partners.

By the end of 1995 the main activities were training in animal traction, clearing and burning of trial plots after taking soil samples, destumping by hand–winch (which turned out to be a much more efficient way of destumping in terms of lower cost and less damage to the upper soil layer), distribution of seed, application for credit and finally the preparation of management notebooks. Destumping by bulldozer is now being carried out, and members of the various organisations are analysing the contract. The critical point will be the decision on credit by the local agricultural bank, which is taking longer than expected.

Farmers' motivations for experimentation

LAET researchers, with their general hypotheses about the appropriateness of animal traction and with the results of their studies in Transamazonia, still felt confronted by a mystery. Why were farmers interested in experimenting with animal traction, a technology which their own experience had shown to be uneconomic under the prevailing circumstances? Why did farmers want to intensify farming, abandon shifting cultivation and try mechanization, even though they still had enough land to maintain soil fertility through traditional methods?

LAET explored this contradiction by analysing the minutes and notes from the various meetings and interviews with farmers. It became clear that the initiative for introducing mechanization was actually taken by local technicians who wanted to attract a concrete project to their area, and by some politicians who wanted to fulfil their election promises. This group put forward a proposal aimed at the majority of smallholder farmers, using arguments based on ecological concerns. The representatives of the farmer organizations and the churches supported this proposal, as they saw it as a way to modernize agriculture. The farmer representatives expressed the following arguments:

- shifting cultivation and fallowing are antiquated practices; farmers cannot continue to work like they did 200 years ago; ways of farming have to be changed
- techniques should be used which bring greater benefits; production capacity must be increased
- deforestation and burning must be reduced; the already cleared and, in part, degraded land must be better used.

The farmers themselves initially showed no great interest in mechanization. This topic was mentioned by only one of nine working groups of the Uruará meeting on alternative economic projects, but it appeared as top priority in the final report (prepared by the technicians and officials in the farmer organizations). Also in a study conducted in 1993 in Transamazonia, only 8% of the interviewed farmers mentioned the lack of mechanization as a major problem. For 77% it was not relevant (Walker et al. 1995). It should be mentioned that a majority of the farmers involved in the action research were strongly linked to union leaders.

Certain farmers appeared to have had an ulterior motive in joining the Altamira mechanization project: to get land cleared for pasture establishment. Other farmers who then expressed interest in experimenting with mechanization probably hoped that a project and subsidies could be attracted to their area. They also seemed to be influenced by technicians and local leaders, for example, by the smallholder union wanting to 'modernize' agriculture. Other farmers, however, had no clear idea of what could really be achieved by mechanization under the farming conditions of Transamazonia. The action research in Uruará allowed this question to be investigated, and to seek possible adaptations or alternatives to the mechanization initially proposed.

During the farm surveys, farmers were asked directly why they were interested in mechanization. This was meant not only to satisfy the researchers' curiosity but also to avoid possible disappointment on account of farmers' unrealistic expectations. Indeed, this was a first step towards formulation of hypotheses by the farmers. During the individual interviews, the reasons mentioned for wanting to experiment with mechanization were, in order of frequency:

- to try something new
- to reduce work, especially in controlling weeds
- to increase yields
- to be able to sow more than once on the same area and not have to clear land each year
- to be modern
- to expand the area cultivated.

These responses were later discussed in a meeting with all the farmers (focus group discussion), in which a researcher from LAET acted as facilitator. During this exchange of experience and problems, some farmers brought in other topics: problems of soil fertility, the importance of soil cover and of incorporating organic matter, crop rotation, changes in labour productivity. As individual knowledge was shared, all became more conscious of the risks involved in mechanization, and their expectations from the new technology became more realistic. However, despite the known risks, the farmers continued to be motivated by an interest in trying something new, in experiencing change. It must be remembered that all these farmers were colonists, most of whom had migrated more than once in search of something better for themselves and their families. Moreover, they had enough land to be able to afford a new experience, risky as it may be. If the experiment failed they could still clear another piece of land and go back to their old system of shifting cultivation. However, they did not want to tackle the risks of intensification alone. They explicitly sought the accompaniment and support of agricultural researchers and extensionists. They preferred to carry out the experiments within the framework of a collaborative research programme.

An analysis of their motivation for participating in the research made clearer their strategies. From the viewpoint of LAET researchers, based on their experiences in carrying out research with farmers upon farmer demand, those participating could be divided into six interest groups:

- those who had carried out mechanized farming in the area before
- those who had always wanted to try it in the region because they had done it elsewhere, and this gave them the opportunity
- those who were not familiar with mechanization but wanted to try out something new and modern
- those who hoped to avail themselves of free clearing services to achieve other private aims, such as making a path or a fishpond, but who withdrew as soon as more was demanded of them
- those who really wanted only to establish pasture
- those who were interested in partially transforming shifting cultivation into a ley system.

Individual farmers pursued different strategies to develop their farms further, and this is not to be condemned. The example illustrates the contradiction between the various private strategies and the collective strategy of the group: the introduction of mechanization. How do researchers deal with this heterogeneity? What strategies do they support? The most suitable partners for introducing mechanization, and thus realizing the collective strategy, are groups 2, 3 and 6, whereas the experience of group 1 can be useful in the process.

Group six is worth reinforcing. A ley system (in this case a regulated ley system) is characterized according to Ruthenberg (1980) by more or less regular rotation between "several years of arable cropping followed by several years of grass and legumes utilized for livestock production" and, in the case of a regulated system, some pasture management, fencing, seeding or planting of grass. Research by Veiga et al. (1995) reveals that there exists some tendency in Transamazonia to plant grass after annual cropping instead of fallowing. Indeed, the action research in Uruará was influenced by the idea of testing a regulated ley system.

In the preparatory stage of the action research, 27 farmers took part in the meetings. However, the emphasis on mutually binding agreements and payment for the services led to a self–selection process. Immediately before the final application for credit, another farmer withdrew because farmers and LAET researchers would not agree to the use of the bull-dozer to clear a road to his property, and he had then wanted to use another plot for the mechanization, even though the soil samples had already been taken. Thus the confrontation between individual and collective strategies reduced the number of experimenting farmers to 14.

Communication and farmer knowledge

Farmer knowledge is embedded in social processes. A basic prerequisite for communication about it is finding a common language. This is possible if people share some common background, such as can be created through interaction (Winograd and Flores 1992). The major advantage of action research is that it allows the partners to gain a common experience. This requires time. A research team which lives and works in the region for a lengthy period has better conditions for such interaction than a team that appears only briefly on the scene to make a rapid analysis.

Things that function as a matter of course are often not consciously perceived. They are recognized only when they no longer function in the usual way. It is not easy to speak, for example, about problems of soil fertility or of transition from shifting to permanent cultivation if these concepts are not consciously perceived by the dialogue partner. If enough land is still available and fallowing is also a possibility in the future, farmers are not likely to be interested in discussing the problems of soil fertility connected with the mechanization of farming.

However, farmers who have already had such experiences in other areas, or who have tried to convert to permanent cropping in Transamazonia by using the knowledge of mechanization brought with them from southern Brazil, can convey these problems in discussions with farming colleagues much better than can researchers. In such cases the researchers have primarily the function of initiating such farmer-to-farmer exchanges.

Discussions with farmers about areas in which they do not yet recognize problems requires considerable time, as experiences must be made in small steps to come to new insights. It was probably for this reason that a slide-show about the possibilities and problems of mechanization brought only the comment from farmers that this was nothing new. Showing slides of draught equipment awakened little interest, perhaps because the time for acquiring the equipment was still far in the future in the minds of the farmers. Later, during the training, when decisions had to be made in choosing equipment for which credit would be sought, it became apparent that some of the farmers knew next to nothing about the equipment. At this point they showed great interest in every detail. They noted down the names of all the pieces of equipment written on the blackboard and tried to arrive at common concepts and descriptions for each and every piece.

Researchers' role in supporting farmers' experimentation

It is an important role for researchers to recognize when farmers need additional information, and to offer it in an appropriate form. The farmers were interested in reducing the risks of experimenting with new technology and LAET researchers were able to provide information which could help to keep credit as low as possible in order to avoid problems with repayment. For example, when the researchers mentioned the advantages of using *fuçadors* in recently cleared fields, and when the testing of the hand–winch led to immediate results, the number of farmers who wanted to hire bulldozers for destumping sank from 12 to 8, and the number who wanted to test the hand–winch themselves rose from one to four. Other possibilities for lowering costs considered by the farmers were training their own oxen (the acquisition of the animals is equivalent to about 80% of the costs for initial investment for animal traction, not including the cart) and having local artisans construct appropriate implements or doing it themselves.

Open discussion among researchers and farmers led to a revision of ideas on both sides. For example, in earlier discussions in Uruará, some farmers had emphasized that, at least in the first year after destumping by bulldozer, the soil would have to be worked with tractors in order to tame it (an acceleration of the taming process mentioned above) before using animal traction. After a discussion about credit and repayment for equipment and services, they obviously reconsidered this argument because of costs. When drawing up their rules of the game for action research, the farmers decided unanimously to exclude the use of tractors for seedbed preparation. A few farmers also wanted to mechanize the sowing operation, but all eventually agreed upon continuing to use the *matraca* (hand–seeder). Here, the researchers' information about the possible advantages of this tool over the fairly complicated and expensive animal–drawn seeders, especially under the conditions in the first years after slashing, may have influenced the farmers' decision.

On the one hand, the very fact that researchers were interested in the farmers' informal experiments and their local knowledge about ecologically–appropriate farming techniques and tools helped to increase the value of these in the eyes of the farmers and their peers. On the other, the searching questions and, in some cases, openly–expressed doubts of the researchers served to sharpen the farmers' awareness of their own limitations in assessing experimental results. Some of these limitations were evident in the following:

- views of cause–effect relations: for example, declining yields of areas cultivated by machine are not always due simply to poor quality seed (example of Altamira project) or to uncontrolled weed infestation
- interviews with farmers and technical advisers gave rise to uncertainties about the basis on which they were making their respective judgements of new technologies: for example, their assessments of using mineral fertilizer (costs, expected increase in yields, market prices) differed greatly. There is a need to check the quantities of fertilizer with which farmers have been experimenting, and the assumptions made by the technicians

- the farmers' ability to quantify factors if it was not done immediately; for example, labour inputs and yields per unit area varied greatly. They knew exactly how much time was worked by hired labourers, but tended to underestimate their own work.
- farmer knowledge does not spread automatically. Some of the farmers encountered can be regarded as individualists. Moreover, colonization has brought together farmers from different regions of Brazil, who have experienced very different agro–ecological conditions. Many of these groups deliberately keep their distance from each other.

A basic question is: What do the farmers want to reveal to the researchers? How willing are they to pass on sensitive information about their farms, families and organizations? To what extent do they make statements which they believe the researchers expect to hear? For example, it was often difficult to obtain information about yields from the farmers involved in the Altamira mechanization project, as the farmers feared that the municipality might then start demanding repayment. The farmers also withheld information about land use, as they had obviously already cleared much more of the 50% forest cover allowed by federal law. Even if the introduction of mechanization seems to be more a technical problem, social factors influence the process considerably. That is why there is a need for more inter-disciplinarity in the research, e.g. in the question of motivation.

Although the farmers are themselves in a position to draw up hypotheses about techniques they experiment with, certain types of hypotheses are more likely to be drawn up by researchers. For example, the hypothesis about the dynamics of farming system development and introducing mechanization had not previously been part of the discussions in Pará about mechanization. According to Pimentel et al. (1992), reasons for the low level of adoption of mechanization were a lack of tradition, the high costs of equipment and the lack of information. A theoretical framework allowed for a greater understanding of those reasons. It brought another way of looking at the matter, facilitated a constructive discussion between all participants, and helped them recognize the possibilities and limitations of mechanization under the conditions prevailing in Amazonia. In a meeting facilitated by LAET researchers it was then possible to crystallize out of the farmers' own arguments the major factors for transition from shifting to permanent cultivation. This brought all participants in the discussion one step nearer understanding the development of farming systems.

On the other hand, the researchers were also forced to reconsider their hypotheses. Several farmers questioned the hypothesis that mechanized cultivation does not increase productivity per unit area and insisted that maize yields increase. Here, the stated yields, soil types and other possible influencing factors must be looked into. A possible hypothesis to explain the farmers' observations is that, two years or more after burning, the potassium content of the soil is low and the maize no longer suffers from an excess. Mechanization can promote this effect by mixing the soil and thus increasing the rate of decomposition. The farmers indicated to the researchers that the seeding rate in destumped areas is higher than under shifting cultivation simply because space is no longer taken up by tree stumps in the field. This alone can lead to a higher yield.

For a balanced partnership, both sides must regard the research as legitimate. This refers particularly to the ratio between short– and long–term demands on research. To be able to collaborate on an equal basis with farmers and their organizations, researchers must seriously consider their suggestions and needs, and must deal with their immediate concerns. This does not mean that participatory research leads to a gradual integration of viewpoints and overcoming all differences. Indeed, Long and Villareal (1994) and Castellanet et al. (1995) emphasize that recognition of the differences between the partners is an essential component for building a partnership. Constant negotiations and keeping mutually acceptable records of the results, such as in the contract between LAET and MPST, form the basis of a constructive partnership. The aims and proposals of researchers and farmers can differ greatly, as was initially the case in the question of mechanization; and the results may not please all partners, such as the farmers in this case.

In providing information and accompanying farmers' experiments, researchers have an ethical responsibility to remain critical, and not to support fictitious 'solutions' in order to attract funds in the form of projects, subsidies or credit, if negative effects on the community or the environment are likely. In negotiations with farmers, their representatives and other politicians, the researchers who are in constant interaction with farming communities are under constant pressure to succumb to these influences. Hébette's warning, in his oral contribution to a seminar about relations between researchers and farmers (*Pesquisas para o desenvolvimento sustentável da agricultura familiar amazônica: Relações entre Pesquisadores e Agricultores*, 04-06/04/95. NEAF/CAP/UFPA, Belém) that "The researcher, even in the function of rendering a service, cannot lose his autonomy for critical thinking", holds true also, indeed especially, in participatory research. This encompasses honest criticism of ideas proposed by farmers or their representatives and awareness of the motives behind them, as well as criticism of the researchers' own assumptions and motives.

Within farmer organizations and groups, homogeneity cannot be assumed. The farmers normally express their interests via their representative organizations. The farmers and their representatives do not necessarily hold the same views of agricultural development. For example, the farmer representatives were long opposed to research and development work in the framework of CAT, part of UFPA's programme of research, training and development about wood utilization or cattle husbandry, as they connected this with other groups (large farmers, wood traders). It did not comply with their understanding of smallholders (Muchagata et al. 1994). Even if farmer representatives adopt some of the arguments of technical advisers about mechanization, they have basic differences in views as soon as 'ideological' questions such as the identity of smallholders plays a role. A large part of the farming communities, particularly the youth and women, are not well represented in the farmer organizations. The farmer leaders develop their own dynamics and often begin to pursue their own political projects, which do not necessarily reflect the basic interests of the majority of farmers. In the case of mechanization, the topic was more strongly advocated by the spokesmen in farmer organizations than by the members themselves. It is worth remembering, as MacArthur (1980) points out, that "From the farmer's point of view, labour productivity and work rationalisation are of great importance, not only because labour is a major input but because its use is the subject of acute personal experience".

In such cases the researchers must negotiate not only with the farmers' official representatives but also with the experimenting farmers themselves, as they are the actual partners in the day–to–day research work. In this connection it is essential that the relationship between LAET and MPST is defined as a 'preferred partnership' but does not exclude links with other institutions. For example, the formation of the GCI was encouraged in order to bypass in some way the MPST for the better dissemination of experiences at the regional level.

Conclusions

To avoid confusion of concepts we suggest that farmers should be characterized less as researchers and more as experimenters and innovators, areas in which they are ahead of formal researchers. This goes beyond Freire (1977), who characterizes the nature of farmers' knowledge as empirical.

Experience with participatory research in mechanization shows that the methods of researchers and farmers are very different. Farmers observe, formulate hypotheses (often not explicitly expressed), experiment, analyse and conclude. But normally they content themselves with few trials and do not proceed systematically in planning and executing experiments or analysing the results. This can be shown in the test with mineral fertilizer, where different rates of fertilizer were applied, but they did not try gradually to reach an optimum.

The farmers also had difficulties in answering the question: "How is the rise in productivity [reported by some of the farmers] related to mechanization?" Neither could they describe the interrelations which are complex because of the influence of various factors. Only after several discussions and interviews did the researchers and other farmers come to realize that there were different views among the farmers about the possible explanations for the increase in productivity: higher seeding rate after destumping, increase in yields of mechanized cultivation of maize and generally higher yields after ploughing.

Further, it is important to recognize that farmers normally abstract only when facts are part of their universe of experience, whereas the researcher is used to working theoretically, beyond direct experience. It was an important precondition for the emerging interest of farmers to participate in action research that some had experience of the problems of mechanization. It allowed them to understand the objections of the researchers and they did not therefore insist on a programme of dissemination of mechanization.

In PTD the researchers' systematic way of working and the farmers' practical experience and capacities to observe, explore and investigate complement one another. Cooperation with farmers enables the researcher to gain insights into the reality of smallholder (family) farming and to benefit from the farmers' accumulated experience and observations, and the farmers are supported in doing their investigations and experiments more systematically. In the process, the individual knowledge of particular farmers is socialized and shared with other farmers. The researchers try, through their persistent enquiries, to analyse the influence of the different factors.

Although the topic of the action research 'Introduction of Mechanisation' appears to be strictly technical, we soon found that farmers' motivations were strongly influenced by local social and political considerations. Various efforts were made to reduce these effects (through a no–subsidy policy and by drawing up formal agreements between farmers and other agencies), but they continued to play a role after two years of interaction. Without an effort to integrate social scientists into the PTD teams who are prepared to spend a considerable amount of time in the field, it is likely that these effects will not be taken into consideration sufficiently. The building of ties of mutual confidence between researchers and local farmer leaders can help to avoid the persistence of misunderstandings, but this requires much time and the more or less permanent presence of the researchers in the area. This experience brings us to question the validity of any type of rapid intervention which is not embedded in a long–term programme with regular monitoring of the process and its results, including the social and political influences and effects.

Acknowledgements

The research was realized in cooperation with members of the technical team: Darcisio Quanz (agricultural technician, EMBRAPA), José Raul dos Santos Guimaräes (agricultural engineer, CEPLAC) and Gilson Barbosa (agricultural technician, EMATER), all from Uruará.

References

Boserup, E. 1972. *The conditions of agricultural growth*. London, George Allen & Unwin.

Castellanet, C., A. Simões and P. Celestino Filho. 1994. Diagnóstico preliminar da agricultura familiar na Transamazônica: Pistas para pesquisa–desenvolvimento. Paper presented at the internal seminar on 20/10/94 of EMBRAPA–CPATU. Belém (in press).

Castellanet, C., J. Alves and B. David. 1995. A parceria entre organizações de produtores e equipe de pesquisadores: a pesquisa participativa como ferramenta de um projeto de desenvolvimento sustentável. *Agricultura Familiar* 1 (1), Belém, NEAF/CAP/UFPA, pp 139-161.

Falesi, I.C. 1972. Solos da rodovia Transamazônica. *Boletim Técnico* No. 55. Belém, IPAN.

Falesi, I.C. 1986. Estado atual de conhecimentos de solos da Amazônia brasileira. In: *Proceedings of First Symposium on the Humid Tropics*. Belém, EMBRAPA–CPATU, Vol. I, pp 168-191.

Freire, P. 1977. *Extensão ou comunicação*. São Paulo, Paz e Terra.

Hamelin, P. 1994. A obrigação da reestruturação do projeto de colonização de Uruará. Belém (unpublished).

Léna, P. and I.M. Silveira da S. 1993. *Uruará: O futuro das crianças numa área de colonização*. Belém, UNAMAZ/UFPA.

Long, N. and M. Villareal. 1994. The interweaving of knowledge and power in development interfaces. In: Scoones, I. and J. Thompson (eds), *Beyond farmer first: Rural people's knowledge, agricultural research and extension practice,* London, IT Publications, pp 41-52.

Martins, P.F. da S., C.C. Cerri, B. Volkoff, F. Andreux and A. Chauvel. 1991. Consequences of clearing and tillage on the soil of a natural Amazonian ecosystem. *Forest Ecology and Management* 38: 273-282.

MacArthur, J.D. 1980. Some characteristics of farming in tropical environment. In: Ruthenberg, H., *Farming systems in the tropics,* 3rd ed., Oxford, Clarendon Press, pp 19-29.

Muchagata, M., V. Reynal and I. Veiga Jr. 1994. La construction du dialogue entre chercheurs et paysans à travers l'expérience du CAT. In: *Symposium international recherches-système en agriculture et développement rural,* 21-25.11.94, Montpellier, CIRAD, pp 768-772.

Pimentel, G.B.M., A.F.S. Reis and R. Palheta de FR. 1992. *Tração animal: Uma experiência piloto no Pará.* Belém, EMBRAPA–CPATU.

Pingali, P., Y. Bigot and H.O. Binswanger. 1987. *Agricultural mechanization and the evolution of farming systems in sub-saharan Africa.* Baltimore, Johns Hopkins University Press/World Bank.

Ruthenberg, H. 1980. *Farming systems in the tropics.* 3rd ed. Oxford, Clarendon Press.

Sanchez, P.A. 1976. *Properties and management of soils in the tropics.* New York, Wiley.

Schmitz, H., W. Sommer and S. Walter. 1991. *Animal traction in rainfed agriculture in Africa and South America: Determinants and experiences.* Braunschweig, Vieweg.

Schmitz, P.A. and C. Castellanet. 1995. Intensificação da agricultura na Transamazônica: experiências de um levantamento nas 'chácaras' e nos travessões em Uruará. Altamira, LAET (unpublished).

Veiga, J.B., J.F. Tourrand and D. Quanz. 1995. A pecuária na fronteira agrícola da Amazônia: O caso do município de Uruará-PA na Transamazônica. Belém, EMBRAPA–CPATU (unpublished).

Walker, R.T., A.K.O. Homma, A.J. de Conto, R. Carvalho de A, C.A.P. Ferreira, A.I.M. dos Santos, A.C.P.N. da Rocha, P.M. de Oliveira and C.D.R. Pedraza. 1995. Dinâmica dos sistemas de produção na Transamazônica. Belém, EMBRAPA–CPATU/FSU/IITF (unpublished).

Winograd, T. and F. Flores. 1992. *Erkenntnis, Maschinen, Verstehen.* 2nd ed. Berlin, Rotbuch Verlag.

13. Empowering farmers to conduct experiments

Edward Ruddell, Julio Beingolea and Humberto Beingolea [1]

A social calamity

1985 was the third year in a row that a population of 211,849 Quechua and Aymara people of northern Potosí, Bolivia, had suffered serious drought and frosts. This combination of climatic factors had once again resulted in harvests of potatoes the size of thumbnails. Without their major staple of potatoes, thousands of mothers and children were forced to abandon their animals and homes in rural areas to migrate to the major cities of Bolivia for

[1] Edward D. Ruddell, Julio Beingolea and Humberto Beingolea, Vecinos Mundiales (World Neighbors), Neuva las Condes 12225 / D4 Casilla 20005, Santiago 20, Chile

three to twelve months of the year. It was a pitiful sight to see Quechua women and their children squatting on urban sidewalks with hands outstretched for money to purchase their food.

The following physical, cultural and geographic factors make the task of helping these indigenous people to improve their food security on a sustainable basis seem even more challenging:

- acute erosion of sandy loams; cultivation on slopes up to 45 degrees; elevations ranging from 2800 to 4000 metres above sea level; average annual temperatures of 9-15°C, with occasional hail; an average rainfall of 500 mm per year; and relatively complex agronomic practices required for potato production
- high rates of functional illiteracy in Spanish, the national language, as a result of only one to three years attendance at primary schools coupled with strong oral cultural traditions mean that the written word is of limited use to communicate ideas
- geographic isolation, no government agricultural research or extension services.

Despite these problems, there was a positive side: the opportunity to participate in the planning and implementation of a people–centred self–help development programme had motivated peasant farmers. They were interested enough in improving their production to walk up to 24 hours on a round–trip to attend monthly seminars. These farmers had planned and conducted hundreds of demonstration trials to improve food security in their own communities. When the rainfall was fairly good and there was no hail or severe frosts, production increased by 50 to 100%.

Searching for a solution

To help search for a solution, the World Neighbors (WN) area representative spent two weeks visiting experimental plots which Quechua and Aymara farmers had planted on their farms in an effort to improve crop production. He hoped that some of these might provide useful clues about the best strategy for improving food security in the area. To his disappointment, all the plots he visited had failed because of the severe climatic conditions.

Up to this point the results from farmer–led demonstration plots of a thousand irregular shapes and sizes planted on their own land had not been documented in a systematic manner. When programme facilitators inquired about results, farmers would report the number of sacks of potatoes harvested for every *arroba* (5.2 kg) of seed planted. Precise measurements of the size of the experiments, the elevation of the sites, the general rainfall, date of planting and harvesting, exact weight of harvests, and the number of people trained were never recorded because of oral cultural traditions and high rates of illiteracy.

In addition, most experiments tested only one new idea at a time. This posed major problems when population pressure and environmental problems were growing faster than the farmers' ability to increase production with indigenous methods of experimentation.

In 1989 Julio Beingolea, former director of the College of Agronomy of the University of Huamanga in Ayacucho, Peru, approached WN for employment. He had a deep respect for the indigenous peoples of the Andes, spoke the local dialect of Quechua, had completed a Masters Degree in agriculture in the USA, and had been in charge of research on Andean crops at the University. With his assistance, WN was able to offer farmer–promoters the opportunity to add another tool to their indigenous kit for documenting the results of their own experiments. It consisted of teaching them how to design, conduct and evaluate small 10 x 12 m experimental field trials. To compare the productivity of four potato varieties under similar conditions, 368 plants, distributed in twelve sub–plots, were sown. It was thought that the results should be sufficient to provide data for predicting similar results on a larger scale.

Since farmer–promoters had gained a thirst for new knowledge from previous site–specific trials they had conducted, the idea appealed to them of learning how to plan, execute and evaluate field trials, in the manner taught at the university. Rural peoples are often looked down upon by city people as backward and unable to learn, and the farmers were eager to show their ability to perform at a professional level.

As Julio Beingolea explained, if such small areas could be used to project results on a larger scale with a reasonable degree of accuracy, it would cost less to test new ideas. In this way no one would lose much in financial terms if they had bad weather, and it also meant that poorer farmers with less land could participate more readily.

How it works

During the annual planning meeting of staff for five programmes, the WN national director introduced Julio Beingolea and told them he had been hired to assist farmer–promoters improve the documentation of their field trials in a systematic way. This was followed by discussion of appropriate dates for holding 3–day seminars on the topic in each of the five programme areas so that promoters interested in the topic could attend.

When seminars began a month later, farmer–promoters discussed the reasons for the importance of documenting the results of their experiments. The reasons included hunger, a growing population, shortage of land, low levels of production, and the need to identify and share the results of new technologies which might increase yields. To achieve the goal of learning the new methods to evaluate their trials as rapidly and efficiently as possible, the national director of WN suggested that seminars be organized. The farmer–promoters embraced the idea with enthusiasm. The seminars gave instruction on the principles of designing and conducting a field trial. The initial treatments (variables) that farmers elected to test in their own trials varied from farm to farm. In some cases they chose to compare the productivity of different types of their own native seeds with varieties introduced and made available through research stations. In other cases they chose to compare the results of different methods of fertilization (see Table 13.1). A 6–page mimeographed handout summarizing their findings was given to participants at the end of the session.

Next, farmers participated in planting two field trials designed by a promoter in the community where the seminar was held. Random replication permitted the use of small sub–plots (3 x 3.2 m) within the trial (see Figure 13.1). In order to improve production under even the worst climatic conditions, Julio Beingolea encouraged everyone to plant their experimental plots on land prepared with deep cultivation, uniform spacing, appropriate seed size and adequate fertilization.

Replication   Treatment

I	2	4	1	3

II	4	1	3	2

III	3	2	4	1

Figure 13.1. Random location of varieties (number) in the three replications

Programme personnel followed this seminar with monthly two−day courses which reviewed agronomic practices for controlling weeds, pests, etc. During these courses farmers visited the field trials of their neighbours; this allowed farmer−to−farmer exchange.

As the crops matured, farmers saw the importance of including a control plot to compare the new with traditional practices. Previously farmers had disliked including control plots with demonstration plots because they felt it was a waste of land and resources. Poorer farmers who visited these sites often felt the increased yields were unattainable on their own land because of poorer soil fertility, climatic variations and other factors beyond their control. With the inclusion of control plots in the field trials, farmers and programme leaders began to observe the importance of accurately comparing the results of new technologies with traditional practices under the same climate and soil conditions.

One month prior to harvest the farmers were invited to attend a second seminar given by Julio Beingolea. He made suggestions about the appropriate data to record. The farmer−promoters liked the ideas and agreed to record the date of harvest, the number of participants, the weight of produce from each sub−plot, and the total weight from the three randomly distributed sub−plots for each treatment. Then they were shown how to determine the average yield of the sub−plots, calculate the yield per hectare, and use statistical formulae to evaluate the results of the trials.

The seminar concluded by harvesting two field trials in the area. Farmers noticed it was much easier to weigh the plant material harvested from the small sub−plots. Hand−held scales used in local stores could weigh it accurately. They also began to notice that in some cases the yield of one replication might be twice that of another. This observation led to a discussion concerning the factors that might be causing such differences. In one case it was due to competition from a tree 10 m away on one side of the trial plot. In another, two of the three repetitions were planted on a 20 degree slope. The third, at the bottom of the hill, had received additional rainfall and fertilizer from the run−off from the two treatments above.

Next, the farmers collected the yields from each treatment in separate piles. These piles gave a much more accurate visual comparison of the yields of each of the four treatments and varieties or fertilizer applications. Each of these treatments always included a test plot using traditional technology.

For the first time farmers had the opportunity to appreciate the impact of combining deep cultivation, appropriate seed size, better spacing, and much higher rates of fertilization when conducting variety trials. Julio also encouraged the farmers to group the potatoes according to size, since larger potatoes were more valuable when sold.

Increasing yields to secure food supply

Bolivia

Between 1991 and 1993 farmer–promoters, elected at community assemblies in their communities, planned and conducted 342 experimental field trials in a wide variety of elevations for 89 varieties of eight crops, including potatoes, corn, wheat, barley, quinoa and legumes. A minimum of three fertilization regimens were also tested repeatedly for each crop (see Table 13.1). It was a satisfying experience for Julio Beingolea as a professional agronomist to watch the farmers plan their experiments at the annual planning meetings. The farmer–promoters were always coming up with new native varieties of plant material we had never heard of before. They also continued simultaneously to test other ideas for improving food security. For example, one farmer had the idea of applying ash to potato leaves to protect them during severe frosts. A second developed the idea of building underground hot–houses. Temperature variations were reduced when vegetables were planted in pits 2 m wide, 4 to 8 m long and 2 m below ground level. The plastic required to cover a small area of 2 x 8 m, for example, was minimal. In addition, farmers tested new ideas for water and soil conservation to protect the environment and improve their production.

The 800 field trials planned and conducted by over 80 farmers during the past six years have enriched everyone's knowledge about the best site–specific agronomic practices for improving the food security of small farmers living in the Andean mountains of Bolivia, Ecuador and Peru. A tiny sample of some of the unique results follows.

Table 13.2 shows that, in farmers' field trials, the introduced varieties Waycha, Colombiana and Qorisonqo increased yields from an average of 5000 kg/ha to 24,000 kg, when the seed bed was prepared with deep tillage (0.45 m) as compared to the normal 0.1 to 0.15 m, fertilized with the equivalent of 10,000 kg of animal manure per hectare, and seed size of a minimum of 40 g. Native varieties followed in importance with yields of 18,000 kg/ha with adequate rainfall. In contrast, the introduced varieties of Cardinal and Desiree produced 50% less than native varieties under these conditions.

The results in Table 13.1 also proved invaluable to a government agency which had encouraged farmers of the area to multiply all the introduced varieties Waycha, Colombiana, Qorisonqo, Cardinal and Desiree. All five had demonstrated comparable yields at lower elevations, but the farmer–led, site–specific field trials showed that this was not the case at higher elevations. Thanks to this documentation the organization soon stopped recommending the last two varieties for multiplication at these elevations.

Table 13.1. Farmers' field trials in Bolivia, 1993-94. Number of experiments planned and conducted by small farmers

Crop	Experiment	S. Pedro	Sacaca	Chiro	Pairu-mani	Toro Toro	Sub-totals	Totals per crop
potato	varieties	14	14	4	7	7	46	
potato	org. & chem. fertilizer	3	4	8		15		
potato	seed size	1	9	1		11		
potato	green manure		3	4			7	
potato	amount of chem. fertilizer			2	2		4	
potato	plant density		1	2			3	
potato	planting date	2					2	
potato	variety & density	2					2	90
corn	varieties	9				12	21	
corn	org. & chem. fertilizer	2					2	
corn	plant density	2					2	25
barley	varieties				3	1	4	
barley	method of planting				1		1	5
wheat	varieties	10				6	16	16
peas	varieties	4					4	4
h. beans	varieties				1		1	1
quinua	varieties		2				2	2
TOTAL		49	24	29	15	26		143

Table 13.2. Comparison of potato varieties summarizing 24 experiments in 20 communities of the programme of Chiroq'asa, northern Potosí, Bolivia

Variety	Waycha	Colombiana	Qorisonqo	Natives	Cardinal	Desiree
Yield kg/ha	24,491	24,306	23,241	18,380	11,343	10,926

Another interesting finding from the Chiroq'asa field trials was that averages alone were an inadequate measure of progress. Yields ranged from 8333 kg/ha to 44,444 kg/ha (Table 13.3). Learning which community had the highest and lowest yields provided an opportunity to promote cross-visits to discuss why such major differences were occurring.

A third finding concerned an experiment to confirm optimal seed size to maintain basic food security. Andean subsistence farmers living in marginal areas that suffer serious drought frequently harvest so little that they are forced to eat their best potato seeds to survive. What are left to plant are too small to re–sprout if drought or frost strikes early in the next growing season. A vicious cycle of diminishing harvests and lower–quality seed ensues. A field trial conducted by Filemon Colque at 3880 m elevation confirmed that egg–sized seeds (60 g) with deep tillage and 10,000 kg of animal manure per hectare would almost double yields from 8333 to 14,352kg/ha .

Table 13.3. Comparison of potato varieties in two Bolivian communities

Community:	Qayastiya	Limaya
Conducted by:	community	Gregorio Chambi
Planted:	15.10.90	18.10.92
Harvested:	12.03.91	23.03.93
Rainfall:	abundant	good
Elevation (m):	3900	3300
Previous crop:	barley and tarwi	fallow
Slope:	inclined	flat
Fertilization:	10,000 kg/ha sheep manure	10,000 kg/ha sheep manure
Seed size (g):	80	60
Soil preparation:	deep tillage	deep tillage
Results	*Yield (kg/ha)*	*Yield (kg/ha)*
Pali	9722	
Waycha	9722	21,518
Qorosonqo	8333	36,808
Cardinal	4629	
Desiree	2777	
Colombiana		44,444
Runa Blanga (native)		18,519
Qharan (native)		17,824

Ecuador

In an effort to achieve quicker results from a new programme in Ecuador, Julio Beingolea visited the regional government field station to inquire if they had new varieties of corn that they felt would improve local production in the province of Bolivar. As these seeds are often in great demand and difficult to obtain, he was pleased to acquire them. When he met with the local farmers they expressed interest in testing this new variety so he distributed it to 75 farmers from 6 communities. They enthusiastically planted it in 75 demonstration plots. To everyone's dismay the native varieties of corn exceeded every single demonstration plot.

There was also excessive rain in that year which also wiped out 169 green manure field trials planted with sweet peas. These covered 22,296 square metres of land in the same communities. Fortunately Julio's reputation was protected because he had helped the farmers plant other small field trials of their own. The experience taught World Neighbors Andean Area staff that field trials must precede all demonstrations. Once the trials are completed and farmers agree on what works best, demonstration plots become important for disseminating results.

Julio also helped leaders of an NGO called Centro de Desarrollo Ecuatoriano para El Indígena test barley varieties in field trials in the province of Chimborazo, Ecuador. In this case the new varieties increased yields from 736 kg to 5299 kg/ha. This was very important in an area where many men are forced to leave their families and work in the city to improve family income.

Influence on neighbouring programmes

Systematic documentation of field trials conducted by the farmers themselves has influenced other farmers as well as government agencies, research stations, universities and other NGOs.

Box 13.1. Field trials improve the life of Encarno Fernández in more ways than one

"I am 35 years old, married, with 5 children, 3 girls and 2 boys. The oldest is a boy of 15. My father died when I was only a baby. I suffered from lack of food in my community so I decided to go to Cochabamba where I worked as a labourer in construction for 3 years. Then I had to return to my community because of my mother, who was alone and had insufficient help.

I heard about World Neighbors in 1985, when I was nominated by my community to be trained as a volunteer agricultural promoter. There, in San Pedro, I started learning how to improve the production of my crops. Engineer Alcibiades Oporto helped me very much.

While I continued to attend the training courses in San Pedro in 1991, Don Claudio Miranda, a WN extensionist and at present a member of the Congress of Bolivia, got me a post in Literacy as a Yuyaypurichic Andean educator. Thanks to the training and education received from WN I worked in this project for 2 years. I was hired for one year and the second year I remained as a volunteer.

I raised very little food before attending WN classes on food production. Production improved after I started applying the technologies I was learning in the short courses,. I did not have enough land and just now I am buying some with the profit of the sale of some food production and small animals.

During the training courses in San Pedro I learned about green manure. I was doubtful so I tested it in a field trial. The results of the first trial with green manure convinced me, because it doubled production compared to sheep manure fertilization. After seeing the results I increased the area.

In Saucine, my community, we always planted lupines. Most families planted a little lupine to harvest the bean and eat it as mote, we did not know it could be used as a green manure. If it weren't for World Neighbors' short courses and demonstrations, I think we still wouldn't know how to use it as a green manure..

I did not have much land before and I planted little lupine. Now I am buying small plots and I will increase food produced for my family. I will also sell part of the production to have some money for clothing and other types of food we need to buy in the market... I still continue planting trials. I have observed that lupines increases not only the production of potatoes but also that of corn and wheat".

For the first time programme leaders from adjacent areas that reported results at biannual meetings believed the results of the trials and began repeating these trials in new areas. The Bolivian Government made a grant through its social investment fund to train local leaders in 120 communities in the Provinces of Charcas and Alonzo Ibañez how to use appropriate technologies developed by local farmers during a 10–year period. This included exposure of how to design and conduct experimental field trials of their own choosing. This benefited 1936 men and 794 women farmers during an 18–month period. The grant covered the cost of producing five different pamphlets that summarized the results of farmers' experiments over three years. After seeing the first edition of these pamphlets, Unicef Proandes reprinted and distributed them to functional literacy classes being conducted in 600 communities. The Ministry of Education has assigned ten teachers to work full time in the programme area in response to the farmers' demand for more education. This has opened the doors to including scientific field trials in the new curricula for rural schools.

In addition, programme leaders helped seven agronomy students, who speak the indigenous languages of the area, complete their theses for their professional degrees. This has produced a small pool of young agronomists originally from this area who are interested in remaining in the area to work. To our surprise, farmer–promoters in Bolivia insisted this year that they also be taught how to design field trials that would enable them to test four varieties and four planting dates at the same time. This is proof that once human development starts, thirst for new knowledge never stops.

Lessons learnt

WN believes that its people–centred methodology ensures the farmers' willingness to adopt the documenting of the results of site–specific field trials. This methodology consists of:

* selecting marginal communities based on need and opportunity
* establishing a relationship of mutual trust
* strengthening local capacity to identify problems, analyse root causes, and identify and prioritize possible courses of action to address the problems
* working with the people to try out new ideas by starting small and staying practical to generate early enthusiasm
* strengthening local capacity to access additional resources from the outside world, and
* building on experience so that the role of World Neighbors changes from being a direct programme partner to a catalyst for wider impact through replication, dynamic programme transformation, influencing other agencies and policy reform (World Neighbors 1993).

When systematic documentation of simple site–specific field trials were introduced with this methodology, farmers felt even more empowered since they were learning professional, university–level concepts and techniques. In contrast, those organizations which have introduced farmers to these ideas without the participatory, people–centred methodology have generally failed. A second key for success was that the facilitator, Julio, had respect for both local culture as well as people–centred methodology, in addition to being recognized for his expertise.

Empowerment and development of farmers' skills in farmer–based experimentation has led to growth in the area. This has included a greater demand for literacy classes, people completing their high school education and continued technical training. Publication of the results of farmer–led experiments has also improved the understanding by academic and research institutions of the vital role farmers play in testing, adapting and disseminating technologies appropriate for diverse micro–climates and soils found throughout the Andean region.

Most of the poorest areas of the world have never had, nor will ever have, professional research or extension services. WN's methodology offers an approach to the development of these regions on a sustainable basis that empowers the beneficiaries and has the potential of being linked with the rural educational system. This approach would cost the national governments a fraction of the cost of the traditional research and extension systems.

Challenges for the future

Recent semi–structured interviews with a sample of 28 women from the 120 communities served by this programme demonstrate that the women are appreciative of the results of the site–specific field trials, but that they also want to have more access to the training itself.

We are encouraged that one–third of the promoters who have begun training in two new programmes are now women. Experience has proven that it takes time to integrate women into this effort because mothers are already overloaded with frequent childbirth, feeding the family, gathering wood, collecting water, in addition to helping plant and harvest the crops. Younger girls have more time to participate but almost never possess land of their own to conduct field trials. Furthermore, since these activities are generally considered the domain of men, it takes time for young girls to gain the courage to try them.

Because rural children of today will soon be the farmers of tomorrow, WN hopes that the small 12–page pamphlet it has developed as a training manual will someday be incorporated in rural school curricula so that each community can begin to think of itself as an experimental research station. WN Andean Area staff believe that this approach offers the only hope for adaptation to rapid economic integration in today's world.

References

World Neighbors. 1993. World Neighbors strategic planning conference report. Oklahoma City, World Neighbors.

photo: Hans Sas

14. Farmers' laboratory

Marius Broekema, Jan Diepenbroek and Luppo Diepenbroek[1]

Research is done by scientists in their laboratories and farmers work the land. A logical division of labour, or so it seems. But not so. Our group of 23 potato growers proved this by establishing our own farmer laboratory back in 1992. Through this laboratory we are able to monitor nematode infection intensively at very modest costs. This has played a key role in our efforts to develop a flexible system of soil fumigation, and has helped us to cut the use of fumigation chemicals by more than 50%.

Historically, research and experimentation has always been part of farming. Research by specialist institutes is relatively new. Of course, such research has greatly contributed to the development of Dutch agriculture, and will continue to do so. But, one should not forget that

[1] Marius Broekema, Jan Diepenbroek and Luppo Diepenbroek, Borgercompagnie 109, 9631 TE Borgercompagnie, The Netherlands

the same is true for research and experimentation by farmers. In fact, farmers' and scientists' research should be complementary. In the recent past, however, the balance has been greatly disturbed. A great deal of money has been put into formal research, especially since the Second World War, often without providing farmers with the expected practical solutions.

The Farmer Laboratory initiative of 23 farmers in the area of Borgercompagnie, North Netherlands, is an effort to restore that balance. Farming conditions in this area are generally much more difficult than in other parts of the Netherlands. Although the average farm size of 37 hectares is not far below the Dutch average, soil conditions are such that farmers depend very much on one or two crops, potatoes and sugarbeet, for their income. In the past few years this income has been negative as costs of production in both the larger and smaller farms have been higher than the income generated. Where potato cultivation is characterised by a high use of synthetic inputs, mostly soil fumigants, the present government pressure to reduce the use of such inputs is felt particularly hard, as is the case in the Borgercompagnie area. The possibilities to switch to other crops or agricultural enterprises, however, remains very limited.

Inadequate research recommendations

The history of the laboratory goes back to the early 1990s when the local Borgercompagnie farmers' association asked one of us, a former office–holder in the association, to explore ways to reduce production costs. Initially the feeling was that N–fertilization and nematode control would offer possibilities.

A neighbouring farmer was asked to help collect information and to review most of the recent research suggestions, and shortly after, his son, who was studying at the Agricultural University, also became involved. A variety of organizations were contacted by the three of us and the son's network was used extensively. With the type of soil prevailing in the area, it quickly became clear that little could be achieved with N–fertilization. But there was increasing evidence of deep groundwater being polluted through the intensive use of soil fumigants. A revealing insight for many of us.

Our study, and the various discussions we held, indicated that existing soil fumigation regulations and recommendations on nematode treatment were often not effective. Soil fumigation was carried out at regular intervals, as required by Dutch law, to cultivate potatoes once every two years on the same plot. This had to be done, even when infection was only very limited, or when weather and soil conditions prevented effective application. Such practices are not only bad for the environment but also an unnecessary financial burden for farmers. In 1992, the 23 members in Borgercompagnie were each spending annually some Dfl15,000 (US$8,800) on soil fumigation. If this could be reduced by 50%, and we know now that even more is possible, this would have a considerable impact on overall farm profitability.

A 50% reduction is very much in line with current government policy (known as MJPG, *Meer Jaren Plan Gewasbescherming*, or Longer–Term Crop Protection Plan), and fortunately coincides with a lifting of the government regulation on compulsory annual soil fumigation. This provided the room to manoeuvre for farmers in all parts of the Netherlands, to develop alternatives to be able to remain in potato cultivation, to reduce the harm to the environment, and to improve their financial situation.

Soil Laboratory – slow and costly

We thought a considerable reduction would be possible by changing the present practice of treating whole plots at regular time intervals, to more localized treatments as and when required. To do so, however, a better insight into nematode infections was needed. We had to be able to find localized infections with a diameter of little more than five metres. Soil sampling methods by the Soil Laboratory of, for example, three samples per hectare, are not an effective way of finding such infections. A much more intensive sampling approach was needed, and at a much lower cost per sample if the soaring costs of total sampling were to be avoided.

Monitoring of nematode infection by the Soil Laboratory has another disadvantage: a long time interval between the sampling and communication of results. More timely feedback would help in judging the effectiveness of different practices, such as localised treatments with fumigants. Knowing the results of soil tests within three weeks of harvesting, for example, enables one to treat infested locations before the winter starts, and thus to take advantage of more favourable weather conditions.

Timely feedback is also important in the cultivation of seed potatoes. Every year, farmers obtain certified seed for multiplication and later use on their farms. If new varieties could be screened effectively for nematode infection and the results obtained soon after the harvest, one could avoid buying again certified seed of susceptible varieties, thus saving one full season.

Developing the farmer laboratory

Thus the idea for a farmer laboratory grew, to make possible the intensive and timely monitoring of the effects of different practices. As a first step a machine was developed, on the basis of an old design, to collect soil samples. It had to be adapted to allow for sampling of the first 25 cm – rather than the normal 5 cm sampling – while at the same time enabling sampling of every 5 m within a relatively short period of time. To reduce costs, quite a few of the old parts scattered around the different farms were used to construct the sampling machine. The resulting machine is simple, yet effective, and mounted on a tractor, it can sample a hectare in less than four hours.

We applied the same philosophy in building the laboratory. A centrifuge apparatus was developed and constructed based on the well–known 'Schuiling design', and microscopes were modified versions of existing, relatively simple, microscopes. After careful consideration, part of an old farmhouse was chosen to host the new laboratory. We wanted it to be sited in the area itself. Several wives volunteered to run the lab. They receive a salary, higher in fact than if we had hired young personnel from elsewhere. But when we now pay for the services of the laboratory, the money is staying within the area, and some of the 'idle' labour hours of our colleagues are being put to effective use. It helped a great deal that one of them had worked at the Hildebrand Laboratory, a leading research institute in the north of the Netherlands, studying among other things, a number of soil–based diseases.

All in all, the sampling machine and the laboratory has helped to reduce sampling and testing costs to less than Dfl4 per sample, much lower than the Dfl27.5, plus value added tax (BTW), asked by the soil laboratory. This allows 20 samples per hectare (each consisting of 20 sub–samples) as compared to the conventional practice of three samples per hectare, without any increase in costs. At the same time the interval between sampling and communication of results has gone down from three months to less than two weeks.

Recognition emerges

The quality of our work is, of course, a major point of concern both for ourselves and the various government and service organisations. We have therefore decided to participate in a research–exchange programme with the Soil Laboratory in Oosterbeek, the Netherlands General Inspection Agency (NAK), and the Hildebrand Laboratory. Participating laboratories study the same soil sample every year, then results and possible differences are compared and discussed. Through this programme, and existing links with the Agricultural University in Wageningen, we are able to maintain good contacts with a number of relevant institutes. The Department of Nematology of the University studies, for example, the virulence of the nematodes encountered by our members, and four of our members participate in a research programme which studies the effect of crop rotations on the control of nematodes.

The laboratory has never asked for formal government recognition through the National Crop Protection Agency. This would enable us, for example, to obtain export permits for our potatoes on the basis of our own research data. So far, we have not felt the need for this. This situation might change, however, if we should decide to start work for non–member farmers. What is more important for us at this stage is to have our results accepted under the 'TBM' regulation, a Dutch regulation that requires 50% of the area under potatoes to be tested for nematode infection. This is a general provision, paid for by a compulsory contribution from farmers through the large cooperative potato processing company AVEBE. It took quite some lobbying to have our testing accepted as an alternative procedure, and to be exempted from the TBM contribution.

The laboratory makes a difference

Our involvement with the laboratory has now created its own momentum. It has shown us that disinfecting is not necessary to achieve zero infection levels. The laboratory now helps us to find appropriate 'infection thresholds', at which fumigation becomes an economic necessity. As far as we know, little information is available on this elsewhere. Close monitoring of infection levels under different practices and related yield developments should give us the required insights.

Laboratory work also revealed that certain cysts containing a fungus did not contain eggs or larvae of the nematodes. Could this fungus play a role in controlling the nematodes biologically? Further investigation indicated that the samples containing these cysts were collected from a limited number of plots. We now feel that the development of the fungus may perhaps depend on the content of the organic matter of the soil. It goes beyond our capacity to follow this up, but through our existing contacts, we understand that the Institute for Agrobiological Research (DLO-AB) in Haren is interested in taking this up.

One of the main reasons for our success is that all members are committed to the work of the laboratory. The sampling machine, for example, was been developed by two members in their own time. It cost them more than two months' work, but compensation was never asked for. A lot is being done in a similar way. The commitment is the result of the direct involvement of all concerned in the development and management of the laboratory. Moreover, a truly democratic structure has been chosen for the group in which the ideas and opinions of each member count. This is the advantage of a relatively small group. There is a lot of discussion within the group in which the expertise of each member becomes evident. The Borgercompagnie area has a long history of self-help and farmer collaboration, and the local farmers' association has been a pioneer in many situations. This has no doubt provided a fertile ground for the laboratory initiative.

Scaling up?

We do not see the laboratory as a competitor to professional research institutes. But it is now evident that we can quite effectively carry out practically-oriented experimentation involving the monitoring of nematode infection, and at relatively low cost. But as the example of the fungus in cysts shows, our experimentation generates questions that need further investigation by specialists under the controlled conditions of a research centre. But this is only one example of the questions we meet which could be taken up by the research centres. And would it not also be in their interests to link up with ideas and questions that farmers come across in their day-to-day work?

Initially the research institutes were not happy with our initiative in Borgercompagnie. Maybe they feared the competition. Possibly there was a doubt as to whether we could maintain test quality. However, we were more surprised by the lack of support from the regional farmers' association. Regional associations could in fact play an important role in promoting this and similar initiatives from their members. Fortunately, the attitude of both research institutes and farmer organizations is gradually changing. The NLTO, the largest regional farmer organization, has already offered financial support, and breeders of potato varieties have been especially alert. They have been quick to offer us new varieties before their official release, so that we can test their performance under normal field conditions. In this way we have a wider role to play than just supporting the members of our group.

The question is how to proceed from here. Quite a few farmers have been applying for membership of our group. We have decided, however, to continue with the original group for a few years before considering further expansion. If the group grows too fast and becomes too large, commitment of members to the group is bound to decrease and the laboratory will almost certainly lose its momentum, its speed of work and flexibility. A feeling of direct ownership is crucial. A large group will slowly become an institute in itself, and there are good reasons why larger institutes are often slow and expensive.

For the same reasons we discussed intensively whether or not to accept sampling and analysis for non−members, at the same or possibly at a price higher than for group members. In the view of the group, there is room for many more relatively small, farmer−initiated laboratories in the region, owned and controlled by the members themselves. A government body such as NAK, mentioned earlier, could be asked to advise the laboratories and monitor quality control in each of them. This would allow for the maximum initiative and involvement of the growers themselves.

Farmer research and the quest for sustainability

The experiences of our Farmer Laboratory show that practically−oriented field research can well be done by farmers themselves. Such research enabled us in Borgercompagnie to experiment with a diversity of measures to decrease the costly and often poisonous use of synthetic inputs. These included lower overall levels of application, location−specific application, and a critical assessment of varieties on their resistance to nematodes. We could also assess the effect of a different timing of soil fumigation as compared to the conventional autumn application, or the longer−term impact of continuous potato cultivation now that the AVEBE is urging an increase in the area under potatoes.

This leaves the important task of further research, based on what is found at field level, to the formal research sector. Several of our ideas conflicted with official government regulations at the time. A government policy giving farmers more flexibility and responsibility to determine when and how to treat their land, based on their own field observations, is needed to allow farmers to play their role in the search for sustainability. And farmers do have their own financial interests in this matter. The role of the government would then be more in terms of ensuring that the total reduction of input use is being achieved. This might require a different sort of regulation, for example, an average litre−allowance of input use per farmer per year. Whatever the form, it would bring responsibility closer to the growers, the people directly concerned.

Acknowledgements
This is an expanded version of the article 'Farmers' Laboratory' by Rudolf van Broekhuizen and Han Wiskerke in *Pioneers op het platteland*, 1993, published by Agripers, Netherlands. With kind permission of the publisher.

Sustaining the process

photo: Peter Gubbels

15. Strengthening community capacity for sustainable agriculture

by Peter Gubbels[1]

In the West African Sahel, knowledge about effective ways to promote agricultural technology development through community–based organizations is limited. There is little documentation of institutional arrangements, methods and strategies to strengthen farmers' capacity to achieve food security and a more equitable and sustainable agriculture. In this connection, several questions arise that are rarely posed explicitly:

---

[1] Peter Gubbels, Voisins Mondiaux, Strengthening Community Organization for People's Empowerment (SCOPE), 01 BP 1315, Ouagadougou 01, Burkina Faso.

- Is a process of technology development and dissemination sufficient to mobilize the widespread local support needed to establish and sustain new forms of collective action and organization?
- Is a more organized and scientific approach to technology development more effective than existing, informal mechanisms?
- What factors in the local institutions inhibit or favour the emergence of more organized and systematic approaches to technology development? What magnitude and type of benefits would a new form of organization have to generate to overcome such inhibiting factors?
- What arrangements will ensure that poorer households will benefit from locally organized action to develop and promote new agricultural technologies?

This chapter addresses such questions by drawing on the experiences of World Neighbors (WN) in Sanando in the Segou Region of Mali. It gives particular attention to identifying principles and strategies to strengthen the capacity of farmer organizations to promote sustainable agriculture. As the WN Area Representative for West Africa, I supported the Sanando programme for over 8 years. In 1995-1996, I worked with programme staff and village leaders during three field visits involving a series of Participatory Rural Appraisal (PRA) exercises in four study villages. The field data were supplemented by a review of WN programme documents, interviews with other agencies and a review of research carried out in another district of Segou Region (Toulmin 1992).

The chapter is divided into six sections. Section 1 explores the context of the Sanando programme: the physical environment, the class structure and the local social, cultural and political institutions which mediate the process of agricultural development.

Section 2 describes the objectives, strategies, evolution and outcomes of the agricultural development activities of the Sanando programme. Particular attention is given to the work in community-based experimentation and extension (CBEE).

Strategies to sustain CBEE are described in Section 3. The interplay of the technical and organizational changes promoted by WN are analysed in the light of 8 community capacities strengthened by the programme in its different phases. Particular attention is given to critical issues in capacity-building: mobilizing village volunteers, transforming community organization and promoting intervillage collaboration.

In Section 4 the impact of the programme's agricultural development activities is considered in terms of adoption rates, benefits to different socioeconomic groups, and change in number of households that fail to produce enough food for the whole year. The effects on richer and poorer households are compared, and reasons for the differences analysed.

Section 5 explores the lessons and implications of the Sanando case for agencies seeking to promote, strengthen and institutionalize processes for developing an equitable and sustainable agriculture under similar conditions. Some conclusions are then drawn on the Sanando case in Section 6.

1. Context of the World Neighbors programme

The WN programme in Mali covers the Sanando District, about 60 kilometres south–west of Segou, the country's second largest city. It lies in the northern savannah zone of West Africa, where the natural vegetation is a mixture of grasses and woody species. The land is generally flat, with a few hills or rocky outcrops. Most soils are sandy and gravelly, with some clay in low–lying areas. Run–off is not extensive, and erosion is localized.

Temperatures are high year–round, with a mean of 28°C. A single wet season from June to September is followed by 8 to 9 dry months. Mean annual rainfall in Sanando is between 620 and 680 mm. Fluctuations around this mean can be as great as 30% for extended periods. Recent examples are the droughts in the early 1970s and 1983-84. The great variability in amount and distribution of rainfall within the wet season and within a local geographical area can have devastating effects on harvests and livestock populations. Droughts trigger off massive selling of assets and extensive seasonal migration.

Agriculture is the dominant economic activity. Cereals (millet and sorghum) are the staple crops. Secondary crops are cowpea, groundnut, bambara earthnut and cotton. Minor crops grown on small patches are maize, various vegetables, cassava, fonio and watermelon.

Sanando District is inhabited by over 33,000 people (mainly Bambara) living in 70 villages. The population density is 30 persons per square kilometre. Farm land is relatively abundant. Customary land tenure arrangements prevent land sales. Renting or loaning land is very uncommon. Newcomers wishing to farm within a village territory must apply to the village council for consent. Such requests are usually granted, if the council is convinced that the immigrants plan to settle permanently and become part of the community.

Sanando households have two types of fields: village fields, permanently cleared plots around the settlement, where fertility is maintained by applying animal manure; and more distant bush fields, where shifting cultivation is practised to maintain fertility. Beyond these fields is a zone of communal bushland where cattle, sheep and goats are grazed, and bush products collected.

Class structure

Traditionally, Bambara society consisted of three social classes: the nobles, who fought and farmed; the slaves, who worked for their masters; and the blacksmith–griots, who worked with metal, wood and leather, made pots and sang the nobles' praises. In rural areas, the legacy of these social divisions persists to some extent, particularly in marriage, but they are being superseded by economic differentiation (Toulmin 1992).

Using local criteria of wealth, key informants identified four broad economic categories:

A   the rich (29% of the 143 households in the four study villages) keep substantial numbers of cattle and small ruminants, own complete farming equipment (plough, cart, seeder, in some cases also a cultivator) and sometimes even more than one plough and pair of oxen, and produce a grain surplus in all but the worst years

B   the less wealthy but well–off (28% of the households) own fewer cattle, have only a basic set of farming equipment (a plough and cart for two oxen), are grain self–sufficient in most years, and produce a small surplus in good years;

C   the poor (18%) own no cattle except, at most, one ox; are grain–deficit in most years; and may own a plough, but need to borrow or rent the other ox or both

D   the poorest (25%) are chronically food–deficit households which grow enough food to last only 6 to 8 months in good years; they have no farming equipment, cattle or small ruminants.

Of the richest households, 85% have more than 10 members. In contrast, only 3% of the poorest households have more than 10 members. Bigger households are often richer because a large domestic group can diversify its production and income–earning activities. They benefit from economies of scale in using productive assets, such as oxen and ploughs, and can spread over more people the risk of labour loss from sickness or other causes. They can thus generate more surplus than smaller households. The wealth is invested primarily in livestock. Richer households in the study villages own up to 50 head of cattle in addition to their sheep and goats. Toulmin (1992) also found that larger households tend to have more animals per person.

Smaller households, often consisting of a man, his wife and children, and perhaps an unmarried brother, have a labour force of only 2 or 3 adults and are more vulnerable to the sickness or death of a member. These households with less labour find it more difficult to acquire and make effective use of farming equipment. There is less scope for specialization and division of labour within each gender–defined set of tasks.

Household size is a key determinant of farm productivity, farm investment decisions and food security. Household members are kept together by the advantages of belonging to a larger domestic group. The tendencies for a household to split is reduced because the members are aware of the vulnerability of smaller domestic units.

The ability of the household head to minimize internal disputes and to revise household arrangements of rights, responsibilities and use of assets is critical to maintaining larger domestic units. Individual well–being and food security often decline when poor management leads to conflict, the breakup of the household and the division of assets.

Social organization

Men and women are classified into a system of age–groups which span 3 to 4 years. All men who are circumcised at the same time form a single age–group, the members of which have a special relationship of trust and mutual help with each other. Women's age–groups are determined by their date of marriage (Toulmin 1992). Age–group status often determines membership in wider village groups called *ton* (associations). The *ton* are diverse in nature and membership, but most cut across normal social divisions based on household wealth or lineage. Each *ton* is led by two or three leaders, who apply rules and sanctions, organize group activities and manage the *ton's* assets.

In the traditional sense, the *ton* is the village youth association, a work group that includes several male age–groups from 14 to 30 years of age. These *ton* hire their labour out to perform farming tasks such as clearing land, weeding, harvesting, making bricks and building houses. Each household must send the members of the appropriate age–group to participate in *ton* activities or risk paying a fine. Until recently, the *ton* earnings in many villages of Sanando were used to hold a village festival, during which all village members were provided with meat and other food.

The Bambara also append the term *ton* to other types of village groups. Some are self–help groups that provide mutual support to members. The main purpose of *ton* formed around social functions, such as marriage, baptism and circumcision, is to share the expenses between members. These socially–oriented *ton* are organized into male and female sections, with separate leaders but mutual objectives.

Leadership structure

A Bambara village is made up of several households, some of which belong to the founding clan while others are later arrivals from other clans. Each village has a chief, whose position is usually hereditary. The chief is assisted by elders, or advisers, who form the village council. On occasion, the council convokes all household heads for a village assembly. The primary roles of the chief and council are to deal with the local government authorities on issues such as taxes and to receive official visits by outsiders.

In Bambara society, the system of age–groups and *ton* promotes an egalitarian ethic which greatly influences the leadership structure. Village leaders are drawn from the senior age–set in each *ton*. This ensures a change in leadership every 3 or 4 years. Leaders tend to be selected on criteria of merit. An analysis of leadership structure in the 4 study villages indicated representation from all wealth categories, although the poorest households were less involved.

2. Community–based experimentation and extension

In the wake of the devastating 1983-84 drought in the Sahel, WN established the Sanando programme to help rainfed farmers improve their food security. Work began in 4 pilot villages, following the WN principle: start simple and small. The entry point was the testing of short–cycle crop varieties, in direct response to a priority concern expressed by farmers when WN assessed community needs in 10 villages in early 1986. Farmers were keen to find seeds that would reduce risk of crop failure when rainfall is low and irregular, and would produce an early harvest to shorten the hungry season.

This innovation proved useful for introducing what WN West Africa staff call the community–based experimentation and extension (CBEE) process. Short–cycle seed met the minimalist approach espoused in *Two Ears of Corn* (Bunch 1982): a simple technology that meets a strongly felt need, requires no external inputs (apart from the seed itself), is easy to understand, involves low risk, entails no increased labour or time to apply, and produces immediate, visible results.

After the first year (1986), the Sanando programme spread quickly. When the programme organized the first intervillage session of the 4 pilot villages in early 1987 to assess the experiments, 7 new villages sent delegates and 4 of them decided to work with WN. In successive years, the outreach of the programme grew until 1991, when 20 villages were involved. The programme also widened the range of community development activities it supported, to include dry–season gardening, well digging, tree growing, functional literacy training, local production of improved seed, and collective grain storage and marketing.

Long–term objectives of the agricultural programme

The objectives of WN's agricultural programme in Sanando evolved over time. In 1986, in the context of reducing vulnerability to drought, the stated aim was "helping farmers learn a process of solving their own agricultural problems by identifying, testing on a small–scale [in their own fields under local conditions], evaluating the results of [new agricultural] techniques". In the 1989 programme document, this CBEE process was extended to include "exchanging experiences with other villagers ... and taking responsibility for training interested farmers through village–based and managed extension...." The programme team called itself SAFADR (*Service d'Appui et de Formation pour l'Auto–Développement Rural*, support and training service for rural self–development).

By 1990, the long–term objective shifted to promoting sustainable agriculture:

1. to "identify, develop, adapt to local conditions and extend a number of agroecological innovations leading to sustainable agriculture that will significantly increase agricultural production and income of farmers". This was further specified as:
   - developing one or more agroecological technologies to improve soil fertility that have been proven by community–based experimentation to increase crop yields by more than 20%
   - developing one or more agroecological innovations (not related to soil fertility) to either significantly
     - reduce risk of crop failure due to poor rains, or
     - increase total food production during the year, or
     - increase cash income or productivity per unit of labour.

Annual targets and activities referred to the number and type of experiments undertaken, and increase in adoption rates of technologies selected for extension by communities based on their evaluation of trial results.

Although the early programme plans also mentioned improving food security as a long–term goal, specific objectives or indicators related to food security were not formulated. It was assumed that increased adoption of tested technologies would increase food production and thus improve food security. By 1993, the SAFADR team had been taught participatory methods to assess household food–security status, and added a new long–term objective to the agricultural programme:

2. to reduce the number of households that chronically experience hunger in the lean season (i.e. are not self–sufficient in food production) in each of 14 villages from the current level (48%) to 25% by:

- increasing food–production capacity via technologies accessible to poorer households
- developing a community–based food–security system (cereal banks).

Community–based experimentation

Initially, SAFADR placed great emphasis on teaching volunteer farmer experimenters simple but rigorous scientific methods to compare new technologies with their existing practices. This involved drawing up detailed protocols for each trial, accurately marking the test and control plots, collecting important agronomic data such as plant density, number of days to flowering, number of days to maturity, cropping history of test plots, and yield weight. Since none of the farmer experimenters was literate, SAFADR devised visual aids to assist in data recording. At village and intervillage meetings, the farmer experimenters used these visual records to report their results to the assembly. On the basis of these reports, the villagers evaluated the results and drew conclusions.

The innovations tested in Sanando from 1986 to 1995 are shown in Table 15.1. During this period, the farmer experimenters recruited by their communities conducted over 68 sets of experiments to address priority problems identified by their communities. Generally, these experiments entailed four to ten replications spread across several villages. Experiments with only one replication were those in collaboration with the Cinzana Research Station; the other replications were done by farmers beyond Sanando. (Unfortunately, Cinzana did not inform SAFADR about the results of these replications.)

Immediately after the drought, farmers were most interested in testing short–cycle varieties. This interest waned after 1988, when the rains were the heaviest for over 40 years. Formal experimentation with new seed continued, mainly in collaboration with the Cinzana Research Station, but not as a farmer–driven programme. The farmers began to give higher priority to improving soil fertility, and tested technologies to improve the quality and quantity of organic manure, as well as alley cropping with leucaena and *Bauhinia reticulata*, direct seeding of *Faidherbia albida* (formerly *Acacia albida*) and growing cover crops such as *Mucuna utilis*, *Crotolaria* and *Canavalia ensiformis*. Two improved methods of producing organic manure (better bedding in animal kraals, compost/manure pits) generated the best results. By 1993, richer farmers were giving priority to increasing feed production, particularly for oxen and milk cows.

Evolution in the experimentation

Over the years since 1986, the approach to conducting trials changed. As WN became concerned with transferring responsibility for experimentation to local structures, it became clear that many farmers (including farmer experimenters) did not judge the more scientific approach, with its emphasis on measurement, written data collection and analysis, as worth the effort. However, the idea of seeking and testing new ideas remained popular. Left to their own devices, farmers did not continue to apply many of the methods designed to improve their informal experimentation. Most farmers felt they could test and judge the value of new technologies on the basis of their practical experience and careful observation.

Table 15.1. Innovations tested by farmers with support of WN/Yèrènyèton Programme in Sanando District (1986-1995)

	1986		1987		1988		1989		1990		1991		1992		1993		1994		1995	
	V	R	V	R	V	R	V	R	V	R	V	R	V	R	V	R	V	R	V	R
Adapting staple cropping to irregular/reduced rainfall																				
Short-cycle millet	4	8							1	1	4	14	1	1					3	3
Short-cycle sorghum	4	11					1	1	2	2	4	14	1	1			1	1	4	4
Short-cycle cowpeas	4	18	3	4	6	24					4	15	3	8			1	1	2	2
Groundnuts																	1	1		
Improving soil fertility																				
Improved organic manure: kraal							6	8												
Improved organic manure: pit							6	8												
Composting							6	8												
Method of applying organic manure													3	8			4	4	3	3
Crop diversification																				
Upland rice							3	7	2	2	3	9	4	31						
Short-cycle yam							4	9	1	2			2	4			6	7	4	12
Short-cycle maize			3	4	5	20	6	20												
Soybean	4	30																		
Improved cultural techniques																				
Testing sowing dates: soybean					4	16														
Intercropping millet with legumes							1		1	1	1	4	6	2	2	11	11			
Cover crops									5	11	5	14	2	4	3	3	3	4		
Micro-catchment *Zai* with yams																				
Crop protection and storage																				
Chemical pesticides									4	4										
Natural/local methods																	5	8		
Mildew/fungus control																	4	4	4	4
Promotion of mixed farming																				
Fodder crops															7	15	3	3	4	6
Animal feed production: 3 methods																				
Live fencing (against animals)																	3	3	5	10
Improved poultry husbandry																			8	10
Agro-forestry																				
Crop yields under fertilizing trees									5	13										
Protection natural regeneration																				
Alley cropping																	3	3		
Direct seed of *Faidherbia albida*																	4	8		
Windbreaks															6	9	6	11	5	5
Dry-season farming																				
Berebere sorghum from Chad									3	3	3	5								

Key: V = Number of villages
R = Number of farmers with 1 farmer doing 1 replication

224

By 1994 the experimentation programme had evolved into three tiers:

Tier 1: Farmer Experimenter Collective. In 1994 a collective was formed by a group of 15 experimenting farmers from the member villages of *Yèrèynèton*, an association formed upon the suggestion of delegates to the annual intervillage sessions organized by SAFADR (see Section 3). An Agricultural Programme Coordinator manages the experimentation and extension activities of the association: organizing training sessions, managing supplies and administering the budget for agricultural development, including the Farmer Experimenter Collective.

The collective is made up of men who are innovators interested in more scientific experimentation. Most are relatively young but experienced farmers from the B and C wealth categories. The richest households are less keen to be involved, as they already produce a food surplus. The collective is responsible to *Yèrèynèton,* not to the village leaders of the members. It has a district–wide mandate to develop technologies for sustainable agriculture. The members have been trained in diagnosing problems and conducting on–farm trials using more rigorous experimental methods.

Because the members of the collective often have greater interest in innovation than normal farmers, they are more likely to test technologies, such as live hedges or alley cropping, which differ significantly from the local farming system. Because most members are from relatively large households, they can better afford the time and resources to experiment.

Tier 2: Community-based experimentation. Not all agricultural experiments are conducted by the collective. Some are done by interested farmers at the community level. *Yèrènyèton* encourages its member villages to continue to identify and test innovations at their level, and to report the results at association meetings. These trials, however, are often not as rigorous and well–documented as the trials conducted by the collective.

Tier 3: Informal farmer experimentation. Individual farmers continue to devise and test innovations and spread the word informally. When initiating the programme, WN had documented several innovations developed by local farmers to respond to drought, but had not tried to understand farmers' methods of experimentation or how these could be strengthened. By 1991, SAFADR had become aware that many farmers were not keen on the more scientific approach proposed by WN. This prompted WN to sponsor an in–depth study of indigenous forms of farmer experimentation. The study provided a better understanding of farmers' adaptive rationality or what Stolzenbach (1992) has termed learning by improvisation.

Stolzenbach found that most farmers give low priority to hypothesis testing, the basis of the scientific approach. They prefer explorative (move–testing) experiments, in which the design and execution are adapted to new factors during production. Implicitly, farmers consider flexibility, spontaneous variation and learning from action within a context of practice to be better suited to their needs than the more rigid and systematized scientific approach.

The study and other anecdotal evidence suggest that informal experimentation by individual farmers has become more widespread in Sanando as a result of WN's work in promoting the concept of 'testing new ideas' and in facilitating farmer–to–farmer exchange in and between villages. Although the SAFADR staff recognize and encourage informal farmer experimentation, they have not devised methods or indicators to assess its impact on overall change in agricultural technology.

Extension and adoption of innovations

Of the innovations shown in Table 15.1, sixteen became part of a community–based extension effort supported by SAFADR. Table 15.2 presents adoption rates of these innovations as a percentage of all households in the case–study villages. Adoption means that the household applied the innovation at least once between 1992 and 1995. The innovation of planting *Faidherbia albida* is not included because of lack of data.

The most popular innovations, with adoption rates of 50 to 75%, are two techniques for improving the quantity and quality of organic manure. Short–cycle cowpea, soybean and tree planting are also popular. The next range of innovations, with adoption rates between 8 and 25%, are short–cycle millet and sorghum and the new crop, upland rice.

Although the adoption rates of specific varieties of short–cycle millet and sorghum promoted by *Yèrènyèton* are low, almost all households in the study villages have changed the

Table 15.2. Ranking of agricultural innovations by level of adoption by all 143 households in four study villages in Sanando District, Mali (1992-1995)

Agricultural innovation	DJELA n=35 No.	% of HH	DJOLE n = 44 No	% of HH	SAWU n= 31 No	% of HH	FANU n=33 No	% of HH	Total = 143 HH	Total = 143 %Total HH
Improved organic manure: kraal	27	77	38	86	19	61	22	67	106	74
Short-cycle cowpea	25	71	16	36	25	81	31	94	97	68
Improved organic manure: pit	27	77	12	27	15	48	29	88	83	58
Fertilising trees	21	60	15	34	16	52	31	94	83	58
Soybean (women)	15	43	19	43	19	61	24	73	77	54
Soybean (men)	11	31	22	50	0	0	0	0	33	23
Short-cycle millet	3	9	4	9	6	19	20	61	33	23
Upland rice	0	0	0	0	5	16	13	39	18	13
Short-cycle sorghum	4	11	7	16	0	0	0	0	11	8
Intercropping	6	17	3	7	0	0	0	0	9	6
Feed: forage crops	5	14	3	7	0	0	0	0	8	6
Feed: urea/straw	0	0	5	11	0	0	0	0	5	3
Feed: silage	0	0	2	5	0	0	1	3	3	2
Live fences	2	6	0	0	0	0	0	0	2	1
Composting	0	0	0	0	0	0	0	0	0	0
Average% adoption all innovations by village		28		22		23		35		26

Key: No. = total number of households;
HH = households

main crop varieties they cultivate in the past ten years. This suggests that the informal system (third tier) of experimentation and exchange is more dynamic and effective for identifying, testing and disseminating new varieties than the more formal experimentation conducted by *Yèrènyèton* (which tests varieties primarily from Cinzana Research Station).

Moreover, data obtained from farmer delegates at an intervillage session revealed that SAFADR is not the primary source of agricultural change in Sanando (see Section 4 on programme impact). However, by strengthening local capacities to undertake a process of agricultural development, SAFADR facilitated adoption of new technology promoted by other formal development agents and through informal farmer–to–farmer exchange. Part of this process of strengthening local capacity entailed helping new, functionally literate leaders to emerge. Another element was enabling the association to enter into direct collaboration with other research and development agencies (see Section 3).

Factors contributing to increased outreach

Several factors contributed to SAFADR's success in spreading the CBEE process to new villages in the first four years of the programme. Firstly, the short–cycle varieties generated strong enthusiasm and quickly attracted widespread attention. By 1989 the seeds had spread beyond Sanando District, partly because promoting short–cycle crops requires little village–level effort.

Secondly, the informal participatory style of the SAFADR team contrasted strikingly with the villagers' prior experience with the formal, often coercive approach of the Malian administration of the day. Team members sometimes stayed overnight in the villages, ate the local food and conversed informally over tea. They respected local leaders and customs, and treated the villagers as equals. They listened and responded flexibly to other development needs of the community. This helped establish trust and a good working relationship early on.

Thirdly, the initial four pilot villages were strategically chosen to facilitate outreach. The criteria for selecting the villages included:

* lack of internal conflict
* good level of organization and dynamic leadership
* relatively small population
* location within different clusters of villages linked by kinship or other ties
* accessibility
* little or no commercial, political or administrative authority over neighbouring villages.

Fourthly, SAFADR's strategy of organizing intervillage meetings enabled farmer delegates to discuss development problems, activities and results, and helped expand the programme's outreach. At these sessions, held for 2-3 days once a year on a rotating basis by the participating villages, delegates from new villages quickly learned about the key elements of the WN approach: testing new ideas, applying low–cost technologies, using local resources, training village promoters and functional literacy. Since this approach was substantiated by the practical experience and results of other villagers, its credibility was far greater than if it had come from WN staff alone.

3. Sustaining the CBEE process

The evolution of the agricultural programme's long–term goals was described above. From the start, however, SAFADR aimed to sustain the CBEE process by strengthening farmer organization and by placing agricultural technology development in a broader context of community self–development. This was expressed already in the long–term goal stated in the programme plan of 1986: "to promote and strengthen local structures at the village level and on the intervillage level so they will be more effective in undertaking self–help development projects in ... agriculture and other sectors." Nevertheless, the programme plans from 1986 to 1989 contained neither activities relating to this goal, nor means to assess progress towards it. The assumption was that, by achieving the long–term technical objectives, the local organizational capacity to continue CBEE would be strengthened.

In 1990, when SAFADR staff realized that the CBEE process remained heavily dependent on them, they included an additional sector in the programme plan: community organization and management. This contained goals to strengthen capacities deemed necessary for villagers to plan and implement CBEE (and other) activities themselves.

Community capacities needed to sustain CBEE

SAFADR began to assess village–level organization more systematically in terms of capacities required to sustain the CBEE process, and eventually identified eight key capacities (see Box 15.1). The strategy was to link capacity–building to the on–going agricultural (and other sectoral) activities determined by the community. Using a transfer–of–competency framework, SAFADR staff annually reviewed the roles and tasks they had assumed and what had been done by each community, and planned how to shift more responsibilities (and the competencies required) for the next year's activities to community structures. In this way, SAFADR gradually developed methods for strengthening each of the capacities indicated in the box, as well as means of assessing progress.

Phases of capacity strengthening

SAFADR did not address all these capacities at once. After analysing key programme events, the team identified three major phases in the capacity–strengthening process, each of which marks a significant transition in the transfer–of–competency framework:

i) Initiation and growth phase. From 1986 to 1991 the primary responsibility for management, training and facilitation of the agricultural development programme rested with SAFADR. In the absence of appropriate community structures, SAFADR focused on generating local support for CBEE, facilitating village planning and evaluation meetings, organizing the technical training of farmer experimenters and agricultural promoters, providing follow–up in the field, and negotiating technical support from outside agencies. Later in this phase SAFADR helped form *comités de développement villageois* (CDV) with a view to gradually transferring responsibilities to them.

Box 15.1: Community capacities critical for agricultural self-development

1 Capacity to identify, develop and extend improved technologies and practices
2 Capacity to mobilize local (human and financial) resources: to recruit and motivate farmer experimenters and agricultural promoters, and to generate revenue to cover core operating expenses
3 Capacity to negotiate with external agencies (e.g. research and extension services, credit institutions, donors)
4 Capacity for intervillage collaboration: coordination of villages in the same area and communication with farmer organizations in other areas for mutual learning
5 Capacity for programme management: diagnosing problems, assessing needs, planning, setting objectives, budgeting, monitoring and evaluation, reporting
6 Capacity to organize itself (i.e. have appropriate structures) for implementing self-development activities, such as identifying, testing and evaluating new technologies, and farmer-to-farmer extension
7 Capacity for broad-based leadership with a mobilizing vision, initiative and ability to conceptualize and raise awareness
8 Capacity for democratic, transparent and representative decision-making, which takes the needs of different socioeconomic groups and genders into account.

Source: World Neighbors West Africa Area Office Strategic Planning Conference Reports, Participatory Evaluation Reports, and Annual Programme Report 1989-1994.

---

ii) Co-management stage. In 1992-93 SAFADR started systematically transferring its technical, training and facilitation responsibilities to peasant animator–trainers (*paysans animateurs–formateurs*, PAF) and to the newly–created intervillage association *Yèrènyèton*. SAFADR support shifted to strengthening organization and management at both CDV and association levels. It focused the functional literacy training on PAF and *Yèrènyèton* leaders. These shifts enabled the CDV and *Yèrènyèton* to assume some (but not all) responsibilities for programme management, including planning, budgeting and controlling funds, hence the term 'co–management'.

iii) Autonomy phase. In 1993-96 *Yèrènyèton* and SAFADR drew up separate annual plans and budgets, based on distinct but complementary responsibilities. *Yèrènyèton's* plan contained technical objectives that addressed priority problems related to food security and agricultural development, including CBEE activities. SAFADR's plan contained support objectives to strengthen the organizational and managerial capacity of village and association structures to implement CBEE and related technical activities. *Yèrènyèton* became autonomous in terms of assuming control over planning, evaluation, training and budget management, and negotiating collaboration with external agencies, including funders.

Key elements of the capacity–strengthening process

The actual pattern of events in Sanando did not fall neatly into such distinct phases, nor did SAFADR staff have these phases in mind when they started intervening. However, it is convenient to use this descriptive model to clarify the capacity–strengthening process.

Table 15.3. Key elements in strengthening local organizational capacity

	Initiation/Growth	*Co–Management*	*Autonomy*
Focus of capacity strengthening	- Technical training	- Organization and management - Broad–based leadership - Intervillage collaboration	- Planning and evaluation - Negotiation with outside agencies
Mobilizing village human resources	- Farmer experimenters - Agricultural promoters - Tree growers	- Village–level peasant animator–trainers (PAF)	- Association agricultural coordinators - Association–level PAF
Transforming village and intervillage organization	- Technical volunteers	- Village Development Committees (CDV)	- Intervillage association - Management sub–committees

Only key elements of SAFADR's strategy to strengthen these eight capacities are discussed here: mobilizing village volunteers, transforming community organization and promoting intervillage collaboration. The discussion supports a central argument of this chapter: embedding and sustaining a CBEE process requires an understanding of local institutions and forms of social cooperation, and the development of strategies to incorporate new activities into the existing sociocultural system.

Mobilizing village–level human resources

Farmer experimenters and agricultural promoters. In the first year, most volunteer farmer experimenters were household heads. They had come forward mainly because of their interest in the new seed, not in the idea of experimentation *per se*. As they had the decision–making authority to set up trials on the family field, the experimentation generally went well.

The next year, SAFADR asked for volunteers to be trained more intensively in experimental methods and literacy. Their function would be to test innovations on behalf of the community and to promote selected innovations within the village. This request attracted people of a different social category, often younger men. The households' heads had many responsibilities and, although interested in new technologies, many were not interested in committing their time as volunteers to assume this additional responsibility. The results of the experiments in 1987 and 1988 were of much poorer quality than in 1986. Many volunteers had problems in obtaining the support of the household head to conduct the trials and to provide follow–up to other farmers. Ways of helping communities mobilize their human resources had to be sought.

The key was to obtain the sanction of the village chief and council, the local institutions which regulate most collective action. Instead of asking for volunteers, SAFADR asked the council to select the individuals best suited for the task. This change marked a milestone in the programme. The motivation of people in the newly-created posts was shifted from self-interest to community service. In Bambara society, fulfilment of one's community obligations brings social recognition. Failure to do so can mean social disapproval, particularly if one is removed from office for neglect of duty.

When a person is appointed by the village council for community tasks, the household head must free that person from certain family obligations. During the busy rainy season, most agricultural promoters were liberated from otherwise obligatory *ton* work so that they could support fellow farmers in applying new techniques or carrying out experiments.

Broadening the local leadership base. By 1989 the number of agricultural development activities had increased to encompass gardening, tree growing, and producing seedlings and improved seed. SAFADR encouraged each participating village to recruit two new promoters for each additional activity. During each dry season these people attended two or three 15-day sessions, which combined functional literacy with practical training in how to conduct experiments, plant trees, etc. The literacy training permitted the promoters to weigh yields, fill in data sheets, conduct simple surveys and monitor activities. These sessions, which brought together people from several villages, offered a forum for exchanging experience, mutual support and building informal links between villages.

As discussed earlier, traditional social rules among the Bambara tend to inhibit concentration of power. However, the emergence of new village-level development roles, coupled with a shortage of persons who can be spared from essential production tasks and who meet other important criteria (willingness to become literate, volunteer spirit, etc.) can lead to a situation in which a few people are given multiple functions. SAFADR tried to avoid this by:

- facilitating the emergence of a new cadre of potential leaders (mostly male). Over the first years the less serious ones dropped out, migrated or were replaced. To those who remained, SAFADR provided opportunities to broaden their vision, self-confidence and knowledge. The best moved on, in later stages of the programme, to more responsible positions at village or association level
- building on the community service ethic, rooted in Bambara society, as the main dynamic to mobilize people for development. If given too many tasks, individuals would have had too much work and the difficult question of remuneration would have risen prematurely, before local capacity to generate resources to provide such compensation had been developed
- preventing a concentration of responsibility and control. With many posts to be filled, it was less likely that one lineage could dominate. At this stage SAFADR was not injecting significant material or financial resources into the villages. By the time such resources could be increased the principle of one person, one role had been established
- preventing dependence on one or a few dynamic leaders. Communities in which most responsibilities lie in the hands of one leader are very vulnerable if this person's performance, for whatever reason, begins to fail.

Most new leaders come from the larger, wealthier households which can free one of their younger men from household tasks to perform community tasks. The social institution of the *ton* already prevents excessive socioeconomic differentiation. Each *ton* member is, in principle, the equal of his or her peer, regardless of wealth status. Households therefore tend to avoid economic relations of indebtedness, wage employment and cash transactions among themselves. In this context, the selection of promoters and new leaders from wealthier households in the villages constituted another mechanism for community redistribution of (human) resources.

Recruiting and training peasant animator-trainers (PAFs). In 1990, to lay the groundwork for the co-management phase, SAFADR encouraged each village to recruit two PAFs, who were meant to:

- facilitate meetings and give technical training in their own and neighbouring villages
- make simple surveys and collect data on agricultural experiments and extension activities
- fill in simple information forms as a basis for quarterly activity reports.

The villagers generally selected PAFs from among the most dynamic agricultural promoters. SAFADR then concentrated its training activities on the PAFs, who eventually took over technical training and follow-up support for the farmer experimenters and agricultural promoters.

Transforming community organization. SAFADR had initially worked through the village chief, who usually asked a councillor to organize activities. As the number and scope of development activities increased and their management required more intensive and varied input, this arrangement became inadequate. SAFADR facilitated a discussion among the traditional leaders about the organizational requirements for self-development. The existing local structures were identified and their strengths and weaknesses for assuming new development tasks were analysed. In most cases, the village leaders identified these weaknesses:

- concentration of functions in one or two persons
- lack of trust in certain cases (for handling funds)
- villagers' lack of support or understanding for certain collective activities.

The key question asked by SAFADR was: "Who or what structure in your village is now responsible for activities related to community development?" Often, the answer was that the village chief informally delegated one or two of his councillors to take responsibility for development (as distinct from administrative) issues as they arose. SAFADR suggested that they formalize this informal structure and add more people so as to de-concentrate the responsibilities. The catch phrase was 'one person, one role'. Another innovation was the introduction of a simple management system, particularly for accounting for the community development fund.

These organizational innovations resulted in establishment of *comités de développement villageois* (CDV). Most CDV consisted of four members: a president, a secretary, a treasurer and an organizer (responsible for calling meetings and assigning tasks to implement decisions). In many villages, the assembly appointed the original one or two councillors already responsible for development to be president and treasurer, and added two men to take the roles of secretary and organizer. The latter were often those who had gained numeracy and literacy skills though the WN programme, and who met other criteria set by the assembly.

The Bambara name given to the CDV has the suffix *ton*. This implies community recognition that the structure is charged with development responsibilities, in the same way that other *ton* are responsible for other village activities. The CDV members are accountable to the village chief and council.

Thus, SAFADR's approach to embedding CBEE into local structures started with identifying how traditional organization functioned. By attracting villager interest in low-cost technologies that addressed priority problems in farming and brought quick results, SAFADR could:

- enable villagers to gain practical experience with the approach, principles and basic steps of CBEE
- create a range of new technical positions in each village (including farmer experimenters, agricultural promoters, tree growers, dry-season gardeners, improved-seed producers) to test, apply and disseminate innovations
- provide an opportunity for a new cadre of potential leaders to emerge to take up these new positions
- reinforce and begin transforming traditional leadership structures to be able to oversee these new activities.

Promoting intervillage collaboration. The idea of an intervillage structure to sustain the CBEE process was already expressed in the 1986 programme plan. At that time, the aims were to facilitate a deeper analysis of the trial results obtained in different villages and an exchange about informal experimentation. Gradually SAFADR realized that an intervillage association was essential also for other reasons. It had become clear that costs for individual villages to seek new technologies and obtain technical support from research stations and extension agencies would be high. Moreover, a single village would not have sufficient clout to negotiate with outside agencies, or to obtain funding, credit or inputs. An intervillage association would have greater negotiating power and could coordinate planning and provide follow-up services as WN phased out its support.

In Sanando, no indigenous intervillage structure existed, so the approach taken at village level of building on existing forms of organization could not be applied. To catalyse the emergence of an association, SAFADR developed a two-pronged strategy:

- sponsor annual or biannual meetings of farmer delegates to evaluate results of trials and to coordinate planning for the next agricultural season
- select motor villages in which to concentrate SAFADR support and capacity-building.

The motor villages were to serve as centres for diffusing new ideas and techniques to a cluster of 4-5 nearby villages. Before choosing motor villages, SAFADR made a survey to identify which villages had strong ties with others (going to the same market, intermarriage, etc.). By selecting the more dynamic villages within each cluster of related villages, SAFADR aimed at forming a 14–member village association that could eventually reach all 70 villages in Sanando District. Although not without problems, the intervillage association *Yèrènyèton* eventually came into being in 1992. Literally, the name means:

yèrè = oneself or one's own efforts
nyè = well–being or progress
ton = association.

SAFADR began transferring its tasks to the newly–elected members of the association. Although it gave some training in establishing management systems and procedures, SAFADR primarily tried to transfer competencies and responsibilities gradually through accompanied learning–by–doing.

In the autonomy stage, *Yèrènyèton* achieved recognition of its status by several outside agencies. SAFADR played a role behind the scenes to facilitate *Yèrènyèton's* collaboration with CMDT and the local bank in Segou. In 1993 *Yèrènyèton* negotiated that Cinzana Research Station attach a person to the association headquarters to help coordinate on–farm trials in several villages in Sanando, primarily through the farmer experimenter collective. This collaboration included sending several delegates from the association to Cinzana to be trained in fodder–production techniques.

By 1994 *Yèrènyèton* was one of five farmer organizations which became part of Segou Region CRU (committee of users of research results). With the support of the World Bank these committees were established in different regions of Mali to provide a forum for enabling organized farmer groups to participate in setting research priorities and assessing the benefits of new technologies.

Principles for sustaining a CBEE process

The key lessons that emerge from SAFADR's experience in Sanando are:

* Ensuring sustainability of CBEE is a long–term, phased process which must start from the outset of intervention, not just be added near the end
* This requires an understanding of local social structures and forms of cooperation, and an assessment of the strengths and weaknesses of local structures in terms of capacities needed to continue CBEE
* Programme plans must contain explicit activities to strengthen the capacities identified as necessary for a gradual transfer of responsibility. This entails developing strategies to incorporate new (or more effective) activities into local structures
* Strengthening local organizational capacity to continue CBEE must be integrated with the process of technology development. Benefits generated by developing and adopting inno-

vations must be strategically leveraged to bring into being new or stronger forms of social organization and cooperation

• Preconceived organizational structures should not be imposed. It is critical to engage the villagers in adapting existing structures. New roles should be proposed only after the community perceives the need and utility. Otherwise structures or positions may be created as an artificial and temporary mechanism for collaboration with the intervening agency

• In traditional societies where much power and authority is concentrated in the hands of household heads and village chiefs, it is important to broaden the leadership base. One strategy is to promote a high degree of task specialization and division of responsibilities. In Sanando, this approach helped generate a new cadre of leaders with a broader vision of, and strong commitment to, community development.

4. Programme impact

Assessing the impact of the agricultural programme deserves high priority because the CBEE process can become self-sustaining only if it can generate tangible benefits. The case study sought to find out to what extent SAFADR's long-term agricultural objectives (see Section 2) had been achieved.

Assessing impact entails more than evaluating progress on objectives. Adoption rates are only one piece of the puzzle. The question of attribution (i.e. to what extent are the measured changes due to programme intervention) was also addressed. Exercises that were particularly useful in this regard were focus-group impact discussions, before-and-after wealth ranking, and exploring sources of change in agricultural practices. In general, these exercises set out to determine:

• the nature and magnitude of benefits gained by the adopting households

• the extent to which poorer households were benefiting and improving their food-security status, and the magnitude of these benefits in comparison to those of wealthier households

• the impact on women within the adopting households

• the extent to which the changes in agricultural practices could be attributed to the WN programme or to other forces of change in Sanando District.

Particular attention was given to assessing whether SAFADR's work had reduced the number of households in each village that experience grain deficits.

Finally, the study tried to determine SAFADR's impact on strengthening local organizational capacities to tackle problems such as food insecurity, especially for low-income farmers, and to what extent the strengthened capacity contributed to the material benefits achieved.

Economic impact

Table 15.4 indicates the extent to which the innovations promoted by SAFADR are benefiting rich and poor households. Certain innovations, like the improved technique for obtaining kraal manure, have been adopted by over 90% of households in the A and B wealth categories but by only 36% in the poorest D category. Interviews revealed that not only did a higher percentage of richer households adopt these innovations; they also gained greater benefits from them than did poorer households.

Table 15.4 Percentage of households adopting agricultural innovations by wealth category: Synthesis of four villages (143 Households) in Sanando District, Mali (1992-1995)

Agricultural innovation	*A Category* =42		*B Category* =40		*C Category* =25		*D Category* =36		*All Categories* =143	
	No of HH	% HH	No of HH	% HH	No of HH	% HH	No of HH	% HH	No of HH	% all HH
Improved organic manure: kraal	38	90	36	90	19	76	13	36	106	74
Short–cycle cowpea	22	52	30	75	16	64	29	81	97	68
Improved organic manure: pit	26	62	27	68	14	56	16	44	83	58
Fertilising trees	27	64	24	60	15	60	17	47	83	58
Soybean (women)	27	64	21	53	13	52	16	44	77	54
Soybean (men)	9	21	9	23	6	24	9	25	33	23
Short–cycle millet	12	29	11	28	4	16	6	17	33	23
Upland rice	11	26	2	5	1	4	4	11	18	13
Short–cycle sorghum	1	2	6	15	3	12	1	3	11	8
Intercropping	5	12	2	5	1	4	1	3	9	6
Feed: forage crops	4	10	4	10	0	0	0	0	8	6
Feed: urea/straw	4	10	1	3	0	0	0	0	5	3
Feed: silage	2	5	0	0	1	4	0	0	3	2
Live fences	2	5	0	0	0	0	0	0	2	1
Composting	0	0	0	0	0	0	0	0	0	0
% of HH per wealth category	29		28		18		25		100	
Average % adoption by wealth category	30		29		25		21		26	

Key: 1) A, B, C and D: A category are richest households; D are poorest; B and C are intermediate
2) HH = household

On average, the richest (A) households doubled the amount of manure produced and the land surface manured per year. Most of them now obtain 50-100 carts of manure using the improved kraaling technique. The poorer households that adopted this technique have not quite doubled the quantity of manure produced. Because they have fewer animals or rely primarily on compost pits, they produce only 5-20 cart–loads of manure per year. Moreover, they did not have their own carts to transport the manure to the fields.

On the other hand, the adoption rates of some innovations are higher in poorer households. The most striking case is short–cycle cowpea, which was adopted by 81% of the poorest (D) as compared to 52% of the richest (A) households. In interviews it emerged that poorer households adopted short–cycle cowpea because it can be harvested sooner and sold to buy grain, thus reducing the length of the hungry season. This is not as important to richer households, which already grow enough grain to last until the regular harvest.

Moving from the effects of individual innovations to the overall pattern of food security, Table 15.5 shows the changes in household–level food security and economic progress in the four study villages: 40% of households are better off now than five years ago, 32% are about the same and 18% are worse off. Most of the households whose economic situation has improved were already relatively rich: 31 (74%) of the 42 households in category A had progressed. Not a single rich household became worse off in the last five years.

Table 15.5. Change in household wealth and food security status from 1991-1996 by wealth category: Synthesis of four villages (143 Households) in Sanando District, Mali

Change in status	Wealth category									
	A Category =42		B Category =40		C Category =25		D Category =36		All Categories =143	
	No of HH	% HH	No of HH	% HH	No of HH	% HH	No of HH	% HH	No of HH	% all HH
Families better off	31	74	15	38	7	28	4	11	57	40
Families remaining same	11	26	21	53	12	48	16	44	60	42
Families worse off	0	0	4	10	6	24	16	44	26	18
% of total HH per wealth category		29		28		18		25		100

Key: 1) A, B, C and D: A category are richest households; D are poorest; B and C are intermediate
2) HH = household

Among the 36 poorest households in category D, only 4 (11%) advanced economically, the situation of 16 households was about the same, and the situation of the remaining 16 (44%) had worsened. Looking at the poorest households in each village, Djela fared best. Of the seven poorest households, none had regressed. In Sawu, four of the ten poorest households (40%) had regressed. In Djole and Fanou, five of seven (71%) and seven of 13 (54%) poorest households, respectively, were worse off than five years ago.

The pattern that emerges can be visualized as an upward economic spiral for rich households and a downward spiral for poor ones. Richer households improve their situation because the large families have more labour, allowing a pooling of resources to reduce the risk of losing labour on account of sickness or death. They can thus produce a surplus more consistently. This surplus is invested initially in ruminant livestock, which increases the amount of manure available to fertilize the fields, which in turn increases the potential for a grain surplus. Once a household manages to produce a substantial surplus, part of this is used to acquire implements such as ploughs, seeders, cultivators and carts. Many of the wealthier households which have progressed in the past five years have bought a second set of farming equipment and oxen. This increases their production potential still further.

Another use of grain surplus is to finance dowries so that the men in the household can marry one or more wives. This long-term investment increases the labour force of the household and reinforces the accumulation of surplus. In bad years a well-off household can sell animals to buy grain. A very wealthy household can sustain itself for many years merely from the natural increase in its animals. This explains why so few of the richer households slide down the economic spiral.

Poorer households experience more difficulties in maintaining their production levels in the event of sickness, disability or death of an economically active member. Other factors

Table 15.6. Contributing factors to change in household wealth/food–security status cited by key informants in 4 study villages, Sanando District, Mali (March 1996)

Village	DJELA	DJOLE	SAWU	FANOU
	Number of times cited in interviews			
Factors: improvement food security/wealth				
1 Younger sons become older; able to work on farm	1		2	
2 Application of improved organic manure technique	3	3	6	1
3 Credit for agricultural equipment and oxen (programme)	4			
4 Credit for agricultural equipment (bank)		1	1	1
5 Purchase of 1st set of equipment/oxen from savings		2	1	4
6 Purchase of 2nd set of equipment/oxen from savings		3		5
7 Remittances from relatives in the city/Côte d'Ivoire	1	2		
8 Remittances from sons on seasonal migration		1	1	8
9 Mastery of agricultural techniques			2	2
10 Assistance from clan member or relative		2		1
11 Commerce/trading		1	1	
12 Herder for village: rents out animals			1	
13 Inherited wealth: sale of animals		2	1	
14 Move away to earn money to buy equipment and return		2		
Factors: worsening of food security status				
15 Increased age of older men/few or no sons			1	3
16 Sickness/blindness/accident		1		1
17 Death of one or more men: reduced labour force		1		2
18 Death of one or more women			1	
19 Son left on seasonal migration; no remittances		2		3
20 Poor management (inexperienced new HH head)			1	1
21 Loss of husband (female head of HH)		1		
22 Debt due to dowry expenses		3	3	
23 Hiring oneself out to earn money: abandon own field			1	
24 Debt Cotton Development Board: forced sale of assets		3		
25 Split up of family: division of assets		1		

that contribute to decline in economic fortunes are: the emigration of young adults (increasing the workload on remaining older persons), especially if they fail to earn or send money home; the sale of assets to pay debts or to finance a son's marriage; and the poor management or inexperience of a new household head. Even moderately well–off households can fall into the downward spiral if a major shock upsets production and forces them to sell productive assets to make up for grain deficits. Table 15.6 summarizes the principal factors affecting the economic fortunes of families in Sanando as cited in the interviews.

The impact of SAFADR's agricultural programme must be seen within this larger pattern of economic, social and demographic forces which affect the economic well–being and food security of households. The study data suggest that most of the agricultural innovations have brought far more benefits to the better–off households, which have more livestock, labour and equipment, than to poorer households.

This does not mean that the poor have not benefited from the programme. The short–cycle varieties and compost pits, in particular, have helped poorer households to develop better coping mechanisms and to become less vulnerable to food insecurity. Other programme activities, such as the village cereal banks, have also improved the food security of the poor. The situation of households whose fortunes regressed because of factors beyond the control of the programme would have been worse in the absence of the programme. Moreover, some of the above–mentioned redistribution mechanisms within Bambara society are likely to have enabled poorer households to benefit indirectly from economic gains of better–off households. None the less, the cumulative impact of new agricultural technology promoted by SAFADR appears to have been insufficient to enable most poorer households to enter an upward spiral towards increased food security.

Impact of agricultural credit on food security

What can bring poorer households into the upward spiral? The study data suggest two possibilities: cash generated by sons who migrate during the dry season; and credit to purchase oxen and equipment. Although most loans came from CMDT, SAFADR also provided some credit via the CDV. Seven households in Djela village which received loans had been chronically short of food five years ago, but five of them have now risen from the D category to the relatively food–secure C and B categories. They bought farming equipment, repaid their loans and can grow sufficient grain in good years. One household could not use the loan to become food–secure because two sons died, leaving only one son and the aging head of household to work the fields. The other poor household improved its situation, but was judged to have remained in the same wealth category.

It is by no means certain that Djela's positive experience with agricultural credit can be replicated in other villages. A number of enabling factors specific to Djela converged to generate greater community capacity for collective action than elsewhere. A major factor is the high level of solidarity between Djela's two principal clans, the Diarra and the Traore. Also, it must be noted that the situation of some poor households worsened because of the necessity to repay the credit after they failed to gain the expected increase in production.

Table 15.7. Changes in agricultural practices in Sanando by order of importance, adoption level and source of change

Adoption level	Rank	Change in practice	Source of change					
			CMDT	WN SAFADR	Water and forests	Cinzana	Animal husbandry	Peasant farmer
Most important changes:								
A	1	Multicultivator	X1					
D	2	Forage crops	X2	X1		X		X
D	3	Making animal feed	X1	X2	X	X		
A	4	Compost/manure pits	X1	X2	X	X		
D	5	Composting		X2		X1		
C	6	Animal vaccination				X1		
A	7	Ridging technique						X1
A	8	Harrowing	X1					
A	9	Short–cycle varieties	X	X1		X2		
A	10	Insecticides	X1	X2		X		
B	11	Seeder	X1					
D	12	Hiring of equipment	X2					X1
C	13	Ploughing	X2					X1
A	14	Intercropping	X	X2		X		X1
A	15	Hilling						X1
D	16	Agricultural testing	X	X1		X2		
A	17	Grain storage treatment	X	X1		X2		
B	18	Collective grain storage	X	X2				X1
D	19	Live fencing						
D	20	Stalk contour bunds						
D	21	Stone contour bunds						
Moderately important changes:								
B	22	Improved kraal						
C	23	Planting *Faidherbia albida*						
A	24	Fertilizer						
D	25	Sowing in dry soil						
D	26	Fallowing						
Least important changes:								
D	27	Manual sowing technique						
D	28	Herbicides						
A	29	Thresher						

Key:
A = Adopted by most   X = a source of change
B = Adopted by majority   X1 = the most important source of change
C = Adopted by about half   X2 = the 2nd most important source of change
D = Adopted by a few

CMDT   Malian Cotton Development Agency
WN   World Neighbors programme

Sources of agricultural change

During a session with *Yèrènyèton* the study team facilitated an exercise in which delegates from 14 villages identified the main changes in agricultural practice over the past ten years, and the primary source of each change. This exercise was then repeated in one of the study villages (Djole). Some of the changes, such as the use of compost/manure pits and live fencing, are introduced technologies; others are modifications or significant increases in adoption of existing farming practices.

As evident in Table 15.7, many changes were not a result of the WN programme. Other sources of agricultural technology also made significant contributions: CMDT, Cinzana Research Station and informal farmer–to–farmer exchange. Even if the specific innovations cited above were introduced by SAFADR, other agencies or forces of change may have enhanced their success.

5. Implications

Stepping back from the details about the evolution and impact of the agricultural pro-gramme in Sanando, what insights can be gained about how to sustain a CBEE process?

Farmer organizations

Local organizations established solely to undertake CBEE are unlikely to become self–sus-taining. It is questionable whether a process of technological innovation can provide an adequate basis on which to build farmer organization. WN's classic approach is essential-ly a technology–driven one in which technology development and dissemination form the leading edge, and organizational development is the contingent process.

In Sanando this approach gave the programme a very rapid start. The first wave of tech-nologies, the short–cycle varieties, responded to a deeply–felt need and produced tangible, immediate results. The second wave, involving ways of increasing the quantity of manure, also addressed a fundamental agricultural problem and had substantial impact, although it tended to favour wealthier households. It also gave the programme a substantial boost.

When the experimentation programme no longer generated new technologies that were ideally suited to the local social and physical environment, the enthusiasm and commit-ment appeared to flag. This suggests that farmers' interest in testing new ideas may have had more to do with acquiring new ideas than a genuine interest in the more scientific approach to experimentation proposed by WN.

If agricultural technology development is continued by *Yèrènyèton*, it is due to SAFADR's skill in leveraging early technical success for strengthening local capacities and organiza-tional development. As the stream of well–suited technologies started to run dry, other activ-ities were in place to generate benefits to sustain the process. Also, *Yèrènyèton* had devel-oped sufficient human, managerial and financial resources to carry the costs of technolo-gy development.

If an agricultural programme is fortunate enough to have a set of low–cost technologies that are well suited to the local social and physical context and require only local adaptation, then CBEE can serve as an entry point. In marginal and risk-prone areas, however, CBEE may not be able to generate sufficient benefits quickly enough, and for enough people, to become self-sustaining. Few agricultural programmes can maintain a constant stream of appropriate technologies indefinitely. If it is to be sustained, CBEE must either strengthen existing mechanisms of informal experimentation and diffusion of innovations, or become part of a broader development programme that provides other tangible benefits to the local people.

Scale of operation

An appropriate scale of operation is important in sustaining the CBEE process. The Sanando case suggests that CBEE can continue when undertaken or coordinated by a district-wide, intervillage association. It will be difficult to sustain CBEE in only one or a few villages which cannot bear the high costs of participation compared to the uncertainty of benefits. CBEE is more likely to be sustained if the process and costs can be spread over several villages. The scale is also important to enable farmers to negotiate effectively to obtain technical services and to influence formal research and extension policy.

Autonomous linkages

To sustain CBEE, farmer organizations must have the capacity to make autonomous linkages with government and external agencies. A significant aspect of SAFADR strategy is that it encouraged *Yèrènyèton's* leadership to develop its own linkages with Cinzana Research Centre, CRU and other technical bodies, as well as with funders other than WN.

Multi-tier experimentation

A CBEE process can be effective if a more formal scientific approach is folded into a multi-tier approach to experimentation, with each tier tailored to the practical interests of different types of farmers. An emphasis on teaching farmers more rigorous methods of experimentation may be misplaced, at least in certain contexts. In Sanando most farmers preferred to maintain their own way of experimenting, which was more informal and less rigorous but, in their view, more practical. The Sanando programme eventually encompassed three tiers of agricultural experimentation. The implication is that a vigorous programme to promote CBEE should recognize, promote and monitor technology development at several levels.

Access to information

The Sanando case suggests that providing farmers with greater access to information, ideas and experiences about new technologies may generate the same (if not higher) overall impact as promoting scientific on-farm trials. The implication is that high priority should be given to strengthening communication and access to information and sources of new technologies. In Sanando the technology development process benefited particularly from intervillage sessions that enabled farmers to discuss problems and analyse experiences, and from participation of farmers in workshops and excursions to learn from other farmer organizations, research stations and technical agencies.

Socioeconomic factors

To improve rural livelihoods, production and income, it will be necessary to go beyond a CBEE focus. New technologies create new opportunities, but the problems preventing adoption by poorer households are not technical but rather social and economic in nature. Poorer (and smaller) households lack the labour, cash, animal power and manure to make effective use of new technologies and to achieve more sustainable agriculture. Lack of access to resources is a far greater constraint to agricultural improvement than is lack of technical knowledge. To complement technology development, innovative forms of social cooperation and organization to enable poorer households to pool local and outside resources and to decrease vulnerability to food insecurity need to be explored with village leaders.

6. Conclusions

The introduction of CBEE contributed to the adoption of improved agricultural technologies in Sanando and to increased capacity for technology development. Technologies promoted by SAFADR generated some benefits for households in all wealth categories. These benefits have contributed to the increased viability and legitimacy of new organizational roles and structures responsible for CBEE. However, the agricultural technologies developed have provided only indirect benefits for women's economic status and productive capacity. The sole exception is the introduction of soybean, which has provided some women with a new source of personal income.

SAFADR's work in strengthening the capacity of village and intervillage structures to undertake a process of agricultural development has also had indirect benefits: it has facilitated more effective collaboration of local organizations with CMDT, Cinzana Research Station and other outside technical agencies. Encouraging farmers to seek and test new technologies has also bolstered informal systems for experimentation and information dissemination, particularly in identifying and testing new crop varieties.

The case study revealed that appropriate technologies for more sustainable agriculture already exist for the Sanando area. For example, according to the interviews, the increase in manure production has led to less land being cleared and more land left fallow because better–off households can use their manured fields longer. The critical issue is not that poorer households need new technologies to improve production and food security. They know what technologies they need. Over 50% of the better–off households are already using these technologies to increase production, while making their farming system more sustainable. Poorer households simply do not have the resources to apply these technologies.

Promoting innovation through CBEE is necessary, but not sufficient, to achieve equitable and sustainable agriculture. It must be coupled with interventions to provide poorer households with additional means to reduce their vulnerability. Many richer households are food–secure because they have developed forms of cooperation, based on extended kinship groups, that enable them to spread risk, pool resources and achieve economies of scale. What poorer households need, as much as new agricultural technologies like short–cycle cowpeas, are new social technologies (i.e. forms of cooperation) that enable them to link up with other poorer families to spread risk, pool resources and achieve economies of scale.

Merely testing and extending new agricultural technologies, particularly in marginal and risk–prone areas, will not have adequate mobilizing power to change patterns of social cooperation and to catalyze appropriate forms of local organization, leadership and management to sustain the development process. CBEE can be consolidated and spread if strengthening local organizational capacity is part of the programme strategy from the start. Analysis of local institutional structures should be done concurrently with the technical steps of CBEE, and the information integrated into programme decisions throughout. Strategies are needed to ensure that increased capacity to generate improved technology is matched with increased organizational capacities required to sustain it. To be effective, the strategies must take into account contextual factors, not only of national policies and operations of technical agencies, but also of village–level institutions.

Social analysis of the impact of the WN programme in Sanando strongly suggests that the dynamics of the CBEE process favoured richer households, which are better able to take risks and deploy resources, than poorer households. A deeper analysis of root causes of poverty in Sanando showed that CBEE had limited impact in reducing the number of chronically food–deprived households. It may slow down, but not reverse, the slide down the spiral into greater vulnerability, unless it is accompanied by other types of interventions that help poorer farmers gain increased access to resources.

Because of differences in context, village capacity and local institutions, not only between but also within countries, an intervening agency must be able to adapt its approach to new situations. This implies that it will need to recruit and train staff capable of analysing local social institutions and taking a strategic view.

Acknowledgements

I am greatly indebted to the SAFADR team and the leaders of *Yèrènyèton* in Sanando. Denise Caudill, Fatoumata Batta, Mick Howes and NOVIB are also thanked for their support during the research. I gained many valuable insights from Camilla Toulmin's study in another part of Segou Region.

References

Bunch, R. 1982. *Two ears of corn: A guide to people–centered agricultural improvement.* Oklahoma City, World Neighbors.

Stolzenbach, A. 1992. Learning by improvisation: The logic of farmers' experimentation in Mali. Paper prepared for IIED/IDS Beyond Farmer First workshop, Brighton, UK.

Toulmin, C. 1992. *Cattle, women and wells.* Oxford University Press.

16. Supporting local farmer research committees

*Jacqueline A. Ashby, Teresa Gracia, María del Pilar Guerrero,
Carlos Alberto Patiño, Carlos Arturo Quirós and José Ignacio Roa* [1]

Delegating responsibility to local organizations is becoming increasingly attractive to governments worldwide. Decentralization gives local agencies the responsibility for decision–making and payment for services. This is expected to improve and democratize the provision of services at the local level (Putnam 1993). Strengthening farmer experimentation, which represents a local capacity for adaptive agricultural research and technology development, is an example of delegation which can improve the effectiveness of agricultural research and development to serve resource–poor farmers (Ashby and Sperling 1994).

---

[1] Jacqueline A. Ashby, Teresa Gracia, Maria del Pilar Guerrero, Carlos Alberto Patiño, Carlos Arturo Quiros and Jose Ignacio Roa, International Centre for Tropical Agriculture (CIAT IPRA Project), AA 6713 Cali, Colombia.

Farmer experimentation requires organizational, as well as methodological support. For example, an evaluation of World Bank agricultural development projects ten years after they were completed found that the support they gave to developing strong farmer organizations able to assume responsibility for managing project activities was vital (Cernea 1987). However, strengthening the farmer's capacity to experiment and develop technology is different from including farmers in programmes run by agencies external to the farming community. There are some important questions about how best to develop and strengthen local institutional arrangements to promote farmer-led research and technology development. For example: What procedures are useful for identifying the experimenting farmers, and how well can the research they undertake serve different needs in the local community? How should experimenting farmers and external agencies be linked? What are the appropriate financial mechanisms to promote local research capacity and responsibility? What research methods strengthen the capacity of experimenting farmers to do locally useful research?

This chapter addresses these questions through an account of a five-years' action research (1990-94) carried out by the IPRA project of the International Centre for Tropical Agriculture (CIAT) with support from the Kellogg Foundation. The project attempted to assess whether community-based committees of experimenting farmers help to strengthen local technology development, how well such committees serve a numerous, diverse population, and at what cost.

We describe the process through which farmer research committees were developed, from the first pilot phase in 1990, to the present. We Then discuss, by way of a case study, some of the difficulties encountered and how these were addressed, and present some of the results obtained by monitoring the committees. To summarize the implications of the project's experience to date, we return to the questions outlined above.

Development of farmer research committees

Background to the project strategy

During the period 1985-90, IPRA had been carrying out research, developing methodology and producing training materials to demonstrate to the international scientific community that participatory evaluation of technologies with farmers, before their recommendation to extension services, would accelerate adoption. By 1990, it was clear that many governments were reducing investment in state-run agricultural research and extension services. Most state services could not afford to involve farmers in adaptive research. As a result, it was essential to decentralize or pass to the farmers the major responsibility for local technology development (Ashby et al. 1995). The experiment with grassroots farmer research committees was designed in this context. Its main objective was to assess whether community-based committees could take over adaptive research from formal research systems, and improve on this service by making it more relevant to farmers' needs.

Pilot area

The project was initiated in a pilot area in Cauca Department, in southern Colombia. Cauca is one of the poorest provinces in the country, with the lowest wages. The area is characterized by hilly terrain, poor roads and markets, and small farms averaging 5 ha (the average cultivated area is less than 3 ha). All farmers engage in a mix of commercial and subsistence production. This is a marginal coffee–producing area, with infertile acid soils, often badly eroded. Most farmers cultivate coffee and cassava as cash crops; some maize and climbing beans are grown traditionally for subsistence. Livestock is scarce: only 13% of farms have any cattle, although the typical farm may have as much as 40-60% of its land under pasture or secondary bush growth, a feature of the commonly–practised rotation of crops with fallow.

Literacy is quite common (heads of household have an average of 3 years of primary school), as is typical of rural Colombia. The ability to speak, read or write in Spanish is, however, less widespread in the Indian population than among the mestizos. Women and children participate in all aspects of farm labour except for heavy physical work such as preparing land or harvesting cassava; as income levels rise, women's work is concentrated increasingly around the household and its tree garden and vegetable plot, while young children attend school.

Farmer experimentation

In 1986-88 IPRA studied farmer experimentation in this pilot area. A systematic random sample of 30% was drawn from a household census covering 16 communities in the area. The 551 heads of household interviewed were asked whether they had done any kind of experimentation on their own, independently of any external agency; how long ago the experiment took place; its purpose; and whether it was useful. Most farmers did not describe the informal tests they had done on their own as research, or even as experiments, but they did refer to obtaining results from 'trying things out', and viewed knowledge as something requiring a special effort to generate, which needed to be jealously guarded (Patiño 1990). The survey documented over 1000 informal experiments recalled by farmers: of these, 51% involved new crops and varieties; 29% new inputs, especially agrochemicals; and 20% cultural practices, in particular crop associations, land preparation, planting distances, planting dates and comparison of different types of soil, as illustrated in Figure 16.1. The communities were classified into three types: primarily subsistence production; mixed subsistence and commercial production; and primarily commercial. The study found that the average number of informal experiments per farmer was not very different in the different types of community: 5 per farmer in the commercial communities and 4.4 per farmer in the subsistence communities, for example.

It was also investigated whether farmers would identify individuals in their communities as 'experimenting farmers'. Each farmer in the random sample was asked to name up to 5 farmers whom he or she considered both knowledgeable and to be continually testing new practices. A total of 25 farmers, whose names were mentioned repeatedly in the interviews, were identified, and this group was compared with the total sample on a number of key socioeconomic characteristics, as illustrated in Table 16.1. Farmers identified locally as experimenters tended to be slightly better off, with more contact with credit and technical assistance agencies, and were more likely to have bought land in the past 5 years (Patiño 1990). One of the marked differences was that a higher percentage of the experimenters wanted to continue living in the area (60%) as compared to the total sample (44%).

Table 16.1. Socioeconomic characteristics of locally–identified experimenters in subsistence–oriented communities

	Characteristic		
	Farm size (ha)	Age (years)	Bought land in last 5 years (%)
Experimenters	4.3	33	30
Total Sample	3.8	38	26
	Employ farm labourers (%)	Desire to remain (%)	Used credit 10 years ago (%)
Experimenters	60	60	45
Total Sample	57	44	33
	Receive technical assistance (%)	Own a backpack sprayer (%)	
Experimenters	40	25	
Total Sample	22	12	

Experimenters (N = 10);   Total sample (N = 78)

In sum, the study showed a wealth of informal experimentation by farmers who were not linked to formal research and extension. Neither were these farmers in touch with each other, even informally. When the project began to facilitate visits among farmer–researchers, the most common reaction was surprise at the inventiveness of their neighbours.

The project thus identified a need to mobilize local leadership among experimenting farmers, and to encourage them to work together and exchange their research and its results. In order to assess the effects of different linkages with external institutions, the project formed farmer research committees in three different institutional contexts: directly in local communities; with already existing informal groups formed by NGOs for credit and extension purposes; and with farmer associations or cooperatives.

Formation of farmer research committees

The process of forming committees began in Colombia in 1990, in four farmer associations or cooperatives and in one community which had no cooperative. Some time was spent exploring methodology and developing training materials with the 5 pilot committees. By late 1991, the number of committees in the pilot area had increased to 18, to 32 by 1992-93 and to 55 by early 1994. A further 36 committees were then formed in Bolivia, Ecuador, Brazil, Peru and Honduras, bringing the total to 91 by mid–1995.

We discuss here some of the significant issues that emerged during the process of forming the 55 committees in Colombia. The committees covered an area of approximately 1605 km², involving an estimated 50,000 families, and had direct contact with over 4000 farmers, of whom 220 participated in training as members of such committees. Forming these farmer research committees involved action research and was a learning process. The development of each committee was continuously monitored and evaluated by both the project team and the committees themselves. The discussion of the general points is illustrated by the case of the agricultural research committee El Diviso Rosas in northern Cauca.

The learning process and the case of El Diviso Rosas

Formation of a committee
The El Diviso committee was formed in late 1990 by the farmer association of that name, which then numbered 54 farmers. The association is one of several in the pilot area sponsored by the National Federation of Coffee Growers (FEDECAFE) to promote the commercialization of alternative crops in marginal coffee areas. In 1990, the El Diviso association, like many others, was struggling to keep its membership from declining in the face of top–down management by FEDECAFE. The cooperative was failing to identify viable markets for alternatives to coffee, in particular the fruit and vegetables FEDECAFE was promoting.

The El Diviso association already had a marketing committee, so IPRA's proposal that it form a research committee was readily accepted by its members. IPRA proposed that the association identify at least four farmers known as experimenters to make up the committee. In a plenary meeting, after a discussion about what 'research' meant, what qualities were needed to be a member of a research committee, and the steps involved in participatory on–farm research (i.e. diagnosis, planning, experimentation and evaluation), four farmers was elected. The committees were baptized CIALs (Comité de Investigación Agropecuaria Local, or committees for local farming research). In addition to the elected farmers, other association members were interested in joining. Like other CIALs, El Diviso usually included other farmers in its activities, with the four elected members providing continuity.

The general debate over selection versus election is an ongoing one in the IPRA team and in the committees. Mestizo farmer associations and communities in Colombia are accustomed to electing representatives, although in the Indian communities committees have been formed in closed session by the *cabildo* (local governing body). One concern is that election does not create a group of experimenting farmers unless the criteria for eligibility are well discussed and understood by the community. The committees were designed to mobilize local research capacity; the emphasis was on forming a group of experimenting, rather than representative, farmers.

Participatory diagnosis
The first task of any CIAL is to call a meeting to carry out a participatory diagnosis in order to identify a topic for experimentation perceived as important by the group it serves. In El

Diviso, the CIAL visited all the members of the farmers' association to motivate them to attend the gathering. IPRA facilitated the discussion; it was assumed that, at this early stage, participatory diagnosis would require the skills of external moderators. Working in small groups, the members discussed their most important questions or doubts about farming; how their practices were changing and the causes of these changes.

The El Diviso farmers identified four priority topics for research, each related to a different farm enterprise (maize, beans, tomatoes and chickens). IPRA asked them to choose the top priority by ranking each topic against a set of criteria, including cost, risk and who would benefit from the research. On this basis the group prioritized their research question: Can we solve the problem of maize lodging in the summer winds, spoiling the cobs and reducing the yields? Maize is of interest to all the farmers: to feed the labourers who pick the coffee; to prepare traditional dishes; and to feed the chickens. In contrast to FEDCAFE's agenda, which prioritized fruit and vegetables, the El Diviso farmers opted for research on a staple subsistence food crop.

Table 16.2 illustrates the diversity of crops submitted to farmer experimentation in the CIALs. Many of these crops were never considered by extension and credit agencies. For example, peas are an entirely new crop to the area, introduced by the CIALs. As a result many new cropping systems have appeared in farmers' fields: for example, tomatoes intercropped with peas; raspberries planted as contour barriers; maize, beans and peanuts.

Priority–setting

Our experience so far underlines the need to be attentive to the issue of equity and diversity in the priority–setting by the committees. Priority–setting is sometimes undesirable if it does not allow attention to different client groups. It may mean, for example, that women's topics get pushed into second place (the project has experimented with setting up women's committees in response to this dilemma), or that highly innovative ideas of less interest to the majority do not get tested first. In El Diviso in 1994, there were women in the committee who wanted to experiment with peanuts, though this had not appeared as a topic in the

Table 16.2. Number of CIAL experiments, by type of crop/animal

	Peas and related cultural practices	Potato	Maize and related practices	Peanuts	Fruits and related fertilizer dosages, pest control	Beans	Snap–bean	Tomat
				TOPIC				
PHASE I	1	6	7	1	3	6	0	1
PHASE II	3	5	8	3	6	4	1	1
PHASE III	1	1	2	1	7	1	1	1

¹ less than no. of CIALs, not all CIALs yet experimenting

previous participatory diagnosis. Generally, however, topics of general significance to the community emerged from priority–setting; this was important for developing local ownership of the research.

Planning and planting experiments

After the participatory diagnosis, the El Diviso research committee met with the IPRA agronomist to plan their experiment on the maize–lodging problem. They first defined their objective in response to the question: What do we want to learn from our experiment? In the planning meeting, the agronomist listened to all the suggestions and questions. It may be important at this stage for the group to collect more information. This might involve a visit to another CIAL or community; to a research station or NGO with a relevant programme, in the region or elsewhere; alternatively, the CIAL members may visit agricultural banks or other credit services, NGOs, or agricultural schools and extension offices. In the case of El Diviso, the agronomist provided the CIAL members with information about new maize varieties still being developed and tested for the coffee region by the national agricultural research service in other parts of the country. He put them in touch with communities where farmers were experimenting with local and farmer–introduced maize varieties, for example, a local variety called Doña Julia which had been developed in another community.

Using this information El Diviso defined the objectives of its experiment as follows: to compare the local maize with other varieties to find out which ones would best resist lodging by the wind; which would mature earlier; and which would be less susceptible to pests and disease. The committee was looking for a commercial maize with large–sized cobs and grain.

With these aims in mind, the CIAL selected the six most desirable grain types from the seed available for testing from the research service and from other communities. Together with five other interested farmers, and with the agronomist acting as moderator, the committee planned the selection of plots, the information to be collected from the plots, the cultural practices, who was to be responsible for different tasks, the planting date, and the distribution of the harvest.

a bean	Sugar cane	Vegetables	Chicken feed mixes	TOPIC Forage grasses	Cover crops (green manure)	Guinea pigs	TOTAL[1]
1	4	1	1	0	0		**32**
1	7	1	1	0	0		**42**
1	6	0	1	1	1		**43**

Ownership and self-evaluation

The IPRA team was working at the time with five CIALs. Planning experiments in such a way that responsibility for them could be assumed by farmers turned out to be more complicated than expected. When farmers are involved in on-farm testing programmes by external agencies, the research field staff will often coordinate much of the logistic support (e.g. where, when and how to obtain, store and use inputs). The collective management of such tasks by the farmers was not straightforward, and plans were often disrupted by unexpected calls on the farmers' time. A period of weaning from dependence on top-down management by outsiders was often necessary before farmers began to feel and take ownership of their experiments.

In the case of El Diviso, the farmers took ownership of their experiments only after several experiences of seeing the IPRA team deferring to their decisions and accepting any consequences resulting from delegating tasks to them. Delegation became a reality only when it was clear that what mattered was that they, the farmers, should learn for themselves from their experiment and that what outsiders wanted did not matter. For example, the farmers first planted the maize experiment on plots that became waterlogged, so the seed rotted. It was a sign that they had relegated the experiment to sub-optimal plots for the rainy season, presumably because it had been perceived as belonging to outsiders. As a result, the five farmers who had been accompanying the CIAL lost interest, and it looked as if the committee would lose its motivation and fold. At this time, the IPRA sociologist introduced a procedure for self-evaluation by the CIALs, which enabled the members, either individually or collectively, to address a series of questions about their progress. In the case of El Diviso, this self-evaluation enabled the CIAL to identify that the experiment had been poorly managed because the farmers thought the outsiders would take care of it.

After this experience the El Diviso committee decided to plan their maize trial again, this time with a new appreciation that the outsiders had no vested interest in the experiment itself. From this understanding, they formulated the basic principle that CIAL members would reassure each other, especially when new committees were forming, that there was no such thing as a failed experiment, for it was always possible to learn from mistakes.

Introducing routine self-evaluation by CIALs, and the principle of allowing mistakes to happen in order to encourage learning, was a watershed experience in the management of the committees. This required a shift in professional values (see Chambers 1983). The IPRA agronomists had been trained to give farmers their best advice. To allow farmers to make decisions that were known to have negative consequences agronomically was fundamentally contrary to their professional ethos. Yet strengthening farmer experimentation meant that sometimes the farmers' learning experience and establishing the principles of decision-making, responsibility and accountability had to be given more importance than rescuing any particular experiment. As the CIALs grew in number, these principles were transmitted from group to group and farmer to farmer, and it became unnecessary for professionals to return to the difficult choice between strengthening decision skills and good agronomic advice. However, the early stages of committee formation sometimes requires outsiders consciously to reinforce weaning from dependence on outsiders even at the expense of good agronomy.

Our experience contradicts conventional wisdom which says that, with resource–poor farmers, efforts to innovate must bring success in the short–term, that on–farm technology testing must include tried and tested innovations: otherwise farmers will be discouraged from experimenting. The CIALs demonstrate the importance of farmers and outsiders together defining success as learning, and strengthening the capacity of the groups to take ownership of an experiment. Success means generating knowledge, and disproving or descrediting unreliable recommendations, rather than proving that an innovation is better than local practice. In this context, the loss of an experiment is not demoralizing. Our experience showed truly impressive persistence by some CIALs in the face of several experiments which failed to show that a promising innovation compared well in comparison to local practice. In this respect, contact among CIALs is an important ingredient of success; one CIAL benefits from the other's experimentation and is motivated by it.

Method of experimentation

The El Diviso group went on to conduct its experiments on six farms, involving farmers from outside the committee. The seven treatments (varieties), including the local check, were replicated on each farm, where uniform planting practices planned by the farmers were used. In planning the experiment, the farmers decided what information to collect from it, and throughout the season they compared height, lodging, yield, disease and pest susceptibility, plus the size of the cobs and grain. They also cooked each variety separately to compare the flavour. They chose five of the seven varieties with which to continue experimenting. By 1993, El Diviso was multiplying and selling seed of several maize varieties selected in their experiments. This was done exclusively at first through the traditional seed system; as more farmers began to request the seed, the selection was officially recognized by the national research programme under the category of 'farmer–improved seed'.

Maize varieties were progressively selected by different CIALs who shared their results by visiting each other. CIAL Pescador did a varietal trial with 7 materials in the spring of 1991 and identified MB258, MB254 and MB251 as locally adapted lines with desirable grain types. Despite their initial setback CIAL El Division, a hundred kilometres away to the south, continued in the autumn of 1991 with additional materials. In that same autumn, CIAL San Bosco, at a lower altitude and further north, also took up maize selection. After four seasons of selection, in 1993, the CIALs identified MB254, MB251, MB258, SWAN 8027, CIMCALI–SA2 (yellow), and a local variety as the preferred varieties and began propagating all six as 'farmer–improved seed'. The Colombian national research programme decided to release MB251 and MB258 in 1993, after conducting 29 trials in the Colombian coffee region over six years. The varieties were released with 80 tons of certified seed. Farmers in the CIAL communities did not obtain any of the nationally certified seed of the new varieties, since it was not yet available locally in the government seed–distribution agencies or commercial outlets, but they were already harvesting the varieties, using seed from the El Diviso community seed enterprise.

One of the major issues which the IPRA team continues to assess is the value of teaching farmers to experiment using formal scientific methods, in contrast to supporting free or informal traditional experimentation. Of course, a better understanding of the nature of 'folk' experimentation shows that farmers do compare the data of different treatments and results from year to year, usually recorded in their heads rather than on paper. They may also compare results in a distant field with those in a nearby one, or the results of adding more fertilizer to one furrow but not in the remainder of the field. Folk experimentation also involves replication, but this is typically undertaken over time, in contrast to replication in space and time as characterized by the scientific method. Folk experimentation also recognizes confounding effects. A small amount of seed of a new variety may first be tried out in the more fertile home garden before it is moved to other areas, of different soil type. Only when performance has been assessed in a variety of environments are conclusions drawn about the likely performance in the farmer's environment. Data obtained through monitoring trials show that, in 90% of the CIALs' experimental plots, farmers consider that they can draw conclusions about the differences among treatments, although only 75% are statistically analysable by scientific criteria. Plots that farmers consider 'not useful for drawing conclusions' are, for example, those damaged by livestock or hail (Ashby et al. 1995).

IPRA has used statistical procedures to analyse trial data recorded in the diary kept by the CIAL on each experiment. Data analysis is done by farmers using units, ratios and the qualitative criteria they decide upon during the planning meeting. Farmers interpret the trials in their own way, but the statistics are useful for outside agencies interested in the results. So far, IPRA has not attempted to teach or use statistical analysis with farmers, other than simple averages and budgets.

An argument for using the scientific method is that it gives CIAL results credibility with outsiders (NGOs, banks, extension programmes, local government and scientists). This credibility has helped the CIALs to use their results to challenge, for example, fertilizer and pesticide recommendations required by credit programmes. CIAL recommendations and seed from their varietal trials are being disseminated by municipal extension services. Farmers who are experienced CIAL members are being contracted by NGOs and municipalities to provide training to form new committees; and CIALs are being contracted by municipal extension services to develop local recommendations. Scientific credibility is, therefore, a source of bargaining power and income–generation for the committees. The case of El Diviso illustrates how, together with other CIALs, the scientific acceptability of their replicated trials convinced the national maize–breeding programme to accept the CIALs' varietal selections for local release as farmer–improved seed. In El Diviso farmers' informal experimentation still continues, sometimes blending in techniques from the groups' formal trials, such as labelling plots or furrows where different practices are being tested. One of the main differences between the CIALs' experiments and free experimentation is that the former involve working in groups, sharing replications made at the same point in time and over several seasons. Some farmers think they can get a feel for the local potential of a new crop or practice more quickly by working in a group across a range of different farms and field types. Although one CIAT agronomist now provides back–up to cover 55 CIALs, and so has infrequent contact with them, the committees have continued to use replicated trials until they plant semi–commercial plots.

From research to development

An important occurrence is that some CIALs, like El Diviso, which successfully selected new locally–adapted crop varieties, have evolved into small seed–production enterprises, delivering seed of these and of local varieties to farmers in the area. To date, six committees have begun to produce seed, for which they receive additional training in simple seed production, processing and quality–control techniques. The CIAL seed is distributed locally in the village stores and at weekend markets. An estimated 281 ha of maize, 3064 ha of beans and 3.5 ha of field peas (an entirely new crop introduced by CIAL experimentation into the pilot area) have been planted with CIAL seed. More than 10 000 farmers have purchased the seed, which over one planting season is estimated to have produced grain to a gross value of over US$2 million. Based on the yield differential between locally available varieties and those selected by the CIALs for seed production, this output represents an additional US$ 765 000 of gross income to local farmers from maize and beans, and a newly introduced income source worth over US$ 8000 to date from peas. On a per capita basis, this is an increment worth about one month's wages in one planting season, to the farmers who purchased CIAL seed.

Developing small enterprises was not part of the original design for the farmer research committees. Not all CIALs evolve into seed producers; indeed many do not test varieties but select cultural practices, fertilizer rates or animal diet as their topic of experimentation. In terms of farmers' criteria, much of the knowledge generated by CIAL experiments shows that local practice is as good or better than outsiders' recommendations. Knowledge generation, therefore, remains the main business of the CIALs.

The income–generation opportunities which the seed enterprises provide are, nonetheless, a powerful incentive to the groups' research. This is the Development part of their R&D, and that which faces the weakest institutional support. It is difficult to obtain venture capital to finance scaling–up from a successful experiment to commercial production, since the CIAL fund supports only small–scale experimentation. In some cases, the existence of NGO programmes linked to CIALs have been an important mechanism for converting a CIAL's experimental result into a recommendation adopted by large numbers of farmers. For example, an NGO bought quantities of El Diviso's maize seed, and distributed it through its cooperative input–purchasing programme. This, and similar experiences with other CIALs, demonstrates the importance of institutional linkages for the success of extension and credit. Farmer research committees generate locally–appropriate recommendations very efficiently, but they are not able completely to substitute for some of the extension services needed to convert new knowledge rapidly into widespread practice.

The evolution of financial arrangements

When planning its first maize experiment, the El Diviso committee decided to contribute one–third of the net value of sales to the CIAL fund, and to share the remainder of the profit among the farmers who had worked on the trials. Planning the distribution of the harvest before planting has proved to be an important step in maintaining the commitment of the participants and in securing contributions to the fund.

The CIAL fund began as an account held by IPRA on behalf of each community, from which the experimental inputs could be financed as determined by the CIAL. Each committee developed procedures for making regular contributions to the fund from the sale of harvests from the experiments; or for recapitalizing if a major loss had to be absorbed (for example, a calf was raffled by one CIAL for this purpose). The fund later evolved into a permanent endowment owned collectively by the CIAL Corporation, a legal incorporation of all the CIALs in the Cauca pilot area (an arrangement described in more detail elsewhere by Ashby et al. 1995). From the beginning, the intention of the fund was to reinforce ownership of the research by the committee, and its sense of accountability. Together with results from the experiment, committee members must explain in a community meeting held each growing season (twice annually in Colombia) expenditures, losses and gains, and the balance of the CIAL fund.

Although at first the financial arrangement with each CIAL was based on the principle that IPRA staff would release and control the petty cash required for purchasing experimental inputs, this soon proved unworkable. The level of independence required for CIAL farmers to plan and implement planting, harvesting and disposal of the product soon resulted in the creation of a petty–cash fund managed by the committee treasurer. At present El Diviso, like the majority of the 55 CIALs in Colombia, operates experiments almost entirely out of the petty cash obtained by selling the harvest, drawing on invested capital only to cover occasional losses in an experiment.

Management by poor people of even small amounts of cash of donated funds is usually viewed with strong disfavour by outside agencies; it is seen as a temptation to abuse funds. One of the early pilot CIALs formed in a very poor village community sold the harvest piecemeal from its first experiment and the committee members collectively forgot to collect the money from the various vendors. IPRA made it clear that there could be no more funds drawn from the CIAL fund until the harvest was accounted for. The CIAL then decided to call its end–of–season community meeting, as there was much disquiet in the community about the committee's status. At the meeting, an account was given of the experiment and the disappearance of the harvest. The collective concern at the implications for the community of discontinuing access to the fund, caused committee members to come up with the missing money (amounting to about 4 days' wages) so that the next experiment could be planned. (This community is now one of six with a thriving seed enterprise.)

This experience caused much soul–searching in IPRA because of the poverty of the farmers involved, and the implications of theft for the viability of decontrolling the financial management of the CIALs. However, establishing the principle that the CIAL fund is a one–time capital donation, owned by the community, with no possibilities of replacement other than through self–generated funds, for which CIAL members are publicly accountable, has resulted in complete honesty in financial management among the existing CIALs in Colombia.

Since 1991 the CIALs in the project area have met informally on an annual basis to exchange results, swap notes and formulate recommendations. At this one– or two–day meeting, financed by raising money in their communities for transportation and lodging,

256

each CIAL gives an oral report on its experiences. In 1993 a coordinating committee (*junta*) was elected and the following year the CIALs decided to form a legally constituted corporation (CORFOCIAL). Money obtained from international and national donors enabled the corporation to establish an investment fund, from which it can draw up to 70% of the interest for operating expenses, the remainder being used to supplement the capital. This has placed the CIALs on a self–sustaining financial basis. Individual communities keep an account or fund with the corporation. With the signature of a paraprofessional they can draw on this fund to cover input costs for experiments. CORFOCIAL pays for the salaries and transportation of farmer paraprofessionals who supervise the community accounts, support existing CIALs and help to form new ones. The paraprofessionals have begun to give courses for the municipal extension services which have contracted them to form a small number of pilot CIALs elsewhere, paying for their salaries and so generating additional income for the corporation.

The potential of the CIAL method to increase the efficiency of the public sector or NGO adaptive–research programmes is shown in Table 16.3 in a comparison of the labour requirements for on–farm trials. Table 16.4 gives the operating cost of the CORFOCIAL. The total annual budget in 1995 amounted to the equivalent of two agronomists, salaried at national programme rates (Ashby et al. 1995). One possible reason why the cost of forming and running CIALs is relatively speaking so low, is that the procedures for creating these groups and producing training materials were laid down before the corporation was formed. The paraprofessionals, with their low salaries and their practical experience in CIAL formation, can form and run new committees with minimal external support and cost.

New CIALs in other countries are being formed with a variety of financial arrangements, in most cases without the capital donation but with self–generated financing: each project is monitoring the experience.

Table 16.3. Comparison of labour requirements for on–farm trials

Organisation responsible for trial m anagement	Labour required [1] (N)	Total cost of salaried labour [2] in US$
Extension/Research	8	62
New CIAL (Cycle1)	11	46
Fully–trained CIAL (Cycle 2)	5	23

Notes: [1] Based on the number of visits for a crop–related on–farm trial, and averages of Phase I and Phase II training and technical support visits to CIALs. Excludes crop management after trial establishment, which is variable depending on the frequency of the crop and group diagnosis meetings.
[2] Paraprofessional farmer's time costed at minimum wage; extension agent costed at 2x minimum wage; agronomist time costed at average current salary in the pilot area.

The experimentation cycle continues

The regular end–of–season community meeting is an opportunity to revisit the diagnosis and prioritization of topics of interest to the community, and conclude whether to continue an experiment on larger–sized plots the following season or to select a new topic for experimentation. In El Diviso, as both association members and others began to acquire new maize seed, other priorities for adaptive research emerged. Women in El Diviso decided to join the CIAL and experiment with peanuts, a traditional food crop which had been squeezed out of the local cropping system as the latter was intensified and commercialized. The original four CIAL members of El Diviso decided to hand on the committee and the work of experimentation to new members. They continued to run the maize–seed enterprise, which still contributes a portion of its sales to the CIAL fund.

Table 16.4. Annual operating costs of the CIAL Corporation (1994)

Annual costs	*US$*
Personnel costs per CIAL[1]	290.00
Cost of experiments per CIAL[2]	90.00
Other operating costs per CIAL[3]	122.00
Total cost per CIAL	502.00
Total cost for the CIAL corporation (55 CIALS)	2,7610.00

Cost per capita (average across the 55 CIALs)	*US$ per capita per year*
Total population (50,000)	0.55
CIAL communities (12,900)	2.10
33% of CIAL communities (4,260)	6.50
Seed purchasers (10,500)	2.60
CIAL committee members (220)	125.50

Notes: [1] Includes agronomist (0.33), farmer coordinator (1.0), paraprofessionals (2.0).
[2] Average of costs per CIAL charged against CIAL funds in 1994.
[3] Average of transportation, supplies, and capital depreciation on 4 motorcycles.

The new committee, trained by the retiring farmers, meets on a regular basis; like other CIALS with experience of at least two cycles of experimentation, El Diviso is supported solely by a *técnico–agricultor* (farming technician) experienced in CIAL methodology. He visits only twice each experimental cycle. The *técnico* meets with a supporting agronomist twice in a cycle for planning and for evaluating the data. The *técnico* also carries out monitoring and facilitates self–evaluation, and attends the end–of–season meeting. Today, El Diviso, with its 54 sister CIALs in Cauca, Colombia, and the three *técnico-agricultores* who attend them, are members of CORFOCIAL. CIAL seed has been purchased by an estimated 10,500 farmers, and CORFOCIAL is now planning, together with the IPRA team, a rapid appraisal of the impact to date of their experimentation on the total population.

The experience of El Diviso and other CIALs demonstrates that, with the aid of suitable handbooks, most of the training and support can be done by farmers experienced in the methodology. The various roles of the *técnico-agricultor* - to facilitate participatory diagnosis, to motivate the formation of new committees, to visit and check on the progress of CIAL experiments, to plan the end–of–season community meeting, to harvest and evaluate CIAL trials - were progressively handed over to farmers with experience in the committees. By 1994, through careful monitoring, quarterly visits to each CIAL and committees' record–keeping, IPRA had established that the farmer research committees could take over most of the running of their own on–farm research trials, producing results from which farmers can draw conclusions to enrich their own knowledge, and to increase the diversity of locally–available innovations (see Ashby et al. 1995 for more detailed figures).

Analysis of the success and failure of the CIALs over the period 1991-94 (5 CIALs or 11% became inactive), suggests several determinants of their success:

- training must impart the principle that the committee's objective is to experiment, to generate knowledge, and to disprove or discredit unreliable recommendations
- at least one literate member should be included on the committee to facilitate the management process
- the group diagnosis must identify for experimentation a problem or question of concern to farmers and of broad interest to the community
- the creation of a sense of community service and responsibility for group welfare, fostered through the periodic evaluation of members' feelings about each other and the community.

Conclusions

The baseline study of farmer experimentation carried out for this project identified an enormous wealth of informal testing carried out by resource–poor farmers in the pilot area. This informal research was unrecognized by the state and the NGO programmes in the area. The knowledge thus generated by scattered individual farmers was perceived by these as something to be jealously guarded, rather than a public good to be shared with the community at large. The local agricultural research committees (CIALs) are a mechanism through which communities can give the local experimenters a public identity and a role which incurs respect and status, and links them with external agencies.

Participatory diagnosis is a crucial feature of the CIALs' work because it identifies the priorities for the research agenda. If the participatory diagnosis captures the topics of importance to the majority of farmers, then the research carried out by the CIAL has a good chance of being widely relevant. Special interest groups, such as resource–poor women or the labouring poor, may require research committees of their own to articulate their special needs.

So far, the CIALs in the pilot area have experimented with a broad range of crops, an expression of the importance local farmers give to diversifying their production systems and generating a broad set of options. Local knowledge generation and technology development in the first four years have involved: testing new crops such as peas, locating these in new niches in the farming landscape and in new intercropping combinations; replacing purchased staples with locally tested and then home–grown alternatives (such as potatoes); discovering new markets such as locally developed and tested seed; and challenging the recommendations of outsiders, demonstrating that, in some cases, local practice is still the best–adapted option.

Teaching farmers to use scientific methods strengthens their own experimentation when these give their results greater credibility among outside agencies. In the pilot area, this credibility has enabled farmers to negotiate changes in credit terms, to obtain support for their projects from state and NGO agencies which buy CIAL–produced seed, and to disseminate information generated by their experiments. They have also appreciated the opportunity to make replications across land types on farms other than their own and compare results.

The financial mechanisms that have promoted responsibility and ownership of the research process for CIALs in the pilot area involve investment in a committee fund, a one–time donation into a type of rotating fund. The experiments are run by CIALs using petty cash from this common fund, into which a proportion of profits is paid. This liberates the community from handouts, as they are responsible for the continuity of their fund.

External agencies have played two roles in this process: the first has been to strengthen farmers' planning, organizing and decision–making skills, and knowledge of scientific methods for conducting experiments. Since training materials are now systematized in CIAL handbooks for farmers, and proliferation of CIALs in the pilot area is managed by farmers themselves, the second role of the agencies - responding to the local demand for information, technology and related services - has become increasingly important. This is articulated through CIAL experiments. Thus the CIALs' innovation with peas stimulated the local NGO programme to include credit and marketing for peas; state extension sought new germplasm requested by CIALs, made a video and held field–days to promote CIAL recommendations.

Supporting farmer experimentation with local agricultural research committees is one way of empowering farmers as researchers. Perhaps the most compelling testimony to this in the pilot area is that the 55 CIALs now organize, among themselves, an annual meeting or agricultural fair. Each year a different community hosts the event, raising support from local authorities for the visitors' meals and lodging, while the visiting communities raise funds for travel of their CIALs to the meeting place.

The CIALs report to each other on their experiments, exchange seed and discuss how to improve their impact in their communities. New communities wanting to form CIALs, and state and NGO representatives, are invited to attend and to inform themselves about the results of farmer experimentation. Perhaps the most useful lesson to be drawn from the evolution of the committees to date is the value of institutionalizing decision–making power, recognising that a sense of efficacy and self–respect is integral to the strengthening of farmer experimentation.

References

Ashby, J. and L. Sperling. 1994. *Institutonalizing participatory, client–driven research and technology development in agricultural development and change.* Agricultural Administration (Research and Extension) Network Paper 49. London, Overseas Development Institute.

Ashby, J., T. Gracia, M.P. Guerrero, C.A. Quiros, J.I. Roa and J.A. Beltran (eds). 1995. *Institutionalizing farmer participation and technology testing with the CIAL.* Agricultural Administration (Research and Extension) Network Paper 57. London, Overseas Development Institute.

Cernea, M. 1987. Farmer organizations and institution building for sustainable development. *Regional Development Dialogue* 8 (2): 1-24.

Chambers, R. 1983. *Rural development: Putting the last first.* Longman, London.

CIAL handbooks:

IPRA/CIAT. *The Trial.* Handbook No. 1.

IPRA/CIAT. *Local Agricultural Research Committees.* Handbook No. 2.

IPRA/CIAT. *Diagnosis.* Handbook No. 3.

IPRA/CIAT. *Planning the trial.* Handbook No. 4.

IPRA/CIAT. *Designing the trial.* Handbook No. 5.

IPRA/CIAT. *Evaluating of the trial.* Handbook No. 6.

IPRA/CIAT. *Things that can happen.* Handbook No. 7.

IPRA/CIAT. *Feedback to the community.* Handbook No. 8.

IPRA/CIAT. *Actual case.* Handbook No. 9.

Patiño, C.A. 1990. La selección de pequeños agricultores para ensayos de evaluación tecnológica. B.Sc. thesis, Universidad del Valle, Cali, Colombia.

Putnam, R. D. 1993. The prosperous community: Social capital and public life. *The American Prospect* (Spring): 35-42.

17. Farmers' study groups in the Netherlands

Natasja Oerlemans, Jet Proost and Joost Rauwhorst[1]

Farmers' study groups in the Netherlands have become an essential part of the national agricultural knowledge and information system. These groups build on a long tradition in Dutch agriculture. In the late nineteenth century, farmers relied mainly on the mutual exchange of experiences and new technologies shown in fairs and demonstrations. In the northern part of the country, for example, farmers' study groups on maize cultivation were

---

[1] Natasja Oerlemans, Jet Proost, Wageningen Agricultural University, Department of Communication and Innovation Studies, Hollandseweg 1, 6706 KN Wageningen, The Netherlands. E-mail: natasja.oerlemans @alg.swg.wau.nl, jet.proost@alg.vlk.wau.nl. Joost Rauwhorst, Dutch Federation for Horticultural Study Groups, PO Box 567, 2675 ZV Honselerdijk, The Netherlands.

common, since this crop was relatively unknown at the time (van Weperen, pers. comm.). Groups were formed locally around new techniques, such as the use of fertilizer and improved ploughs and animal breeds. During fairs, organized by the first farmers' unions or by farmers from the same church, prizes were awarded for the most promising innovations. In this way, innovation, experimentation and exchange of information were encouraged (Nooij 1991).

From the 1880s, formal agricultural research, extension and education, initiated by a liberal government under pressure from the early farmers' unions, began to complement farmer-to-farmer learning. The present agricultural development institutions find their origin in this period. The government and farmers' organizations started to work together to develop a highly productive and intensive agricultural sector with a strong position on the international market (Blokker and de Jong 1986). Throughout all these years, farmers' study groups remained active, although the number fluctuated with the ups and downs of the agricultural sector. In times of recession, competition prevailed over partnership and collaboration. A recent study shows a slight decrease in the number of study groups as a result of the present crisis in agriculture. The problems at the moment are apparently too big for study groups (Proost and Vogelzang 1996).

Study groups are of many types and forms. Many are initiated and organized by farmers themselves, others by the extension services and research and development institutes. It is an effective way for farmers to obtain information, not just on technical matters but also on how to deal with the increasingly restrictive environmental policies of the government (Proost and Vogelzang 1996). The groups' role in developing technologies and in encouraging farmers to experiment with new ideas, either on their own or in collaboration with researchers and extension workers, is less well documented. The experiences of Dutch farmers in horticulture, described here, demonstrate clearly the importance of this role. Their research efforts have had considerable influence on Dutch policies.

The emergence of the NTS

Farmers' study groups are traditionally strong in the horticulture sector. Many groups arose around the cooperative fruit and vegetable auctions. Almost every grower is a member of such an auction for marketing products, which enables him or her to obtain a good price. This positive experience of working together probably provided a good climate for study groups to flourish.

In 1972, a group of active growers established the NTS, the *Nederlandse Federatie van Tuinbouw Studiegroepen* (Dutch Federation of Horticultural Study Groups), a national federation to coordinate the work of the many study groups. Initially the NTS was a group of friends (NTS 1993) and most of the organizing was done by grower-volunteers. Activities focused on the exchange of information among farmers and the organization of on-farm demonstrations and field trips. The federation received support on technical matters from the government extension service while the existing farmers' unions provided administrative support.

In the early 1980s, an additional role emerged. The NTS began to represent growers in government-financed research organizations; it became their voice (NTS 1993). It became institutionalized and established its own secretariat to coordinate the growing number of activities; professional staff replaced grower-volunteers in many areas of support.

In the past few years, the open exchange of knowledge and information has come under pressure as government research and extension has been privatized, and private research institutes have became increasingly important. Knowledge has clearly gained a market value. Loyalty towards the NTS is also no longer so self-evident. Growers consider the NTS as only one of the many sources for their increasing and more specialized information needs. The NTS has therefore started to broaden its activities. Several commercial undertakings have been developed, in which the NTS acts as an intermediary, bringing growers and others together in specialized research projects. At the moment the NTS can be considered as a provider of knowledge and as a partner in coordinating the increasing number of private projects (NTS 1993). Yet, a major task of the federation remains the bringing together of growers to stimulate an exchange of knowledge and the organization of study groups. With 9000 of the 10,000 growers as members, its importance is undisputed. Most of its members have 1-2.5 ha farms with greenhouses, which, in the Dutch horticultural context, is considered a medium to large farm. Smaller growers are under-represented, as are older growers with no successors, and part-time growers who combine horticulture with other agricultural income-generating activities.

Like other agricultural sectors in the Netherlands, horticulture is predominantly a nuclear-family business. Differences in farm size are therefore not as large as in other European countries. Both men and women can become members of the NTS, but so far not many women have become actively engaged in its activities, despite efforts of the federation to motivate them to take part in excursions, meetings and courses. Within the family, it is mostly the men who are interested in new technology and in improving agricultural production. Women tend to give more attention to the administrative aspects of the farm.

The smallest entity of the NTS is an excursion group; its basic structure is formed by such groups (see Fig. 1). Each focuses on a specific crop, cultivation method or topic pertaining to a crop, such as marketing. There are now about 500 such groups with a membership that rarely exceeds 8 persons. This characterizes the NTS: a strong and active base. Other NTS members participate in general meetings, excursions and courses or obtain knowledge from the newsletters and articles of the NTS in the 'agri-press'. They may have various reasons for not joining a group: perhaps the number of growers willing to form a group around the crop of their interest is too small, their farm is being run down (the older growers), they want to protect their mode of production or market segment (competition), or perhaps horticulture is a sideline activity only.

Excursion groups are clustered into study groups, which in turn are coordinated into 11 regional learning clubs (RLCs). Finally, at national level, the NTS has a management board on which the 11 RLCs are represented, together with the three sector committees (for ornamentals, glasshouse and open-field vegetables).

The RLCs are supported by a regional secretariat and a coordinator. He/she is employed to initiate, coordinate and explore new developments in the field of horticulture, and also maintains relationships with the policy and lobby-oriented regional farmer organizations. The secretariat and the coordinator are paid from the annual subscription fee of member growers, an average of Dfl 390 (US$ 223), depending on the sector. Of this money, two-thirds is used by the RLCs and one-third by the NTS.

Issues that need further attention, for example experimentation, are raised by the study groups' leaders; the RLC coordinator than develops these in further detail.

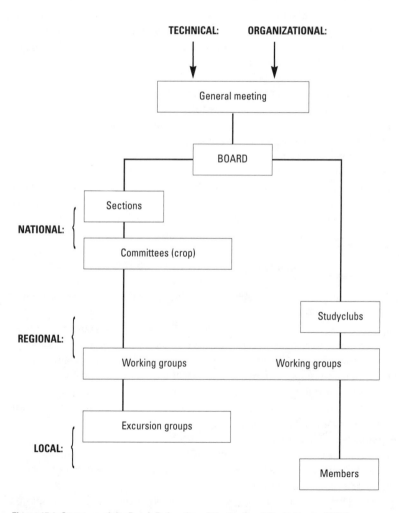

Figure 17.1. Structure of the Dutch Federation of Horticultural Study Groups (NTS)

Learning and experimentation in the excursion groups

Growers are usually motivated and invited to join such a group by the RLC, which also provides administrative and organizational support. The coordinator may organize a meeting or lecture on a particular crop, or arrange an excursion to a research centre, at the end of which the participating growers are invited to study and discuss the topic in depth by joining an excursion group.

Excursion groups take many forms, set themselves different objectives and undertake a range of activities. Central to all these is the development, adaptation, improvement, exchange and application of technologies and techniques. Diversity emerges naturally as the members determine how a group functions and which issues are taken up. Such groups used to be more heterogeneous and changed their composition every few years in response to changing interests within the groups, or as they addressed new issues and problems. Today, however, most groups aim to be as homogeneous (in crop and method of production) as possible in order to refine what are highly specialized modes of production. This is the result also of increasing international competition in horticultural markets, where keeping up with the latest information is a prerequisite to survival.

The following three types of excursion and study groups can generally be distinguished. They reflect an increased intensity in experimentation and learning. In practice, however, groups frequently evolve from one type into the other and back again:

- *Information groups* are engaged mostly in exchange and learning activities of a more general nature, such as trips to experimental farms, visiting each other's farm, inviting extension workers or experts to give lectures, and organizing information evenings. Some groups do not go beyond this point. Their main objective is to gain insight into new developments and technologies and to discuss problems facing their sector.

- *Comparative analysis groups* go a step further and systematically compare members' production results, encouraging each other to monitor, measure and record data on, e.g., climate, yields, the precise amount of water and fertilizer used on their farms. Measuring is knowing, and knowing is the basis for change. All findings are compared over a period of years and analysed as to possible causes for observed differences. Ideas on how to improve individual results are discussed. As one radish grower said:

> *By comparing each others' results over successive years, you get an insight into how you can improve your own cultivation methods. Your own measurements and recordings have value only if you can compare them with others. Together you come to a thorough analysis of the problems and how to solve them. In our group you can actually see this process: in the first years, the results of members differed enormously. This year, the gap between our individual results has decreased.*

Some groups limit their analysis to comparing yields and selected cultivation practices, others include a comparison of costs and benefits. With the present decline in the profitability of horticultural produce, cutting down production costs is seen as extremely important. Exchanging data on costs can help the individual farmer in dealing with this problem and is therefore encouraged by the NTS.

- *Experimentation groups.* Excursion groups may increase their learning further by becoming involved in more systematic experimentation and research. For example, a regional research station lacked the means to perform an experiment desired by a group of growers from Limburg on cultivating freesias, an ornamental, in water. One of the growers initiated an experiment himself and enlisted the support of a researcher from the demonstration farm. Others visited the grower's farm regularly to monitor and evaluate his experiment. The results were published in a growers' magazine (van der Ley and Proost 1992). In another example a group of radish growers undertook an experiment to lengthen the storage period for radishes. As one said:

> *Research on the use and conservation period of new varieties of radishes at the research station is not sufficiently focused on the practical circumstances under which these crops have to grow. We would like to compare varieties already available to the grower. Research done at the station is slow. It takes too long before the results are available to the growers.*

In one year, seven experiments took place on three farms. The conditions under which the seeds were sown were exactly the same on all three. The growers monitored the tests regularly during the cultivation period. When they harvested the crop, the radishes were examined by the quality inspector from the auction. After 5 days' storage in a refrigerator, the inspector judged them again. The results of this test were made available to all radish growers (van Gastel 1995).

A third example concerns a group of enthusiastic growers who felt that water supply was causing problems. The amount of water needed was determined by the driest spots in the soil, which led to an overwatering in places and resulted in loss and a waste of fertilizer. They designed several tests to optimize water supply to the crops using different techniques. They succeeded in their objectives and the research station was very interested in the results. At present, the station is testing the advantages and disadvantages of various techniques so that recommendations can be made to other growers.

Excursion groups get involved in such experiments because they are keen to test new ideas and technologies, such as new varieties, new artificial soils, optimal distance for planting. Group members may have heard of these during lectures or read about them in growers' magazines. They are interested in finding out what works under their own particular conditions. Experiments are also initiated to help address concrete problems experienced by the group.

The ideas for an experiment are either formulated by the farmers themselves or raised in their excursion group. Most groups then ask the staff of a nearby research station to help them design the experiment so that the validity of their tests will be guaranteed. For some of the experiments, where external expertise is needed, a formal contract is set up which states the costs, tasks, responsibilities and liability of the parties involved. In most cases the growers themselves implement the experiment and monitor its developments. Either the farmers or the research station measure the results. Finally, the results are analysed and discussed in the group and conclusions are drawn about the practical implications. For small, low-cost experiments, the members pay for the station employee's time on the experiment. Although such experiments are low-cost, they provide valuable information and knowledge, e.g., the testing of wire netting in freesia production, and an on-farm trial of new tomato varieties developed by a research station. The only costs to the grower were labour input and possibly some materials, but they helped the grower decide on which varieties to use.

For larger projects the excursion group may apply, through the RLC, for central government grants from the marketing board for fruit and vegetables, from collective funds (cooperative banks, cooperative auctions, cooperative insurance companies) or from the provincial government. The results of such tests and experiments are made available to all growers by the NTS through its usual channels: farmers' meetings, the newsletter and articles in growers' magazines. The integrated pest management project in lettuce is a case in point. This project will test new crop protection methods in a large 3-ha glasshouse. It will run for 6 months. The costs of the experiment are estimated to be Dfl 20,000 (US\$ 11,750), covering support from the research station, coordination by the NTS, documentation of the results and the extra labour contributed by the participating grower. In addition, Dfl 45,000 (US\$ 26,470) are to be set aside to compensate for possible loss of produce. The total amount will be paid from collective funds (cooperative banks, auctions, insurance and the Board of Agriculture).

Some groups, however, experiment completely alone, without the support of research stations or any other agencies.

The case of the Rose Cultivators Project Group

The research undertaken by this group is a particular example of farmer-initiated research. Initially the group was formed and organized by five innovative rose cultivators; at present more than 20 growers throughout the Netherlands have joined. The members shared a growing dissatisfaction with the government-financed research practices of the regional research stations, and so in 1990 they started their own research:

> *For us, the government-funded research at these institutes is not specific enough. It lags behind the newest developments in our sector. It is important to keep up with the latest developments because the market for roses is very competitive now that cheap imports from other countries are increasing. We also think the formal linkage between farmers and research, through the NTS, is too long and static.*

Furthermore, the group is convinced that the focus on technical matters (often the case in conventional research on crops) is too narrow to maintain and strengthen their position in international markets. Research on the supply and demand side also provides useful insights into how products can be improved to gain surplus value. As one member said:

Being a grower isn't only cultivating roses in a greenhouse. That way you would lose sight of what you're working for: the market. By exploring consumer demand and the possibilities to improve your product, by looking beyond your own part of the production chain, you can add value to your product and earn extra income.

All members of this group operate highly capital-intensive farms, with glasshouses. As the chairman pointed out, the members are all top cultivators with respect to efficiency of production and the use of modern technology in the production process: "We focus our activities on those cultivators who are innovative and ahead of the majority of rose cultivators".

The members contribute a considerable amount (between Dfl 15,000 - 17,500 a year) to the project group, depending on the size of their farm, out of which most of the activities and projects are financed. For specific projects they receive subsidies from various institutes, such as the marketing board or pesticide industry. At present only 10% of the expenses are covered by subsidies, but this is expected to increase as institutions become familiar with the groups' activities and opportunities.

Members meet six times a year to discuss problems and formulate research topics directly related to their own needs, which in some cases go beyond the technical aspects of cultivating roses. A private consultancy firm has been asked to support the group's activities and to coordinate research. It hires specialized researchers for each experiment or project. In addition, it monitors fields of possible research that are neglected in formal research and keeps the cultivators informed about new developments. During projects and experiments, any member can contact the firm for information and advice.

Based on the ideas and research questions posed by the group, several projects have been started and various institutes selected to assist. For crop-related research, e.g. on new methods of pest control, a research worker will carry out the experiments on the farms belonging to group members, where on-farm conditions are more suitable than those on research stations. The members will be closely involved throughout and are able to monitor and evaluate the results continuously.

The results, like those from the other projects of the group, will not be freely available to all NTS members, or all horticulturalists for that matter. This contrasts with results from government-financed research and those of experiments by the NTS. For the agricultural sector, known for its open exchange of knowledge and information, one could say that this was a small revolution. Of course, it is understandable that those who pay for and invest in new developments should be the first to benefit from them. Yet, it is, or used to be, completely out of keeping with normal practice within the sector and the NTS. In fact, the NTS was initially rather hesitant to support this project, for that very reason. But it realized that a decrease in government funding for agricultural research would lead to new initiatives for developing the necessary innovations and technologies. During its first three years the group operated independently of the NTS, but in 1993 a formal link was set up. This had several advantages: other cultivators became familiar with the groups' activities, membership increased, and the NTS umbrella opened up possibilities for outside funding and subsidies.

At present, the NTS, trying to cope with the consequences of a withdrawing government, has accepted the idea of project groups financing their own research and has created the concept of 'delayed openness': the results of privately financed experiments are made available to all growers after a period of 2-3 years; the federation has also set itself the new objective of acting as an intermediary between agricultural research and the farmers' groups involved in specialized experiments. Knowledge will thus be generated and eventually made available to all farmers.

Farmer research and policy development

The research efforts of farmers' groups not only help to solve their own pressing problems but sometimes have a profound impact on government policy, as the following case of closed–systems research shows.

Some five years ago, the Dutch government decided to implement measures to reduce drastically the emission of chemicals and pesticides from horticultural production into the soil, water and atmosphere. This was in line with new policies to promote sustainable agriculture (Ministry of Agriculture 1990). To meet these new emission levels, several government research institutes, the extension service and the NTS designed a new research programme. Known as 'closed systems' in horticultural production, this focused on the use of independent soil systems (substrate cultivation). This was considered the only way to meet the new emission standards. The programme started in 1990 (Lansink 1993).

As a result, all research activities in soil-based cultivation systems were halted. A group of growers, however, was not convinced. The switch to cultivation on artificial soils, as promoted by the government, required considerable capital investment, the wisdom of which was doubted by many growers. One of the radish growers argued:

> *Technically speaking, one can cultivate almost any crop on artificial soils, but economic feasibility is of course more important to the grower. Cultivation is an economic activity and I have to earn a living for my family.*

Growers felt that the possibility of reducing emissions in soil-based cultivation had never been extensively researched; important opportunities for soil-dependent crops, such as radishes and lettuce, were neglected. "We were convinced," they said, "that an adaption of our present cultivation methods could lead to the desired emission reductions, but we could not prove it since we had no figures or results."

A group of growers decided, therefore, to carry out experiments to study the impact on emission levels of a more precise use of irrigation water and fertilizer. Members of different excursion groups, convinced that their soil-dependent production methods could be made viable by optimizing their existing technology, organized themselves into a RLC. One member of the group told us:

> *For three years we measured the use and loss of water and fertilizer on a few farms, including mine. We analysed the results in cooperation with the NTS and researchers from the experimental station. It turned out that optimalization using our cultivation methods is possible.*

Initially the group received support from the NTS at regional level, and later also at national level. Some of their experiments showed emission results comparable with substrate cultivation (van Gastel 1995). Then, with the support of the NTS, the growers began a campaign to re-establish government-financed research into soil-based cultivation. They invited the important actors in policy development and implementation to visit their farms and see for themselves that soil-based cultivation had a future. When research at the experimental stations also showed that, for some important crops, substrate cultivation was almost impossible or required too much capital investment, the government agreed in 1992, to restart soil-based cultivation research.

This first group triggered the emergence of several other regional groups. Most members have average-sized farms with a relatively low-cost structure compared to growers using capital-intensive substrate cultivation. They all believe that optimalizing their method of production can lead to viable, competitive farms and they are strongly motivated to maintain soil-based cultivation. The groups are coordinated by a national platform within the NTS. At present, approximately 20 farms are continuing to study mineral and water balance to find ways to improve emission levels. Preliminary results are promising. The cultivation of crops in the soil is less polluting than was assumed by researchers and policy makers. A rehabilitation process of soil-dependent cultivation has started.

Institutionalizing farmer research for policy development

With such successes becoming evident, the Dutch government is slowly changing its approach to environmental issues in agriculture. The participation of the growers in the policy-making process is seen increasingly as a prerequisite for success (Ministry of Agriculture 1994a and b). There is also an increasing awareness of the importance of diversity in farming practice. Heterogeneity has become visible, in relation, e.g., to inputs in capital, labour, resources, technology and market links; each farming approach has its own particular advantages in the increasingly competitive markets. The involvement of farmers in policy development is extremely important for dealing with this diversity.

One group of horticulturalists, now joined by four other groups from different sectors, recently took the initiative and proposed a number of experiments to the government to contribute, but on their terms, to policy development. The horticultural part of the proposal is called Horticultural Experiment in Practice. Its main elements are knowledge development, consciousness-raising and cooperation between growers, research institutes and government policy-makers. The group comprises the representatives of the study groups in soil-based horticulture.

The proposed experiments, chosen by the growers, cover three areas: optimalization of water and fertilizer use, a decrease in pesticides and inputs for the control of disease, and the composting and recycling of organic waste. The growers consider these crucial to the development of more environmentally friendly soil-based cultivation. The group analysed the most prominent constraints in their region and examined possible solutions. Priorities were discussed and this led to the three themes. "By discussing and exchanging ideas in a group," a spokesman said, "you get a better picture of the field of problems and which problems have priority."

For each theme, a group of 5-7 growers will implement experiments on their farms. Each group is in fact a study group, since its objectives go beyond the interests of the individual members. Support will be given by researchers from various institutes and it will have an advisory board. The experiments will be financed by the Ministry of Agriculture.

The growers who initiated the plan are all from the same region. They decided to organize themselves regionally for several reasons. As they pointed out, each region has its own environmental problems. In their particular region, pollution of surface water was a major hazard; in other regions, growers have more problems with groundwater. Specific problems require the involvement of the regional government institutes which have an important say in the negotiation process. The choice of regional cooperation has practical advantages, and the organization of meetings is easier. A number of experiments have been designed for each theme. Their aim, the growers claim, is to experiment themselves with new cultivation techniques. The experiments should then give them a better insight into the constraints and opportunities of their use at farm level, and conclusions for policies can be drawn. The farms on which the experiments will take place have been selected to fulfil several criteria so that results are comparable. "The tests and experiments were designed by us", the growers said, "but we consulted several experts to make sure that the test results will be valid." They also thought it important to involve central and regional government and related ministries, so that the design of the experiments and the interpretation of results could be agreed upon in advance, to prevent conflicts or misunderstandings later. The design of the experiment would have to be a compromise, "in which all actors can recognize their ideas."

Experts are to be consulted as necessary, and a list of their tasks drawn up and agreed upon. The experts play an advisory role but will also do most of the measuring so that the results are seen as objective and valid. The experiments are expected to start in October 1996. A committee of growers not participating in the experiments will support the programme; an advisory board on which the NTS, the Ministry of Agriculture and the province are represented will coordinate the administration, eventually translating the results of the experiments into relevant policy recommendations. Financial support is expected from government to pay for the experts, overhead costs and the possible loss of income of the participating growers. Results will be disseminated to other growers through the national NTS network.

Study groups in the horticulture sector: conclusions

Study and excursion groups in the horticultural sector take many forms, set themselves different objectives and undertake a variety of activities. The diversity emerges naturally, as the members themselves determine how a group functions and which issues are taken up. Central to all is the development, adaptation and improvement, exchange and application of technologies and techniques. These study groups and, at national level, the NTS play an important role in technology development in the horticultural sector.

The above cases and research by study groups in other sectors (Proost and Vogelzang 1996) show that membership of a group, rather than working alone, has a number of distinct advantages for farmers:

- members obtain information which is not easily acquired individually or only at relatively high costs, and data can be exchanged and compared, making individual results more meaningful
- membership provides a platform to discuss individual and sectoral problems
- members' opinion on various matters are confirmed or adjusted
- information is disseminated to other members through publication in growers' magazines and in meetings.

Through the coordinating federation, the NTS, farmers' interests are represented in professional research and extension fora. In this way, farmers can influence research and extension priorities, as research stations may set up trials to follow–up the farmers' ideas and experiments. When dissatisfied with these formal linkages, study groups also provide a venue for farmers to be more directly involved in research and extension. They hold joint problem–analysis sessions, organize experiments serving their own interests and priorities, and share the costs of hiring researchers and other experts. The knowledge generated is often available only for members of the group, and this can give them a competitive edge over non–members. But these activities ultimately often go beyond solving the constraints of individual farmers and address issues relevant for the sector as a whole.

The groups' activities can influence policy development. As we saw above, experiments can generate data about specific production methods, illustrating that involving farmers and growers in the policy process can be organized more systematically. The topics dealt with in the groups evolve: moving from an emphasis on what is possible technically to what is desired by society, thus finding an effective way to tune these two perspectives.

Finally, study groups often encourage individual farmers to participate in an activity or experiment that they might never have undertaken on their own. They may feel a mild social control in the group, even competition (van Weperen 1994).

Especially in the horticultural sector, the growers' role in technology development is crucial. The sector has highly specialized, often export–oriented enterprises which need the newest technologies. Large sums are invested in the farms. Research from state institutes generates general recommendations which often need modification at farm level. Because of the rapid development of technology, growers have had to take initiatives to keep up, and the emergence of study groups has been a response to this. Professional research does not always produce results that are applicable at farm level, and it is often the growers themselves, in searching for new ways to solve their own particular problems, who put other issues on the agenda of such research bodies. Working together, they are also capable of developing technology not looked at by the research institutes.

Beginning with a few enthusiastic growers, who are able to gather relevant data, growers are, through their organization, able to exert influence on and change agricultural policy. Of course, the success of the study groups needs to be understood within the local context:

- Dutch farmers have a long tradition of representation on boards and committees of various research, extension, waterscape and polder institutes and agencies.
- Dutch government policy has always been aimed at creating favourable conditions for the agricultural sector. Until 1990, up to 45% of the budget of the Ministry of Agriculture was used for extension, education and research. This has resulted in a strong, open knowledge and information network in which research and technology transfer institutions play complementary roles. However, the increasing commercialization of knowledge and information has put a limit on such openness, and has resulted in the NTS introducing a policy of 'delayed openness'.
- The Netherlands also has a long history of strong cooperative movements, including cooperative auctions, dairies and mills. This has created a good climate for farmers to act jointly.
- Farmers' organizations are well linked to other actors in the agricultural knowledge and information system. The NTS has links at the operational, as well as the research and policy level, in the public as well as the private sector. The growers have become interesting partners for researchers, as better insights into certain technological issues can be gained from on–farm research; financial contributions from farmers increase the resources available for research.

Although the Dutch case shows that farmers' groups can be successful in research and that farmers' organizations can play an important role in technology development, it seems to be an exception rather than the rule. Elsewhere, farmers' organizations, including those that supply inputs, are primarily political groupings whose first preoccupation is not that of ensuring the farmers' access to technology or of influencing research options at national level (Carney 1996).

Building on the tradition of farmers' groups in the Netherlands, the NTS has developed as a strong organization with a sound base and guaranteed representation at all levels. All members are registered and pay their dues. Its membership now provides 50% of the budget of the national and regional experimental stations. The NTS follows the dynamics of its members and takes up new roles when required, such as mediating between farmers' groups and researchers. In this way it maintains its innovative role and serves members' interests. To this end, a well–defined structure, an extensive network, both formal and informal, and the knowledge of who to approach, combined with access to funds, are of vital importance.

Looking ahead

Rapidly changing markets and increasingly tough environmental policies generate new constraints and challenges to agricultural production. There is a need for new technologies and understanding that takes account of not only what is technically possible, but also what is socially and environmentally desirable. The exchange of experiences concerning the integration of the determining factors of production in farming practice is increasingly important.

275

With the recent privatization of the national extension service, study groups are an important means of obtaining and disseminating information at low cost. Besides the free learning from others in the group, the costs of technical assistance by the extension service can be divided among group members; increasing specialization and differentiation in the horticultural sector, and beyond, encourages farmers with similar interests to work together. For the near future it is foreseen that regional activities will become especially important and, as a result, that the RLCs will play a bigger role in defending members' interests. At this level, the RLCs' functions in both policy and technology development will become more intertwined.

Faced with these developments, research institutes and extension services will need to adjust their strategies. Extensionists will become facilitators of a learning process among members of the study groups. In bringing knowledge sources together, social skills will become increasingly important. The linear, hierarchical model of extension as the messenger of science–based technological innovation is being replaced by more horizontal networks in which study groups play an important role (Röling and Jiggins 1994). Researchers likewise must develop more direct relations with the users of technology. With study groups undertaking their own research and hiring in research expertise, research and extension is likely to become much more client–oriented, and the emphasis will shift from providing knowledge and technology to enabling joint development and exchange of knowledge and technology.

Acknowledgements

The section on 'Farmer research and policy development' is based on NTS (1995).

References

Blokker, K.J. and A. de Jong. 1986. *Landbouwvoorlichting*. Muiderberg, Coutinho.

Carney, D. 1996. Research and farmers' organizations: prospects for partnership. Research report, London, Overseas Development Institute.

Gastel, T. van. 1995. Kennis vergaren en kwaliteit telen. *Groenten en Fruit* 44: 16-17.

Lansink, R. 1993. Onderzoek voor iedereen? Onderzoeksvraag en Onderzoeksaanbod in de Nederlandse Bloemisterij onder glas. Unpublished MSc thesis. Department of Communication and Innovation Studies, Wageningen Agricultural University.

Ley, H. van der and M.D.C. Proost. 1992. Gewasbescherming met een toekomst: De positie van intermediairen: Een doelgroepverkennend onderzoek ten behoeve van de voorlichting Meerjarenplan Gewasbescherming. Department of Communication and Innovation Studies, Wageningen Agricultural University.

Ministry of Agriculture, Natural Resource Management and Fisheries (LNV). 1990. *Structuurnota Landbouw*. The Hague, LNV.

Ministry of Agriculture, Nature Resource Management and Fisheries (LNV). 1994a. *Prioriteitennota*. The Hague, LNV.

Ministry of Agriculture, Nature Resource Management and Fisheries (LNV). 1994b. *Sturing op maat: Een andere benadering van milieuproblemen in de land- en tuinbouw*. The Hague, LNV.

NTS (Nederlandse Federatie van Tuinbouw Studiegroepen). 1993. *Beleidstrategie*. Honserlersdijk, NTS.

NTS. 1995. Plan van aanpak: Praktijkexperiment Tuinbouw, Honserlersdijk, NTS.

Nooij, A.T.J. 1991. *Inleiding in de agrarische sociologie*. Leiden, Stenfert Kroese.

Oerlemans, N. 1995. Dutch farmers' organizations and agricultural research: The case of the Netherlands. Unpublished MSc thesis, Department of Communication and Innovation Studies, Wageningen Agricultural University.

Proost, M.D.C. and T. Vogelzang. 1996. Een panacee voor landbouw(kennis)problemen? Studiegroepen: Nuttige interactie op praktijkniveau. *Spil* 1: 137-140; 2: 24-29.

Röling, N.G. 1994. Innovation in the Agricultural Knowledge and Information System. In: *The setting: Background on agricultural innovation*. Wageningen, Peter Linde Productions.

Röling, N.G. and J.L.S. Jiggins. 1994. Extension and the sustainable management of natural resources. *European Journal of Agricultural Education and Extension* 1 (1): 23-43.

Weperen, W. van. 1994. Balancing the minerals, moving boundaries. Unpublished MSc thesis, Wageningen, Department of Communication and Innovation Studies, Wageningen Agricultural University.

Lessons and challenges
for farmer–led experimentation

Introduction

In this chapter, some of the emerging lessons and crucial challenges facing the development, spread and scaling–up of farmer–led experimentation are discussed. The points highlighted here have been raised in the 17 chapters that comprise this book in the field of farmer participatory research. These lessons are coupled with a broad set of recommendations for promoting and extending approaches to support and enhance farmers' research in future.

Farmer–led experimentation: the challenges ahead

The cases in this book, as well as the large number of other contributions which could not be included for lack of space, indicate that interest in PTD approaches is very strong in the field and that results are encouraging. Does this allow us to evaluate the effectiveness and impact of PTD? At this point, the lessons in this book only give circumstantial evidence.

Despite their proven effectiveness, concerns remain about the application of participatory research and development in different agroecological, socioeconomic, institutional and policy contexts. These concerns have resonance in the field of agricultural research and extension, and relate to issues relating to: (1) assessing PTD impacts and judging the trustworthiness of the research findings; (2) influencing policy and policy making; (3) going to scale and institutionalizing participatory approaches in large, government bureaucracies; (4) creating enabling external institutions; and (5) building social capital and setting PTD in a wider regional economic context.

We address each of these challenges below and examine the opportunities for improving the practice of participatory research and extension for farmer–led experimentation.

Challenge 1: Assessing impacts

Participatory Technology Development is part of a growing family of interactive, flexible, people–centred approaches developed to promote participatory learning and action. Like many of these approaches, PTD has been very strong at stimulating discussion, provoking critical reflection and building on local resources and capabilities. It has, however, been much weaker at understanding links between causes and effects, inputs and outputs, and costs and benefits. This makes it more difficult to assess the overall impact of farmer–based experimentation approaches.

Consequently, evaluating the effectiveness of farmer–based experimentation methods in strict statistical terms, where questions of reliability and validity are raised, may not always be appropriate. Instead, it may require an alternative understanding of what the research findings really mean and to whom. This will demand new, innovative means for assessing the impacts of PTD activities.

For example, the emphasis in PTD on facilitating learning processes presents a challenge to the conventional cost–benefit analyses used to measure the physical, quantifiable outputs of research and development activities. Learning outcomes are difficult to assess, especially as they are rarely specified as measurable objectives of participatory research. Moreover, participatory approaches tend to involve a wide variety of participants who have multiple objectives and tend to judge their attainment differently. If there are multiple objectives and multiple value systems for different stakeholders (male farmers, female farmers, development practitioners, researchers, etc.), assessing the overall effectiveness of an approach presents a great challenge.

The interests of the different stakeholders need not be mutually exclusive. Nevertheless, they will tend to place different demands of a research process.

It is also important to note that in a participatory research process there is no single client group that will exclusively use the research findings. For instance, policymakers and planners may enable a PTD effort to take place. In turn an alliance of researchers and experimenting farmers, may aim to influence the thinking of those very decision makers as one outcome of the exercise. In each case there are implications for methodology, although the research is more likely to be useful both as a tool and as a means of influencing policy if it generates information that meets the criteria of 'legitimate' knowledge by each of the stakeholder groups, *and* if it involves them in the generation of that knowledge.

Positive impact in participatory research may be deemed significant if, in the process innovative technologies are developed and the farmers have acquired additional research skills. This has important implications for agricultural research efforts which, in the past, tended to produce only technical innovations to be passed on via extension agents to farmers, coupled with attempts at explaining why the farmers were not adopting them. This suggests that "ways of researching need to be developed that combine 'finding out' about complex and dynamic situations with 'taking action' to improve them, in such a way that the actors and beneficiaries of the 'action research' are intimately involved as participants in the whole process" (Sriskandarajah et al. 1991). In other words, in promoting closer collaboration between formal research, extension agents and experimenting farmers, we are developing a new, multidimensional research framework; one that does not meet the standard textbook definition of 'research', yet appears to be yielding positive outcomes for all those who participate.

Challenge 2: Influencing policy and policy making

One of the primary challenges to PTD is that there are very few experiences in terms of the impact in shifting policies or policy making processes. In this book, there are only two cases in which farmer researchers had a role to play in the policy arena, (Oerlemans et al.; Ruddell et al.).

There are at least two components of a PTD research program that the 'users' of this participatory research might use or be influenced by. One is the final *output* or product such as: research findings, policy recommendations, the reports. The other is the actual *process* of doing the research. Thus, for a group of farmers a PTD research programme might be more interesting for the skills and knowledge that are generated in conducting the research than for its final conclusions. In general, a policymaker is more interested in the outputs (which are generally specified in advance in project objectives or research proposals), but will give them more authority if the process to generate that output meets their criteria of 'trustworthy' research. That said, involving a policymaker in a process of participatory research with local farmers' groups may alter the policymaker's criteria of what is legitimate and credible research. For many policymakers, however, the challenge is rationalizing the costs of introducing PTD approaches to different institutional contexts and scaling up the process beyond project–driven experiences.

Challenge 3: Going to scale

Many PTD approaches were originally intended and developed for use at the community or local level. Recent attempts to apply participatory approaches in national research and development programs and institutionalise their use in large, government bureaucracies have raised new problems and opportunities.

Quite a few cases reported here operate at a relatively small scale, in a few villages or a district. Some of the challenges they raise are easy to recognise but hard to address. In this volume, for example, Scheuermeier shows how farmer–based experimentation is very specific to the individual farmers' situation, especially the poor and marginalised groups which are generally targeted by PTD. On–site experimentation is hard to replicate at a larger scale because of the uniqueness of the most small farmers' complex, diverse, and risk–prone conditions.

Successful cases reported elsewhere also often do not cover more than one or two growing seasons. Only recently have larger, formal, government organisations responding to the challenge to take farmer participation seriously within their national countrywide mandates. The implications of this are only starting to be understood, and they point at the need for a number changes, among others, in the management culture, financial planning, monitoring and evaluation procedures of large institutions (Thompson 1995; Backhaus and Wagachchi 1995; Scheuermeier and Sen 1994).

In other cases, larger–scale coverage is sought outside the government structure, as in the example of the Campesino a Campesino movement in Central America (Holt–Gimenez 1993). A network of farmer trainers, farmer organisations and non–governmental organisations has emerged which implements farmer–led extension approaches to sustainable agriculture development. What remains unclear is how to develop the appropriate institutional arrangements needed to ensure longer–term sustainability of these systems.

Challenge 4: Creating enabling external institutions

A PTD practitioner needs an enabling environment to be able to grow into a new role, gradually gaining participatory skills and attitudes in an apprenticeship or a self–learning process, as described in the contributions by Ishag et al., Hocde and Ruddell et al. The challenge for institutions attempting to employ PTD and other farmer participatory research approaches is create a learning environment which rewards new ways of learning and behaving. Participatory research is not only good for local people, but also good for government agencies and research institutions. It thrives best, however, in a context of democratisation and good governance of organisations. In particular, shifts within agricultural research and extension agencies are therefore inextricably necessary to enable the application of PTD and other participatory approaches.

Many authors struggle with the need to modify the external institutional contexts to allow participatory approaches to be more widely applied and embedded in the institutions. Two key questions arise:

1. Are the tools and methods commonly used to support farmers' research sufficient to address and influence the broader enabling conditions?
2. How can the numerous methods and terms in the literature, sometimes referred to as methodologies for 'participatory learning and action', be best described, promoted and shared with those able to influence change within these institutional dimensions?

The accounts in this book point to the many difficulties encountered when the enabling conditions are not there, which is the most common situation. Authors such as Mapatano and Gubbels describe the challenges they have faced in pushing for a shift away from the conventional 'transfer–of–technology' mode, towards achieving a genuine collaboration of all these actors on an equal footing. Not surprisingly, most of the experiences reported here come from externally–funded projects. As single stakeholders, such projects seem to lack the leverage and legitimacy to influence the broader institutional and policy conditions which enable PTD to flourish.

New mechanisms are needed to stimulate change within government agencies to provide the cornerstones of participatory approaches: development of appropriate skills and reward systems among staff, providing methodological support, securing resources for long–term efforts, and thus allowing the flexibility in pacing that participatory learning demands.

Challenge 5: Building social capital and setting PTD in context

As PTD expands, the concept of social capital (Coleman 1986) is likely to become central. This refers to the capital inherent in relationships, institutions and networks in society, their importance as constituent elements of well–being and quality of life, and the ways in which they are and can be mobilised to foster economic development, social change and government accountability. Creating an effective local institution involves a process of developing a set of working rules on which all stakeholders agree and to which they can adhere.

Local institutions do not operate by themselves; they function in a multi–stakeholder environment. To be able to collaborate effectively, all relevant stakeholders must shape the relationships within among themselves and know how to make them work. This knowledge is part of the social capital that individuals develop over time, when they have the autonomy to do so. A group within which there is reciprocity, cooperation and trust is able to accomplish much more than a comparable group without these reciprocal arrangements (Coleman 1988).

Going through a PTD process, with its emphasis on joint learning and collective action appears to help build this social capital. However, a key lesson drawn from the experiences presented in this book is that PTD needs to be seen in relation to the broader rural economy in which it is practised if we are to understand its role in building social capital. Strengthening other aspects of rural life, especially generating employment in small–scale enterprise, such as input supply, trade, processing; and cottage industries in rural areas, can help take pressure off the land. This can reduce certain environmental problems at least as much as, if not more than, enhancing farmers' ability to experiment. As many rural livelihoods depend on off–farm sources of income, concentrating exclusively on developing resource–conserving technologies, promoting participatory approaches to research and development and farmer–to–farmer extension, address only part of the problem of rural poverty.

It is important that strategies of agricultural research and development do not focus simply on improving productivity, while the unnoticed economic and/or nutritional status of the families involved becomes yet more chronic as a consequence of other changes in the regional economy. Anyone who has been involved in PTD with farmers will know that they do not confine themselves to this simple focus on agricultural production, but they often feel powerless to influence the wider economy. Creating and strengthening institutional arrangements above the level of the individual farmers which can help them secure their livelihoods should be a central thrust of any broad sustainable agriculture policy which recognises the realities of regional economic development and agrarian change.

Conclusions and recommendations

Supporting farmers' research may be only one piece of the whole mosaic of rural development but, for those farmers and development agents who are interested in improving the agricultural aspects of development, this book shows that there are innovative ways of doing this which promise better results than the conventional approach to research and technology transfer. Although success in rural development and social change cannot be measured solely on the basis of the number of farmer–led experiments that spring up across the landscape, these can indicate an increased dynamism in farming that makes some contribution towards improving local livelihoods.

What are the steps to be taken in the future to promote this dynamism in agricultural development? The readers of this book will have to consider which of the previously mentioned challenges for PTD they are in the best position to meet. Those in a position to influence the policy or institutional dimensions will face different challenges than the field practitioners, who are best able to contribute to the areas of developing methods and strengthening social capital and building effective, self–governing, local institutions.

We address ourselves first to readers able to intervene at the policy and institutional levels, as there is need for more attention to these levels than has been given in the contributions to this book. Government policies can have a much bigger impact on farmers' lives than farmers' own localised efforts at technology development. Innovation in forms of social organisation to influence policy will therefore need to become a vital part of participatory research. This requires the collaboration of numerous types of actors, covering both research and extension activities and straddling several sectors, such as in the case of tools research and small–scale enterprise development to produce tools, described by Mellis et. al. The mandates of funding programmes for development–oriented research need to be widened to be able to accommodate such activities.

Formal researchers may recognise the need for further in–depth studies of farmers' informal research in particular areas. Similarly, in their field activities, development workers may recognise the need to focus more attention on the logic and practice of farmer experimentation. These initiatives face the methodological challenges of finding ways to learn about farmers' own research and experimentation, as described, for example, by Stolzenbach in Mali and Levine (1996) in Mozambique.

Those who are able to advance on the methodological aspects will need to seek a more systematic understanding of the differences among farmers within a community, such as between rich and poor, between men and women, or between indigenous people and immigrants. Gubbels' chapter is a good example of one such effort. The tensions between participation and marginalization and the implications of these tensions must be made more explicit in the documentation of PTD in practice. For the field practitioners in agricultural development, there are also challenges in terms of the use of PTD to address improvements in other areas of agriculture and farming: not only field crops but also livestock, fisheries and forest systems; not only production but also processing, storage and marketing; not only in rural areas but also in urban agriculture.

In this book, we have used the term PTD as 'shorthand' to cover various activities which are underway in different parts of the world to support farmer–led development of farming systems. Few of the actors are deliberately referring to their work as 'PTD', but they share common philosophies and face similar challenges. The name given to the activities is not important, but the spirit is. We hope that many more readers with whom we have not yet had contact, no matter what acronym they give to their approach, will recognise that we are seeking similar goals and will also seek to confront the challenges together.

References

Backhaus C. and R. Wagachchi. 1995. Only playing with beans? Participatory approaches in large–scale government programmes. *PLA Notes* 24: 62-65

Coleman J. 1988. Social capital in the creation of human capital. *American Journal of Sociology* 94 (supplement): S95-S120.

Coleman J. 1986. Social theory, social research, and a theory of action. *American Journal of Sociology* 91 (1): 309-35.

Holt-Gimenez E. 1993. Farmer–to–farmer: The Ometepe Project Nicaragua. In: Alders C, B. Haverkort and L. R. van Veldhuizen (eds). *Linking with farmers: Networking for low–external–input and sustainable agriculture*. London, IT Publications. pp 51-65.

Scheuermeier U. and Sen. 1994. *Starting-up participatory technology development for animal husbandry in Andra Pradesh*. Lindau, LBL.

Sriskandaraja, N., R.J. Bawden, and R.G. Packham. 1991. Systems agriculture: A paradigm for sustainability. *Association of Farming Systems Research-Extension Newsletter* 2 (2): 1-5.

Thompson, J. 1995. Participatory approaches in government bureaucracies: Facilitating the process of institutional change. *World Development* 23 (9): 1521-54.